Student Solutions Manual

Financial Accounting:
An Introduction to Concepts, Methods, and Uses

Fourteenth Edition

Roman L. Weil
University of Chicago
University of California, San Diego

Katherine Schipper
Duke University

Jennifer Francis
Duke University

SOUTH-WESTERN
CENGAGE Learning·

Australia • Brazil • Japan • Korea • Mexico • Singapore • Spain • United Kingdom • United States

ISBN-13: 978-1-133-59102-3
ISBN-10: 1-133-59102-7

South-Western Cengage Learning
5191 Natorp Boulevard
Mason, OH 45040
USA

Cengage Learning is a leading provider of customized learning solutions with office locations around the globe, including Singapore, the United Kingdom, Australia, Mexico, Brazil, and Japan. Locate your local office at: **international.cengage.com/region**.

Cengage Learning products are represented in Canada by Nelson Education, Ltd.

For your course and learning solutions, visit **www.cengage.com**.

Purchase any of our products at your local college store or at our preferred online store **www.CengageBrain.com**.

READ IMPORTANT LICENSE INFORMATION

Printed in the United States of America
1 2 3 4 5 6 7   16 15 14 13

PREFACE

This book presents odd-numbered answers and solutions for the questions, exercises, and problems contained in each chapter of the textbook *Financial Accounting: An Introduction to Concepts, Methods and Uses* Fourteenth Edition. We do not attempt to give all possible ways to work a problem, showing the multiple paths to the correct solution. We do not even try to give the most commonly chosen one, even if we know what that is, which is rare. Our students often ask the equivalent of, "Why can't I work the problem this way?" or "Is it OK to work the problem this other way?" In a word, yes. You can work most problems in several different ways. If you get the right final answer, then do not worry if you reached it via a path different from the one we show.

If you have any suggestions as to how this book might be improved in subsequent editions, please feel free to bring them to our attention.

R.L.W.

K.S.

J.F.

CONTENTS

CHAPTER 1: INTRODUCTION TO BUSINESS ACTIVITIES AND OVERVIEW OF FINANCIAL STATEMENTS AND THE REPORTING PROCESS
Questions, Exercises, and Problems: Answers and Solutions.................. 1-1—1-12

CHAPTER 2: THE BASICS OF RECORD KEEPING AND FINANCIAL STATEMENT PREPARATION: BALANCE SHEET
Questions, Exercises, and Problems: Answers and Solutions.................. 2-1—2-7

CHAPTER 3: THE BASICS OF RECORD KEEPING AND FINANCIAL STATEMENT PREPARATION: INCOME STATEMENT
Questions, Exercises, and Problems: Answers and Solutions.................. 3-1—3-37

CHAPTER 4: BALANCE SHEET: PRESENTING AND ANALYZING RESOURCES AND FINANCING
Questions, Exercises, and Problems: Answers and Solutions.................. 4-1—4-15

CHAPTER 5: INCOME STATEMENT: REPORTING THE RESULTS OF OPERATING ACTIVITIES
Questions, Exercises, and Problems: Answers and Solutions.................. 5-1—5-8

CHAPTER 6: STATEMENT OF CASH FLOWS
Questions, Exercises, and Problems: Answers and Solutions.................. 6-1—6-20

CHAPTER 7: INTRODUCTION TO FINANCIAL STATEMENT ANALYSIS
Questions, Exercises, and Problems: Answers and Solutions.................. 7-1—7-26

CHAPTER 8: REVENUE RECOGNITION, RECEIVABLES, AND ADVANCES FROM CUSTOMERS
Questions, Exercises, and Problems: Answers and Solutions.................. 8-1—8-36

CHAPTER 9: WORKING CAPITAL
Questions, Exercises, and Problems: Answers and Solutions.................. 9-1—9-14

CHAPTER 10: LONG-LIVED TANGIBLE AND INTANGIBLE ASSETS
Questions, Exercises, and Problems: Answers and Solutions.................. 10-1—10-10

CHAPTER 11: NOTES, BONDS, AND LEASES
Questions, Exercises, and Problems: Answers and Solutions.................. 11-1—11-18

CHAPTER 12: LIABILITIES: OFF-BALANCE-SHEET FINANCING, RETIREMENT BENEFITS, AND INCOME TAXES

Questions, Exercises, and Problems: Answers and Solutions.................. 12-1—12-16

CHAPTER 13: MARKETABLE SECURITIES AND DERIVATIVES

Questions, Exercises, and Problems: Answers and Solutions.................. 13-1—13-16

CHAPTER 14: INTERCORPORATE INVESTMENTS IN COMMON STOCK

Questions, Exercises, and Problems: Answers and Solutions.................. 14-1—14-14

CHAPTER 15: SHAREHOLDERS' EQUITY: CAPITAL CONTRIBUTIONS AND DISTRIBUTIONS

Questions, Exercises, and Problems: Answers and Solutions.................. 15-1—15-14

CHAPTER 16: STATEMENT OF CASH FLOWS: ANOTHER LOOK

Problems and Cases: Answers and Solutions .... 16-1—16-23

CHAPTER 17: SYNTHESIS AND EXTENSIONS

Exercises and Problems: Answers and Solutions .... 17-1—17-9

APPENDIX: TIME VALUE OF CASH FLOWS: COMPOUND INTEREST CONCEPTS AND APPLICATIONS

Questions, Exercises, and Problems: Answers and Solutions.................. A-1—A-6

CHAPTER 1

INTRODUCTION TO BUSINESS ACTIVITIES AND OVERVIEW OF FINANCIAL STATEMENTS AND THE REPORTING PROCESS

Questions, Exercises, and Problems: Answers and Solutions

1.1   The first question at the end of each chapter asks the student to review the important terms and concepts discussed in the chapter. Students may wish to consult the glossary at the end of the book in addition to the definitions and discussions in the chapter.

1.3   The balance sheet shows assets, liabilities and, shareholders' equity as of a specific date (the balance sheet date), similar to a snapshot. The income statement and statement of cash flows report changes in assets and liabilities over a period of time, similar to a motion picture.

1.5   Management, under the oversight of the firm's governing board, prepares the financial statements.

1.7   Accounts receivable represent amounts owed by customers for goods and services they have already received. The customer, therefore, has the benefit of the goods and services before it pays cash. The length of the financing period is the number of days between when the customer receives the goods and services and when the customer pays cash to the seller of those goods and services.

1.9   A calendar year ends on December 31. A fiscal year ends on a date that is determined by the firm, perhaps based on its business model (for example, many retailers choose a fiscal year end that is close to the end of January). A firm can choose the calendar year as its fiscal year, and many do. Both calendar years and fiscal years have 12 months.

1.11   A current item is expected to result in a cash receipt (assets such as accounts receivable) or a cash payment (liabilities such as accounts payable) within approximately one year or less. A noncurrent item is expected to generate cash over periods longer than a year (assets, such as factory buildings that will be used to produce goods for sale over many years) or use cash over periods longer than a year (liabilities such as long term debt). Users of financial statements would likely be interested in this distinction because the distinction provides information about short-term cash flows separately from long-term cash flows.

1.13   An income statement connects two successive balance sheets through its effect on retained earnings. Net income that is not paid to shareholders as dividends increases retained earnings. A statement of cash flows connects two successive balance sheets because it explains the change in cash (a balance sheet account) from operating, financing, and investing activities. The statement of cash flows also shows the relation between net income and cash flows from operations, and changes in assets and liabilities that involve cash flows.

1.15   U.S. GAAP must be used by U.S. SEC registrants and may be used by other firms as well. International Financial Reporting Standards (IFRS) may be used by non-U.S. firms that list and trade their securities in the United States, and these firms may also use U.S. GAAP.

1.17   The accrual basis of accounting is based on assets and liabilities, not on cash receipts and disbursements. It provides a better basis for measuring performance because it is based on revenues (inflows of assets from customers), not cash receipts from customers, and on expenses (outflows of assets from generating revenues), not cash payments. It matches revenues with the costs associated with earning those revenues and is not sensitive to the timing of expenditures.

1.19   (Capcion, a paper and packaging firm; understanding the income statement.) (amounts in thousands of euros)

     a.   Cost of goods sold = €1,331,292.1 thousand.

     b.   Selling and distribution expenses = €172,033.4 thousand.

     c.   Gross margin percentage = 23.4% (= €405,667.1/€1,736,959.2).

1.19 continued.

    d.   Operating profit = €169,418.2 thousand.

        Profit before tax = €170,863.9 thousand.

        Difference equals €1,445.7 thousand (= €169,418.2 – €170,863.9). The items that constitute this difference are nonoperating sources of income (expense).

    e.   Effective tax rate = €54,289.9/€170,863.9 = 31.8%.

    f.   Profit = €116,574.0 thousand.

1.21   (EuroTel, a communications firm; balance sheet relations.) (amounts in millions of euros [€])

Current Assets	+	Noncurrent Assets	=	Current Liabilities	+	Noncurrent Liabilities	+	Shareholders' Equity
€20,000	+	€29,402	=	€15,849	+	?	+	€17,154

Noncurrent liabilities total €16,399 million.

1.23   (GrandRider, an automotive manufacturer; income statement relations.) (amounts in millions of pounds sterling)

Sales	£ 7,435
Less Cost of Sales	(6,003)
Gross Margin	1,432
Less Other Operating Expenses	(918)
Loss on Sale of Business	(2)
Net Financing Income	221
Profit Before Taxes	733
Less Tax Expense	(133)
Net Income	£ 600

    Odd-numbered Solutions

1.25   (Veldt, a South African firm; retained earnings relations) (amounts in millions of South African rand [R])

Retained Earnings at End of 2012	+	Income for 2013	–	Dividends Declared	=	Retained Earnings at End of 2013
R4,640.9	+	R2,362.5	–	?	=	R5,872.4

Dividends declared = R1,131.0 million.

1.27   (BargainPurchase, a retailer; cash flow relations.) (amounts in millions of US$)

Cash at Start of Year	+	Cash Flow from Operations	+	Cash Flow from Investing	+	Cash Flow from Financing	=	Cash at End of Year
$813	+	$4,125	+	$(6,195)	+	$3,707	=	?

Cash at end of year = $2,450 million.

1.29   (Kenton Limited; preparation of simple balance sheet; current and noncurrent classifications.) (amounts in pounds sterling)

	January 31, 2013
Assets	
Cash..	£ 2,000
Inventory	12,000
Prepaid Rent	24,000
Total Current Assets..	38,000
Prepaid Rent	24,000
Total Noncurrent Assets	24,000
Total Assets...	£ 62,000
Liabilities and Shareholders' Equity	
Accounts Payable..	£ 12,000
Total Current Liabilities...	12,000
Total Noncurrent Liabilities	—
Total Liabilities...	12,000
Common Stock	50,000
Total Shareholders' Equity...	50,000
Total Liabilities and Shareholders' Equity	£ 62,000

1.31 (Hewston, a manufacturing firm; accrual versus cash basis of accounting.) (amounts in US$)

a. Net Income = Sales Revenue − Expenses

= $66,387 million − $62,313 million = $4,074 million.

Net Cash Flow = Cash Inflows − Cash Outflows

= $65,995 million − $56,411 million = $9,584 million.

b. Cash collections may be less than revenues for at least two reasons. First, customers may have purchased on credit and have not yet paid. Second, the firm may have collected cash from customers who purchased on credit last year, but cash collections remain less than cash collected on new credit sales.

c. Cash payments may be less than expenses for at least two reasons. First, the firm may have received goods and services from suppliers, but not yet paid for those items (i.e., the amounts are to be paid in the next year). Second, the firm may have accrued expenses this year that will be paid in cash in future periods; an example would be the accrual of interest expense on a bond that will be paid the next year.

1.33 (ComputerCo, a Singapore manufacturer; balance sheet relations.) (amounts in millions of Singapore dollars [$])

The missing items appear in **boldface** type.

	2013	2012
Assets		
Current Assets	$ 170,879	$ 170,234
Noncurrent Assets	**28,945**	17,368
Total Assets	$ 199,824	$ 187,602
Liabilities and Shareholders' Equity		
Current Liabilities	$ 139,941	$ 126,853
Noncurrent Liabilities	7,010	**7,028**
Total Liabilities	**146,951**	**133,881**
Shareholders' Equity	**52,873**	53,721
Total Liabilities and Shareholders' Equity	$ 199,824	$ 187,602

1.35 (EastonHome, a consumer products manufacturer; income statement relations.) (amounts in millions of US$)

The missing items appear in **boldface** type.

	2013	2012	2011
Sales	$ 13,790	$ **12,238**	$ 11,397
Cost of Goods Sold	**(6,042)**	(5,536)	(5,192)
Selling and Administrative Expenses	(4,973)	(4,355)	(3,921)
Other (Income) Expense	(121)	(186)	(69)
Interest Expense, Net	(157)	(159)	(136)
Income Tax Expense	(759)	(648)	(728)
Net Income	$ 1,738	$ 1,354	$ **1,351**

1.37 (AB Brown, a Swedish firm; statement of cash flows relations.)

Statement of Cash Flows
(amounts in millions of Swedish kronor [SEK])

	2013	2012	2011
Operations:			
Revenues, Net of Expenses	SEK 19,210	SEK 18,489	SEK 16,669
Cash Flow from Operations	19,210	18,489	16,669
Investing:			
Acquisition of Property and Equipment	(4,319)	(3,827)	(3,365)
Acquisition of Businesses	(26,292)	(18,078)	(1,210)
Sale of Property and Equipment	152	185	362
Sale of Short-Term Investments	3,499	6,180	6,375
Other Investing Activities	(573)	663	(1,131)
Cash Flow from Investing	(27,533)	(14,877)	1,031
Financing:			
Proceeds from Borrowings	15,587	1,290	657
Repayment of Borrowings	(1,291)	(9,510)	(2,784)
Sale of Common Stock	94	124	174
Dividends Paid	(8,132)	(7,343)	(4,133)
Other Financing Activities	406	58	(288)
Cash Flow from Financing	6,664	(15,381)	(6,374)
Change in Cash	(1,659)	(11,769)	11,326
Cash, Beginning of Year	29,969	41,738	30,412
Cash, End of Year	SEK 28,310	SEK 29,969	SEK 41,738

1.39   (JetAway Airlines; preparing a balance sheet and an income statement.)

a.   **JETAWAY AIRLINES**
                                  Balance Sheet
                          (amounts in thousands of US$)

	Sept. 30, 2013	Sept. 30, 2012
Assets		
Cash	$ 378,511	$ 418,819
Accounts Receivable	88,799	73,448
Inventories	50,035	65,152
Other Current Assets	56,810	73,586
Total Current Assets	574,155	631,005
Property, Plant, and Equipment (Net)	4,137,610	5,008,166
Other Noncurrent Assets	4,231	12,942
Total Assets	$ 4,715,996	$ 5,652,113
Liabilities and Shareholders' Equity		
Accounts Payable	$ 157,415	$ 156,755
Current Maturities of Long-Term Debt	11,996	7,873
Other Current Liabilities	681,242	795,838
Total Current Liabilities	850,653	960,466
Long-Term Debt	623,309	871,717
Other Noncurrent Liabilities	844,116	984,142
Total Liabilities	2,318,078	2,816,325
Common Stock	352,943	449,934
Retained Earnings	2,044,975	2,385,854
Total Shareholders' Equity	2,397,918	2,835,788
Total Liabilities and Shareholders' Equity	$ 4,715,996	$ 5,652,113

1.39 continued.

b.

JETAWAY AIRLINES
Income Statement
(amounts in thousands of US$)

For the Year Ended:	Sept. 30, 2013
Sales	$ 4,735,587
Salaries and Benefits Expense	(1,455,237)
Fuel Expense	(892,415)
Maintenance Expense	(767,606)
Other Operating Expenses	(1,938,753)
Interest Expense	(22,883)
Interest Income	14,918
Net Income	$ (326,389)

c.

Retained Earnings, September 30, 2012	$ 2,385,854
Plus Net Loss for 2013	(326,389)
Less Dividends Declared During 2013 (Plug)	**(14,490)**
Retained Earnings, September 30, 2013	$ 2,044,975

1.41 (Stationery Plus; cash basis versus accrual basis accounting.) (amounts in US$)

a. **Income for November 2013:**

(1) **Cash Basis Accounting**

Sales	$ 23,000
Cost of Merchandise	(20,000)
Rent	(9,000)
Salaries	(10,000)
Utilities	(480)
Income (Loss)	$ (16,480)

1.41 a. continued.

(2) Accrual Basis Accounting

Sales	$ 56,000
Cost of Merchandise	(29,000)
Rent	(1,500)
Salaries	(10,000)
Utilities	(480)
Interest	(1,000)
Income (Loss)	$ 14,020

b. **Income for December 2013:**

(1) Cash Basis Accounting

Sales Made in November, Collected in December	$ 33,000
Sales Made and Collected in December	34,000
Cost of Merchandise Acquired in November and Paid in December	(20,000)
Cost of Merchandise Acquired and Paid in December	(27,500)
Salaries	(10,000)
Utilities	(480)
Interest	(2,000)
Income (Loss)	$ 7,020

(2) Accrual Basis Accounting

Sales	$ 62,000
Cost of Merchandise	(33,600)
Rent	(1,500)
Salaries	(10,000)
Utilities	(480)
Interest	(1,000)
Income (Loss)	$ 15,420

1.43   (Balance sheet and income statement relations.)

a. Bushels of wheat are the most convenient in this case with the given information. This question emphasizes the need for a common measuring unit.

b.
IVAN AND IGOR
Comparative Balance Sheets
(amounts in bushels of wheat)

| | IVAN | | IGOR | |
	Beginning of Period	End of Period	Beginning of Period	End of Period
Assets				
Wheat	20	223	10	105
Fertilizer..................	2	—	1	—
Ox.............................	40	36	40	36
Plow	—	—	—	2
Land........................	100	100	50	50
Total Assets	162	359	101	193
Liabilities and Owner's Equity				
Accounts Payable	—	3	—	—
Owner's Equity	162	356	101	193
Total Liabilities and Owner's Equity...............	162	359	101	193

Questions will likely arise as to the accounting entity. One view is that there are two accounting entities (Ivan and Igor) to whom the Red-Bearded Baron has entrusted assets and required a periodic reporting on stewardship. The "owner" in owner's equity in this case is the Red-Bearded Baron. Another view is that the Red-Bearded Baron is the accounting entity, in which case financial statements that combine the financial statements for Ivan and Igor are appropriate. Identifying the accounting entity depends on the intended use of the financial statements. For purposes of evaluating the performance of Ivan and Igor, the accounting entities are separate—Ivan and Igor. To assess the change in wealth of the Red-Bearded Baron during the period, the combined financial statements reflect the accounting entity.

1.43 continued.

c.

IVAN AND IGOR
Comparative Income Statement
(amounts in bushels of wheat)

	IVAN	IGOR
Revenues	243	138
Expenses:		
Seed	20	10
Fertilizer	2	1
Depreciation on Ox	4	4
Plow	3	1
Total Expenses	29	16
Net Income	214	122

Chapter 1 does not expose students to the concept of depreciation. Most students, however, grasp the need to record some amount of expense for the ox and the plow.

d.

(amounts in bushels of wheat)	IVAN	IGOR
Owner's Equity, Beginning of Period	162	101
Plus Net Income	214	122
Less Distributions to Owner	(20)	(30)
Owner's Equity, End of Period	356	193

1.43 continued.

e. We cannot compare the amounts of net income for Ivan and Igor without adjustment because the Red-Bearded Baron entrusted them with different amounts of resources. We must relate the net income amounts to some base. The possibilities include the following:

	IVAN	IGOR
Net Income/Average Total Assets	82.2%	83.0%
Net Income/Beginning Total Assets	132.1%	120.8%
Net Income/Average Noncurrent Assets	155.1%	137.1%
Net Income/Beginning Noncurrent Assets	152.9%	135.6%
Net Income/Average Owner's Equity	82.6%	83.0%
Net Income/Beginning Owner's Equity	132.1%	120.8%
Net Income (in bushels)/Acre	10.70	12.20

The purpose of this question is to get students to think about performance measurement. The instructor may or may not wish to devote class time at this point discussing which base is more appropriate.

CHAPTER 2

THE BASICS OF RECORD KEEPING AND
FINANCIAL STATEMENT PREPARATION: BALANCE SHEET

Questions, Exercises, and Problems: Answers and Solutions

2.1 See the text or the glossary at the end of the book.

2.3 Typically, the accountant records journal entries before transferring the amounts to T-accounts. A T-account is used to record the effects of events and transactions that affect a specific asset, liability, shareholders' equity, revenue, or expense account (which the text has not yet introduced). It captures both increases and decreases in that specific account, without reference to the effects on other accounts. It also shows the beginning and ending balances of balance sheet accounts. A journal entry shows all the accounts affected by a single event or transaction; each debit and each credit in a journal entry will affect a specific T-account. Journal entries provide a record of transactions, and T-accounts summarize the effects of transactions on specific accounts.

2.5 Contra accounts provide disaggregated information concerning the net amount of an asset, liability, or shareholders' equity item. For example, the account Property, Plant, and Equipment Net of Accumulated Depreciation does not indicate separately the acquisition cost of fixed assets and the portion of that acquisition cost written off as depreciation since acquisition. If the firm used a contra account, it would have such information. The alternative to using contra accounts is to debit or credit directly the principal account involved (for example, Property, Plant, and Equipment). This alternative procedure, however, does not permit computation of disaggregated information about the net balance in the account. Note that the use of contra accounts does not affect the total of assets, or liabilities, or shareholders' equity, but only the balances in various accounts that comprise the totals for these items.

2.7   (Cement Plus; dual effects on balance sheet equation.)   (amounts in millions of US$)

Transaction	Assets	=	Liabilities	+	Shareholders' Equity
(1)	+$14,300				
	−$ 2,300		+$12,000		
(2)	+$ 3,000				
	−$ 3,000				
(3)	+$ 6,500				+$ 6,500
(4)			−$12,000		+$12,000

2.9   (Balance sheet classification.)

a. SE   h. L
b. A   i. A
c. N/A   j. L
d. A   k. L
e. SE   l. A
f. A   m. L
g. A   (if purchased from another firm)   n. SE (contra; subtract)
    N/A (if created by the firm)

2.11   (Inheritance Brands; dual effects of transactions on balance sheet equation and journal entries.) (amounts in millions of US$)

a.

Transaction Number	Assets	=	Liabilities	+	Shareholders' Equity
(1)	+ $ 550			+	+$ 550
Subtotal	$ 550	=			$ 550
	− 400				
(2)	+ 1,150		+ $ 750		
Subtotal	$ 1,300	=	$ 750	+	$ 550
(3)	− 30				
	+ 30				
Subtotal	$ 1,300	=	$ 750	+	$ 550
(4)	+ 400	=	+ 400		
Subtotal	$ 1,700	=	$ 1,150	+	$ 550
(5)	− 400		− 400		
Total	$ 1,300	=	$ 750	+	$ 550

2.11 continued.

b. (1) Cash.. 550.0

        Common Stock 31.25

        Additional Paid-In Capital......................... 518.75

Assets	=	Liabilities	+	Shareholders' Equity	(Class.)
+550.0				+31.25	ContriCap
				+518.75	ContriCap

Issue 10 million shares of $3.125 par value common stock for $55 per share.

(2) Land.. 250

    Building.. 900

        Cash... 400

        Notes Payable 750

Assets	=	Liabilities	+	Shareholders' Equity	(Class.)
+250		+750			
+900					
−400					

Gives $400 million in cash and promises to pay the remainder in Year 15 for land costing $250 million and a building costing $900 million.

(3) Prepaid Insurance... 30

        Cash... 30

Assets	=	Liabilities	+	Shareholders' Equity	(Class.)
+30					
−30					

Pays $30 million in advance to insurance company for coverage beginning next month.

2.11 b. continued.

(4) Merchandise Inventory 400

Accounts Payable 400

Assets	=	Liabilities	+	Shareholders' Equity	(Class.)
+400		+400			

Purchases merchandise costing $400 million on account.

(5) Accounts Payable 400

Cash.. 400

Assets	=	Liabilities	+	Shareholders' Equity	(Class.)
−400		−400			

Pays cash to suppliers for merchandise on account.

2.13 (Moulton Corporation; recording transactions and preparing a balance sheet.) (amounts in US$)

a. T-accounts.

Cash (A)				Merchandise Inventory (A)				Prepaid Insurance (A)		
(1) 800,000	500,000 (2)		(3) 280,000	5,000 (4)		(5) 12,000		
(6) 300,000	245,000 (4)							
	12,000 (5)							
343,000			275,000			12,000		

Land (A)		Building (A)		Equipment (A)	
(2) 50,000		(2) 450,000		(7) 80,000	
50,000		450,000		80,000	

Accounts Payable (L)		Note Payable (L)		Loan Payable (L)	
(4) 250,000	280,000 (3)		80,000 (7)		300,000 (6)
	30,000		80,000		300,000

2.13 a. continued.

```
            Common Stock (SE)
                      |  800,000  (1)
            _____|_____
                      |
                      |  800,000
```

b.

MOULTON CORPORATION
Balance Sheet
December 31, Year 12

Assets

Current Assets:

Cash	$ 343,000
Merchandise Inventories	275,000
Prepaid Insurance	12,000
Total Current Assets	$ 630,000

Noncurrent Assets:

Land	$ 50,000
Building	450,000
Equipment	80,000
Total Noncurrent Assets	$ 580,000
Total Assets	$1,210,000

Liabilities and Shareholders' Equity

Current Liabilities:

Accounts Payable	$ 30,000
Note Payable	80,000
Total Current Liabilities	$ 110,000

Noncurrent Liabilities:

Loan Payable	$ 300,000
Total Liabilities	$ 410,000

Shareholders' Equity:

Common Stock	$ 800,000
Retained Earnings	0
Total Shareholders' Equity	$ 800,000
Total Liabilities and Shareholders' Equity	$1,210,000

2.15   (Regaldo Department Store; recording transactions in T-accounts and preparing a balance sheet.) (amounts in thousands of Mexican pesos [$])

a. T-accounts.

Cash (A)				Merchandise Inventory (A)				Prepaid Rent (A)	
(1) 500,000	20,000	(2)	(5) 200,000		8,000	(6)	(4) 60,000	
	4,000	(2)			3,200	(7)		
	60,000	(4)						
	156,800	(7)						
	12,000	(8)						
247,200			188,800				60,000	

Prepaid Insurance (A)		Patent (A)			Accounts Payable (L)			
(8) 12,000		(2) 20,000		(6)	8,000	200,000	(5)	
		(2) 4,000		(7)	160,000			
12,000		24,000				32,000		

Common Stock (SE)	
	500,000 (1)
	500,000

2.15 continued.

b.   **REGALDO DEPARTMENT STORES**
                          Balance Sheet
                        January 31, Year 8

Assets

Current Assets:
  Cash .... $ 247,200
  Merchandise Inventory 188,800
  Prepaid Rent.. 60,000
  Prepaid Insurance... 12,000
    Total Current Assets... $ 508,000
  Patent... 24,000
    Total Assets.. $ 532,000

Liabilities and Shareholders' Equity

Current Liabilities:
  Accounts Payable... $ 32,000
    Total Current Liabilities .... $ 32,000
Shareholders' Equity:
  Common Stock.. $ 500,000
  Retained Earnings.. 0
    Total Shareholders' Equity .... $ 500,000
    Total Liabilities and Shareholders' Equity.............. $ 532,000

2.17   (Effect of recording errors on the balance sheet equation.)   (amounts in
       US$)

Transaction Number	Assets	=	Liabilities	+	Shareholders' Equity
(1)	No		No		No
(2)	O/S $ 9,000		O/S $ 9,000		No
(3)	U/S $16,000		U/S $16,000		No
(4)	No[a]		No		No
(5)	U/S $ 1,500		U/S $ 1,500		No
(6)	U/S $12,000		No		U/S $12,000
(7)	No		No		No

[a]Also acceptable to show both O/S and U/S by $1,800, as one asset is
overstated and another, understated.

This page is intentionally left blank

CHAPTER 3

THE BASICS OF RECORD KEEPING AND
FINANCIAL STATEMENT PREPARATION: INCOME STATEMENT

Questions, Exercises, and Problems: Answers and Solutions

3.1   See the text or the glossary at the end of the book.

3.3   The balance sheet and the income statement are linked (that is, they articulate) through the shareholders' equity account, Retained Earnings. Retained Earnings measures the cumulative excess of net income over dividends for the life of a firm; all undistributed earnings are aggregated in Retained Earnings. The following equation describes the articulation of the Retained Earnings:

Retained Earnings (beginning) + Net Income – Dividends = Retained Earnings (end).

3.5   An adjusting entry is used to record the effects of an event or transaction that was not previously recorded. Many adjusting entries result from the effects of the passage of time, for example, interest accrues on amounts owed over time. The accrual of interest at the end of an accounting period is an example of an adjusting entry. A correcting entry is a special case of an adjusting entry. A correcting entry is used to record properly the effects of an event or transaction that was improperly recorded during the accounting period.

3.7   (BigWing Company; analyzing changes in inventory.) (amounts in millions of US$)

Inventory, Beginning of Year 7	$ 8,105
Plus Purchases or Production of Inventory during Year 7	?
Less Cost of Goods Sold for Year 7	(45,375)
Inventory, End of Year 7	$ 9,563

Purchases or production of inventory during Year 7 total $46,833 million.

3.9 (Conima Corporation; analyzing changes in income taxes payable.) (amounts in millions of yen)

Income Taxes Payable, Beginning of Year 7	¥ 3,736
Plus Income Tax Expense for Year 7 (0.43 × ¥73,051)	31,412
Less Income Taxes Paid during Year 7	(?)
Income Taxes Payable, End of Year 7	¥ 14,310

Income taxes paid during Year 7 total ¥20,838 million.

3.11 (Bayer Group; relations between financial statements.) (amounts in millions of euros)

a. €5,868 + €32,385 − €5,830 = a; a = €32,423.

b. €109 + b − €763 = €56; b = €710.

c. €14,723 − c + €2,155 = €12,911; c = €3,967.

d. €6,782 + €4,711 − d = €10,749; d = €744.

3.13 (Journal entries for inventories and accounts payable.) (amounts in millions of yen)

Merchandise Inventories	1,456,412
Accounts Payable	1,456,412

Assets	=	Liabilities	+	Shareholders' Equity	(Class.)
+1,456,412		+1,456,412			

Cost of Goods Sold (= ¥408,710 + ¥1,456,412 − ¥412,387) 1,452,735

Merchandise Inventories 1,452,735

Assets	=	Liabilities	+	Shareholders' Equity	(Class.)
−1,452,735				−1,452,735	IncSt → RE

3.13 continued.

Accounts Payable (= ¥757,006 + $1,456,412 −
   ¥824,825).. 1,388,593
      Cash.. 1,388,593

Assets	=	Liabilities	+	Shareholders' Equity	(Class.)
−1,388,593		−1,388,593			

3.15   (EBB Group; journal entries for prepaid rent.)   (amounts in millions of US$)

a.   **Journal Entries for January, Year 7:**
     January 31, Year 7
     Rent Expense 247
        Prepaid Rent.. 247

Assets	=	Liabilities	+	Shareholders' Equity	(Class.)
−247				−247	IncSt → RE

To record the adjusting entry for the consumption of the prepaid portion of rent expense for the month of January.

January 31, Year 7
Prepaid Rent... 3,200
   Cash 3,200

Assets	=	Liabilities	+	Shareholders' Equity	(Class.)
+3,200					
−3,200					

To record the prepayment of rent for the next 12 months.

3.15 continued.

b. **Journal Entry in December, Year 7:**
December 31, Year 7

Rent Expense 2,933
    Prepaid Rent.. 2,933

Assets	=	Liabilities	+	Shareholders' Equity	(Class.)
−2,933				−2,933	IncSt → RE

To record the adjusting entry for the consumption of the prepaid portion of rent expense for the months of February through December.

Amount of Prepaid Rent consumed = [($3,200/12 months) X 11 months] = $2,933 million.

3.17   (JCM; journal entries related to the income statement.)   (amounts in billions of yen)

Year 7

Accounts Receivable 22,670
    Revenues.. 22,670

Assets	=	Liabilities	+	Shareholders' Equity	(Class.)
+22,670				+22,670	IncSt → RE

To record product sales on account.

Cost of Goods Sold... 18,356
    Inventories 18,356

Assets	=	Liabilities	+	Shareholders' Equity	(Class.)
−18,356				−18,356	IncSt → RE

To record the cost of sales.

3.17 continued.

Cash 22,670
    Accounts Receivable 22,670

Assets	=	Liabilities	+	Shareholders' Equity	(Class.)
–22,670					
+22,670					

To record the cash collected on sales made on account.

3.19   (Bostick Enterprises; journal entries to correct recording error.) (amounts in millions of US$)

Entry Made:

Equipment Expense 120,000
    Cash 120,000

Assets	=	Liabilities	+	Shareholders' Equity	(Class.)
–120,000				–120,000	IncSt → RE

Correct Entries:

Equipment 120,000
    Cash 120,000

Assets	=	Liabilities	+	Shareholders' Equity	(Class.)
–120,000					
+120,000					

Depreciation Expense (= $120,000/10) 12,000
    Accumulated Depreciation 12,000

Assets	=	Liabilities	+	Shareholders' Equity	(Class.)
–12,000				–12,000	IncSt → RE

3-5   **Odd-numbered Solutions**

3.19 continued.

Correcting Entry:

Equipment	120,000	
Depreciation Expense	12,000	
Equipment Expense		120,000
Accumulated Depreciation		12,000

Assets	=	Liabilities	+	Shareholders' Equity	(Class.)
+120,000				+120,000	IncSt → RE
−12,000				−12,000	IncSt → RE

3.21 (COC; preparing a balance sheet and an income statement.) (amounts in millions of US$)

a.

China Oil Company
Income Statement
For the Year Ended December 31, Year 8

Revenues:	
Net Operating Revenues	$ 835,037
Interest and Other Revenues	3,098
Total Revenues	$ 838,135
Less Expenses:	
Cost of Sales	$ (487,112)
Selling Expenses	(41,345)
General and Administrative Expenses	(49,324)
Other Operating Expenses	(64,600)
Interest Expense	(2,869)
Income Taxes	(49,331)
Total Expenses	$ (694,581)
Net Income	$ 143,554

3.21 continued.

b.

China Oil Company
Comparative Balance Sheet

	Dec 31, Year 8	Dec. 31, Year 7
Assets		
Noncurrent Assets:		
Intangible Assets	$ 20,022	$ 16,127
Oil and Gas Properties	326,328	270,496
Property, Plant, and Equipment—Net	247,803	231,590
Other Noncurrent Assets	163,711	132,214
Total Noncurrent Assets	$ 757,864	$ 650,427
Current Assets:		
Inventories	$ 88,467	$ 76,038
Other Current Assets	20,367	13,457
Advances to Suppliers	20,386	12,664
Accounts Receivable	18,419	8,488
Cash	88,589	54,070
Total Current Assets	$ 236,228	$ 164,717
Total Assets	$ 994,092	$ 815,144
Liabilities and Shareholders' Equity		
Noncurrent Liabilities:		
Long-Term Debt	$ 35,305	$ 30,401
Other Noncurrent Liabilities	42,062	36,683
Total Noncurrent Liabilities	$ 77,367	$ 67,084
Current Liabilities:		
Advances from Customers	$ 12,433	$ 11,590
Other Current Liabilities	84,761	90,939
Accounts Payable to Suppliers	104,460	77,936
Total Current Liabilities	$ 201,654	$ 180,465
Shareholders' Equity:		
Common Stock	$ 444,527	$ 354,340
Retained Earnings	270,544	213,255
Total Shareholders' Equity	$ 715,071	$ 567,595
Total Liabilities and Shareholders' Equity	$ 994,092	$ 815,144

3.21 continued.

   c.   Retained Earnings, December 31, Year 7 .... $ 213,255
       Plus Net Income for Year Ending December 31, Year 8......... 143,554
       Subtract Dividends for Year Ending December 31, Year 8
          (Plug) .... (86,265)
       Retained Earnings, December 31, Year 8 .... $ 270,544

3.23   (Patterson Corporation; analysis of transactions and preparation of income statement and balance sheet.) (amounts in US$)

    a.   T-accounts.

	Cash (A)					Marketable Securities (A)		
√	47,150				√	95,000		
(6)	1,206,000	2,400	(1)					
		235,000	(5)					
		710,000	(7)					
√	305,750				√	95,000		

	Accounts Receivable (A)					Receivable from Supplier (A)		
√	0				√	1,455		
(3)	1,495,500	1,206,000	(6)				1,455	(2)
√	289,500				√	0		

	Merchandise Inventory (A)					Prepaid Rent (A)		
√	70,945				√	1,400		
(2)	1,050,000	950,000	(4)				1,400	(8)
√	170,945				√	0		

	Prepaid Insurance (A)					Land (A)		
√	0				√	80,000		
(1)	2,400	100	(11)					
√	2,300				√	80,000		

3.23 a. continued.

Building (A)			Equipment (A)	
√	280,000		√	97,750
√	280,000		√	97,750

Accumulated Depreciation (XA)			Patent (A)	
	0	√	√	28,000
	2,500	(9)		450 (10)
	2,500	√	√	27,550

Accounts Payable (L)			Advance from Customer (L)	
	14,200	√		4,500 √
(7) 710,000	1,048,545	(2)	(3) 4,500	
	352,745	√		0 √

Interest Payable (L)			Income Tax Payable (L)	
	0	√		0 √
	265	(12)		124,114 (13)
	265	√		124,114 √

Mortgage Payable (L)			Common Stock (SE)	
	53,000	√		450,000 √
	53,000	√		450,000 √

Additional Paid-in Capital (SE)			Retained Earnings (SE)	
	180,000	√		0 √
				186,171 (14)
	180,000	√		186,171 √

3-9

3.23 a. continued.

Sales Revenue (SE)					Cost-of-Goods Sold (SE)		
(14)	1,500,000	1,500,000	(3)	(4)	950,000	950,000	(14)

Selling and Administrative Expense (SE)					Rent Expense (SE)		
(5)	235,000	235,000	(14)	(8)	1,400	1,400	(14)

Depreciation Expense (SE)					Amortization Expense (SE)		
(9)	2,500	2,500	(14)	(10)	450	450	(14)

Insurance Expense (SE)					Interest Expense (SE)		
(11)	100	100	(14)	(12)	265	265	(14)

Income Tax Expense (SE)			
(13)	124,114	124,114	(14)

3.23 continued.

b.

PATTERSON CORPORATION
Income Statement
For the Month of February, Year 13

Sales Revenue	$ 1,500,000
Expenses:	
Cost of Goods Sold	$ 950,000
Selling and Administrative Expenses	235,000
Rent	1,400
Depreciation	2,500
Amortization	450
Insurance	100
Interest	265
Total Expenses	$ 1,189,715
Net Income before Income Taxes	$ 310,285
Income Tax Expense at 40%	(124,114)
Net Income	$ 186,171

c.

PATTERSON CORPORATION
Comparative Balance Sheet

	January 31, Year 13	February 28, Year 13
Assets		
Cash	$ 47,150	$ 305,750
Marketable Securities	95,000	95,000
Accounts Receivable	0	289,500
Receivable from Supplier	1,455	0
Merchandise Inventories	70,945	170,945
Prepaid Rent	1,400	0
Prepaid Insurance	0	2,300
Total Current Assets	$ 215,950	$ 863,495
Land (at Cost)	$ 80,000	$ 80,000
Building (at Cost)	280,000	280,000
Equipment (at Cost)	97,750	$ 97,750
Less Accumulated Depreciation	0	(2,500)
Land, Building, and Equipment (Net)	$ 457,750	$ 455,250
Patent (Net)	28,000	27,550
Total Noncurrent Assets	$ 485,750	$ 482,800
Total Assets	$ 701,700	$1,346,295

3.23 c. continued.

Liabilities and Shareholders' Equity

Accounts Payable..	$ 14,200	$ 352,745
Advance from Customers	4,500	0
Interest Payable...	0	265
Income Tax Payable.....................................	0	124,114
Total Current Liabilities........................	$ 18,700	$ 477,124
Mortgage Payable...	53,000	53,000
Total Liabilities......................................	$ 71,700	$ 530,124
Common Stock...	$ 450,000	$ 450,000
Additional Paid-In Capital	180,000	180,000
Retained Earnings..	0	186,171
Total Shareholders' Equity.....................	$ 630,000	$ 816,171
Total Liabilities and Shareholders' Equity...	$ 701,700	$1,346,295

3.25 (Rybowiak's Building Supplies; journal entries, adjusting entries, income statement, and balance sheet preparation.) (amounts in US$)

a. (1) Accounts Receivable 85,000

            Sales Revenue... 85,000

Assets	=	Liabilities	+	Shareholders' Equity	(Class.)
+85,000				+85,000	IncSt → RE

Sales of merchandise on account.

(2) Merchandise Inventory 46,300

            Accounts Payable... 46,300

Assets	=	Liabilities	+	Shareholders' Equity	(Class.)
+46,300		+46,300			

Purchase of merchandise inventory on account.

3.25 a. continued.

(3)   Rent Expense 11,750

        Cash   11,750

Assets	=	Liabilities	+	Shareholders' Equity	(Class.)
−11,750				−11,750	IncSt → RE

Paid rent for July.

(4)   Salaries Payable... 1,250

        Salary Expense 19,350

              Cash   20,600

Assets	=	Liabilities	+	Shareholders' Equity	(Class.)
−20,600		−1,250		−19,350	IncSt → RE

Paid salaries during July.

(5)   Cash 34,150

        Accounts Receivable   34,150

Assets	=	Liabilities	+	Shareholders' Equity	(Class.)
+34,150					
−34,150					

Collected accounts receivable.

(6)   Accounts Payable... 38,950

        Cash   38,950

Assets	=	Liabilities	+	Shareholders' Equity	(Class.)
−38,950		−38,950			

Paid accounts payable.

         Odd-numbered Solutions

3.25 a. continued.

(7) Insurance Expense 50
      Prepaid Insurance...   50

Assets	=	Liabilities	+	Shareholders' Equity	(Class.)
−50				−50	IncSt → RE

Recognize insurance expense for July. $50 = $400/8.
The Prepaid Insurance account has a balance of $400
on June 30, Year 12. Because the firm paid the one-
year insurance premium on March 1, Year 12, we
know that the policy has eight remaining months on
June 30, Year 12.

(8) Depreciation Expense 1,750
      Accumulated Depreciation   1,750

Assets	=	Liabilities	+	Shareholders' Equity	(Class.)
−1,750				−1,750	IncSt → RE

Recognize depreciation for July: $1,750 = $210,000/
120.

(9) Salary Expense 1,600
      Salaries Payable...   1,600

Assets	=	Liabilities	+	Shareholders' Equity	(Class.)
		+1,600		−1,600	IncSt → RE

Recognize unpaid salaries for July.

(10) Interest Expense 25
      Interest Payable   25

Assets	=	Liabilities	+	Shareholders' Equity	(Class.)
		+25		−25	IncSt → RE

Recognize unpaid interest for July: $25 = $5,000 × 0.06
× 30/360.

3.25 a. continued.

(11) Cost of Goods Sold.. 36,500
      Merchandise Inventory.............................. 36,500

Assets	=	Liabilities	+	Shareholders' Equity	(Class.)
−36,500				−36,500	IncSt → RE

To recognize cost of goods sold for July: $36,500 = $68,150 + $46,300 − $77,950.

b. and d.

T-accounts for Rybowiak Building Suppliers

	Cash		
Bal.	44,200	11,750	(3)
(5)	34,150	20,600	(4)
		38,950	(6)
Bal.	7,050		

	Accounts Receivable		
Bal.	27,250	34,150	(5)
(1)	85,000		
Bal.	78,100		

	Merchandise Inventory		
Bal.	68,150	36,500	(11)
(2)	46,300		
Bal.	77,950		

	Prepaid Insurance		
Bal.	400	50	(7)
Bal.	350		

	Equipment	
Bal.	210,000	
Bal.	210,000	

	Accumulated Depreciation	
	84,000	Bal.
	1,750	(8)
	85,750	Bal.

	Accounts Payable		
		33,100	Bal.
(6)	38,950	46,300	(2)
		40,450	Bal.

	Note Payable	
	5,000	Bal.
	5,000	Bal.

	Salaries Payable		
(4)	1,250	1,250	Bal.
		1,600	(9)
		1,600	Bal.

	Common Stock	
	150,000	Bal.
	150,000	Bal.

3.25 b. and d. continued.

	Retained Earnings				Sales Revenue		
		76,650	Bal.	(12)	85,000	85,000	(1)
		13,975	(12)				
		90,625	Bal.				

	Rent Expense				Salaries Expense		
(3)	11,750	11,750	(12)	(4)	19,350		
				(9)	1,600	20,950	(12)
					20,950		

	Insurance Expense				Depreciation Expense		
(7)	50	50	(12)	(8)	1,750	1,750	(12)

	Interest Expense				Interest Payable		
(10)	25	25	(12)			25	(11)
						25 Bal.	

	Cost of Goods Sold		
(11)	36,500	36,500	(12)

c.

RYBOWIAK'S BUILDING SUPPLIES
Income Statement
For the Month of July, Year 12

Sales Revenue		$ 85,000
Less Expenses:		
Cost of Goods Sold	$ 36,500	
Salaries Expense (= $19,350 + $1,600)	20,950	
Rent Expense	11,750	
Depreciation Expense	1,750	
Insurance Expense	50	
Interest Expense	25	(71,025)
Net Income		$ 13,975

3.25 continued.

e.

RYBOWIAK'S BUILDING SUPPLIES
Balance Sheet
June 30 and July 31, Year 12

	June 30	July 31
Assets		
Current Assets:		
Cash	$ 44,200	$ 7,050
Accounts Receivable	27,250	78,100
Merchandise Inventory	68,150	77,950
Prepaid Insurance	400	350
Total Current Assets	$ 140,000	$ 163,450
Noncurrent Assets:		
Equipment—at Cost	$ 210,000	$ 210,000
Less Accumulated Depreciation	(84,000)	(85,750)
Total Noncurrent Assets	126,000	$ 124,250
Total Assets	$ 266,000	$ 287,700
Liabilities and Shareholders' Equity		
Current Liabilities:		
Accounts Payable	$ 33,100	$ 40,450
Note Payable	5,000	5,000
Salaries Payable	1,250	1,600
Interest Payable	--	25
Total Current Liabilities	$ 39,350	$ 47,075
Shareholders' Equity:		
Common Stock	$ 150,000	$ 150,000
Retained Earnings	76,650	90,625
Total Shareholders' Equity	$ 226,650	$ 240,625
Total Liabilities and Shareholders' Equity	$ 266,000	$ 287,700

3.27 (Regaldo Department Stores; analysis of transactions and preparation of income statement and balance sheet.) (amounts in US$)

a. T-accounts.

	Cash (A)		
√	247,200		
(3a)	62,900	32,400	(4)
(6)	84,600	2,700	(5)
		205,800	(7a)
		29,000	(7b)
√	124,800		

	Accounts Receivable (A)		
√	0		
(3a)	194,600	84,600	(6)
√	110,000		

	Inventory (A)		
√	188,800		
(2)	217,900	162,400	(3b)
		4,200	(7a)
√	240,100		

	Prepaid Rent (A)		
√	60,000		
		30,000	(11)
√	30,000		

	Prepaid Insurance (A)		
√	12,000	1,000	(12)
√	11,000		

	Equipment (A)		
√	0		
(1)	90,000		
√	90,000		

	Accumulated Depreciation (XA)		
		0	√
		1,500	(10)
		1,500	√

	Patent (A)		
√	24,000		
		400	(13)
√	23,600		

	Accounts Payable (L)		
		32,000	√
(7a)	210,000	217,900	(2)
(7b)	29,000		
		10,900	√

	Note Payable (L)		
		0	√
		90,000	(1)
		90,000	√

3.27 a. continued.

Compensation Payable (L)			Utilities Payable (L)		
	0	√		0	√
	6,700	(8)		800	(9)
	6,700	√		800	√

Interest Payable (L)			Income Tax Payable (L)		
	0	√		0	√
	900	(14)		5,610	(15)
	900	√		5,610	√

Common Stock (SE)			Retained Earnings (SE)		
	500,000	√		0	√
				13,090	(16)
	500,000	√		13,090	√

Sales Revenue (SE)			Cost of Goods Sold (SE)		
(16)	257,500	257,500 (3a)	(3b)	162,400	162,400 (16)

Compensation Expense (SE)			Utilities Expense (SE)		
(4)	32,400		(5)	2,700	
(8)	6,700	39,100 (16)	(9)	800	3,500 (16)

Depreciation Expense (SE)			Rent Expense (SE)		
(10)	1,500	1,500 (16)	(11)	30,000	30,000 (16)

3.27 a. continued.

	Insurance Expense (SE)				Patent Amortization Expense (SE)		
(12)	1,000	1,000	(16)	(13)	400	400	(16)

	Interest Expense (SE)				Income Tax Expense (SE)		
(14)	900	900	(16)	(15)	5,610	5,610	(16)

b.

REGALDO DEPARTMENT STORES
Income Statement
For the Month of February Year 8

Sales Revenue..	$ 257,500
Expenses:	
Cost of Goods Sold	$ 162,400
Compensation (= $32,400 + $6,700)	39,100
Utilities (= $2,700 + $800)	3,500
Depreciation..	1,500
Rent..	30,000
Insurance..	1,000
Patent Amortization	400
Interest..	900
Total Expenses..	$ 238,800
Net Income before Income Taxes..	$ 18,700
Income Tax Expense at 30%...	(5,610)
Net Income	$ 13,090

3.27 continued.

c.

REGALDO DEPARTMENT STORES
Comparative Balance Sheet

	January 31, Year 8	February 28, Year 8
Assets		
Cash	$ 247,200	$ 124,800
Accounts Receivable	0	110,000
Inventories	188,800	240,100
Prepaid Rent	60,000	30,000
Prepaid Insurance	12,000	11,000
Total Current Assets	$ 508,000	$ 515,900
Equipment (at Cost)	$ 0	$ 90,000
Less Accumulated Depreciation	0	(1,500)
Equipment (Net)	$ 0	$ 88,500
Patent	24,000	23,600
Total Noncurrent Assets	$ 24,000	$ 112,100
Total Assets	$ 532,000	$ 628,000
Liabilities and Shareholders' Equity		
Accounts Payable	$ 32,000	$ 10,900
Notes Payable	0	90,000
Compensation Payable	0	6,700
Utilities Payable	0	800
Interest Payable	0	900
Income Tax Payable	0	5,610
Total Liabilities	$ 32,000	$ 114,910
Common Stock	$ 500,000	$ 500,000
Retained Earnings	0	13,090
Total Shareholders' Equity	$ 500,000	$ 513,090
Total Liabilities and Shareholders' Equity	$ 532,000	$ 628,000

3.29   (Zealock Bookstore; analysis of transactions and preparation of comparative income statements and balance sheet.) (amounts in US$)

a.   T-accounts.

Cash (A)			
√	24,350		
(3)	75,000	1,320	(1)
(4)	8,000	31,800	(2)
(7)	24,900	20,000	(5)
(9)	320,600	29,400	(10)
		281,100	(11)
		4,000	(12)
√	85,230		

Accounts Receivable (A)			
√	5,800		
(7)	327,950	320,600	(9)
√	13,150		

Merchandise Inventory (A)			
√	5,400		
(6)	310,000	286,400	(7)
		22,700	(8)
√	6,300		

Prepaid Rent (A)			
√	10,000		
(5)	20,000	20,000	(13)
√	10,000		

Deposit with Suppliers (A)			
√	8,000		
		8,000	(4)
√	0		

Equipment (A)		
√	14,000	
√	14,000	

Accumulated Depreciation (XA)			
		1,900	√
		800	(14)
		3,000	(15)
		5,700	√

Note Payable (L)			
		30,000	√
(2)	30,000	75,000	(3)
		75,000	√

Accounts Payable (L)			
		5,600	√
(8)	22,700	310,000	(6)
(11)	281,100		
		11,800	√

Advance from Customers (L)			
		850	√
(7)	850		
		0	√

3.29 a. continued.

Interest Payable (L)					Income Tax Payable (L)			
		900	√				1,320	√
(2)	900	3,000	(16)	(1)	1,320		4,080	(17)
		3,000	√				4,080	√

Common Stock (SE)					Retained Earnings (SE)			
		25,000	√				1,980	√
				(12)	4,000		6,120	(18)
		25,000	√				4,100	√

Sales Revenue (SE)					Cost of Goods Sold (SE)			
(18)	353,700	353,700	(7)	(7)	286,400	286,400	(18)

Compensation Expense (SE)					Interest Expense (SE)			
(10)	29,400	29,400	(18)	(2)	900		
				(16)	3,000	3,900	(18)

Rent Expense (SE)					Depreciation Expense (SE)			
(13)	20,000	20,000	(18)	(14)	800		
				(15)	3,000	3,800	(18)

Income Tax Expense (SE)			
(17)	4,080	4,080	(18)

3.29 continued.

b.
ZEALOCK BOOKSTORE
Comparative Income Statement
For Year 5 and Year 4

	Year 5	Year 4
Sales Revenue	$ 353,700	$ 172,800
Less Expenses:		
Cost of Goods Sold	$ 286,400	$ 140,000
Compensation Expense	29,400	16,700
Interest Expense	3,900	900
Rent Expense	20,000	10,000
Depreciation Expense	3,800	1,900
Income Tax Expense	4,080	1,320
Total Expenses	$ 347,580	$ 170,820
Net Income	$ 6,120	$ 1,980

c.
ZEALOCK BOOKSTORE
Comparative Balance Sheet
December 31, Year 5 and Year 4

	Year 5	Year 4
Assets		
Current Assets:		
Cash	$ 85,230	$ 24,350
Accounts Receivable	13,150	5,800
Merchandise Inventories	6,300	5,400
Prepaid Rent	10,000	10,000
Deposit with Suppliers	—	8,000
Total Current Assets	$ 114,680	$ 53,550
Noncurrent Assets:		
Equipment	$ 14,000	$ 14,000
Less Accumulated Depreciation	(5,700)	(1,900)
Equipment (Net)	$ 8,300	$ 12,100
Total Assets	$ 122,980	$ 65,650

3.29 c. continued.

Liabilities and Shareholders' Equity

Current Liabilities:

Accounts Payable..	$ 11,800	$ 5,600
Note Payable...	75,000	30,000
Advances from Customers	—	850
Interest Payable...	3,000	900
Income Tax Payable...................................	4,080	1,320
Total Current Liabilities	$ 93,880	$ 38,670
Shareholders' Equity:		
Common Stock..	$ 25,000	$ 25,000
Retained Earnings.....................................	4,100	1,980
Total Shareholders' Equity	$ 29,100	$ 26,980
Total Liabilities and Shareholders'		
Equity..	$122,980	$ 65,650

3.31 (Computer Needs, Inc.; reconstructing the income statement and balance sheet.) (amounts in US$)

T-accounts.

Cash					Accounts Receivable			
√	15,600				√	32,100		
(1)	37,500	164,600	(4)		(3)	159,700	151,500	(2)
(2)	151,500	21,000	(7)					
		3,388	(8)					
		4,800	(9)					
		6,000	(10)					
√	4,812				√	40,300		

Inventory					Prepayments			
√	46,700				√	1,500		
(5)	172,100	158,100	(6)		(7)	300		
√	60,700				√	1,800		

3.31 continued.

Property, Plant, and Equipment			Accumulated Depreciation		
√	59,700			2,800	√
(10)	6,000			3,300	(11)
√	65,700			6,100	√

Accounts Payable—Merchandise			Income Tax Payable		
		37,800 √			3,388 √
(4)	164,600	172,100 (5)	(8)	3,388	3,584 (12)
		45,300 √			3,584 √

Other Current Liabilities			Mortgage Payable		
		2,900 √			50,000 √
(7)	1,700		(9)	800	
		1,200 √			49,200 √

Common Stock			Retained Earnings		
		50,000 √			8,712 √
					9,216 (13)
		50,000 √			17,928 √

Sales			Cost of Goods Sold		
		37,500 (1)	(6)	158,100	158,100 (13)
(13)	197,200	159,700 (3)			

Selling and Administrative Expense			Depreciation Expense		
(7)	19,000	19,000 (13)	(11)	3,300	3,300 (13)

3.31 continued.

	Interest Expense				Income Tax Expense	
(9)	4,000	4,000	(13)	(12)	3,584	3,584	(13)

COMPUTER NEEDS, INC.
Income Statement
For the Years Ended December 31, Year 8 and Year 7

	Year 8	Year 7
Sales	$ 197,200	$ 152,700
Cost of Goods Sold	(158,100)	(116,400)
Selling and Administrative Expense	(19,000)	(17,400)
Depreciation Expense	(3,300)	(2,800)
Interest Expense	(4,000)	(4,000)
Income Taxes	(3,584)	(3,388)
Net Income	$ 9,216	$ 8,712

COMPUTER NEEDS, INC.
Balance Sheet
For the Years Ended December 31, Year 8 and Year 7

	Year 8	Year 7
Assets		
Cash	$ 4,812	$ 15,600
Accounts Receivable	40,300	32,100
Inventories	60,700	46,700
Prepayments	1,800	1,500
Total Current Assets	$ 107,612	$ 95,900
Property, Plant, and Equipment:		
At Cost	$ 65,700	$ 59,700
Less Accumulated Depreciation	(6,100)	(2,800)
Net	$ 59,600	$ 56,900
Total Assets	$ 167,212	$ 152,800

3.31 continued.

Liabilities and Shareholders' Equity

Accounts Payable—Merchandise	$ 45,300	$ 37,800
Income Tax Payable	3,584	3,388
Other Current Liabilities	1,200	2,900
Total Current Liabilities	$ 50,084	$ 44,088
Mortgage Payable	49,200	50,000
Total Liabilities	$ 99,284	$ 94,088
Common Stock	$ 50,000	$ 50,000
Retained Earnings	17,928	8,712
Total Shareholders' Equity	$ 67,928	$ 58,712
Total Liabilities and Shareholders' Equity	$167,212	$152,800

3.33 (Forgetful Corporation; effect of recording errors on financial statements.) (amounts in US$)

Note: The actual and correct entries appear below to show the effect and amount of the errors, but are not required.

a. **Actual Entry:**

Cash	1,400	
Sales Revenue		1,400

Assets	=	Liabilities	+	Shareholders' Equity	(Class.)
+1,400				+1,400	IncSt → RE

Correct Entry:

Cash	1,400	
Advance from Customer		1,400

Assets	=	Liabilities	+	Shareholders' Equity	(Class.)
+1,400		+1,400			

Liabilities understated by $1,400 and shareholders' equity overstated by $1,400.

3.33 continued.

b. **Actual Entry:**

Cost of Goods Sold 5,000

    Cash 5,000

Assets	=	Liabilities	+	Shareholders' Equity	(Class.)
−5,000				−5,000	IncSt → RE

Correct Entries:

Machine 5,000

    Cash 5,000

Assets	=	Liabilities	+	Shareholders' Equity	(Class.)
+5,000					
−5,000					

Depreciation Expense 500

    Accumulated Depreciation 500

Assets	=	Liabilities	+	Shareholders' Equity	(Class.)
−500				−500	IncSt → RE

Assets understated by $4,500 and shareholders' equity understated by $4,500.

c. **Actual Entry:**

None for accrued interest.

3.33 c. continued.

Correct Entry:

Interest Receivable (= \$2,000 X 0.12 X 60/360) 40

    Interest Revenue 40

Assets	=	Liabilities	+	Shareholders' Equity	(Class.)
+40				+40	IncSt → RE

Assets understated by \$40 and shareholders' equity understated by \$40.

d.   The entry is correct as recorded.

e. **Actual Entry:**

None for declared dividend.

Correct Entry:

Retained Earnings 1,500

    Dividend Payable 1,500

Assets	=	Liabilities	+	Shareholders' Equity	(Class.)
		+1,500		−1,500	Dividend

Liabilities understated by \$1,500 and shareholders' equity overstated by \$1,500.

f. **Actual Entries:**

Machinery 50,000

    Accounts Payable 50,000

Assets	=	Liabilities	+	Shareholders' Equity	(Class.)
+50,000		+50,000			

3.33 f. continued.

Accounts Payable	50,000	
Cash		49,000
Miscellaneous Revenue		1,000

Assets	=	Liabilities	+	Shareholders' Equity	(Class.)
−49,000		−50,000		+1,000	IncSt → RE

| Maintenance Expense | 4,000 | |
| Cash | | 4,000 |

Assets	=	Liabilities	+	Shareholders' Equity	(Class.)
−4,000				−4,000	IncSt → RE

Correct Entries:

| Machinery | 50,000 | |
| Accounts Payable | | 50,000 |

Assets	=	Liabilities	+	Shareholders' Equity	(Class.)
+50,000		+50,000			

Accounts Payable	50,000	
Cash		49,000
Machinery		1,000

Assets	=	Liabilities	+	Shareholders' Equity	(Class.)
−49,000		−50,000			
−1,000					

| Machinery | 4,000 | |
| Cash | | 4,000 |

Assets	=	Liabilities	+	Shareholders' Equity	(Class.)
+4,000					
−4,000					

Assets understated by $3,000 and shareholders' equity understated by $3,000.

3.35 (The Secunda Company; working backward to cash receipts and disbursements.) (amounts in US$)

A T-account method for deriving the solution appears below and on the following page. After Entry (6), we have explained all revenue and expense account changes. Plugging for the unknown amounts determines the remaining, unexplained changes in balance sheet accounts. A "p" next to the entry number designates these entries. Note that the revenue and expense accounts are not yet closed to retained earnings, so dividends account for the decrease in the Retained Earnings account during the year of $10,000.

	Cash					Accounts Receivable			
Bal.	20,000				Bal.	36,000			
(7)	85,000				(1)	100,000	85,000	(7p)	
		2,000	(9)						
		81,000	(10)						
		3,000	(11)						
		10,000	(12)						
Bal.	9,000				Bal.	51,000			

	Merchandise Inventory					Prepayments			
Bal.	45,000				Bal.	2,000			
(8p)	65,000	50,000	(2)				1,000	(5)	
Bal.	60,000				Bal.	1,000			

	Land, Buildings, and Equipment				Cost of Goods Sold		
Bal.	40,000			Bal.	0		
				(2)	50,000		
Bal.	40,000			Bal.	50,000		

	Interest Expense				Other Operating Expenses		
Bal.	0			Bal.	0		
(3)	3,000			(4)	2,000		
				(5)	1,000		
				(6p)	26,000		
Bal.	3,000			Bal.	29,000		

3.35 continued.

Accumulated Depreciation				Interest Payable		
	16,000	Bal.			1,000	Bal.
	2,000	(4)	(9p)	2,000	3,000	(3)
	18,000	Bal.			2,000	Bal.

Accounts Payable				Mortgage Payable		
	30,000	Bal.			20,000	Bal.
(10p) 81,000	26,000	(6)	(11p)	3,000		
	65,000	(8)				
	40,000	Bal.			17,000	Bal.

Common Stock				Retained Earnings		
	50,000	Bal.			26,000	Bal.
			(12p)	10,000		
	50,000	Bal.			16,000	Bal.

Sales		
	0	Bal.
	100,000	(1)
	100,000	Bal.

SECUNDA COMPANY
Cash Receipts and Disbursements Schedule

Receipts:		
Collections from Customers..........................		$ 85,000
Disbursements:		
Suppliers of Merchandise and Other		
Services	$81,000	
Mortgage...	3,000	
Dividends	10,000	
Interest...	2,000	
Total Disbursements...............................		96,000
Change (Decrease) in Cash		$(11,000)
Cash Balance, December 31, Year 7....................		20,000
Cash Balance, December 31, Year 8....................		$ 9,000

3.37   (Preparing adjusting entries.) (amounts in US$)

a. The Prepaid Rent account on the year-end balance sheet should represent eight months of prepayments. The rent per month is $2,000 (= $24,000/12), so the balance required in the Prepaid Rent account is $16,000 (= 8 × $2,000). Rent Expense for Year 6 is $8,000 (= 4 × $2,000 = $24,000 – $16,000).

Prepaid Rent.. 16,000
    Rent Expense   16,000

Assets	=	Liabilities	+	Shareholders' Equity	(Class.)
+16,000				+16,000	IncSt → RE

To increase the balance in the Prepaid Rent account, reducing the amount in the Rent Expense account.

b. The Prepaid Rent account on the balance sheet for the end of Year 7 should represent eight months of prepayments. The rent per month is $2,500 (= $30,000/12), so the required balance in the Prepaid Rent account is $20,000 (= 8 × $2,500). The balance in that account is already $16,000, so the adjusting entry must increase it by $4,000 (= $20,000 – $16,000).

Prepaid Rent.. 4,000
    Rent Expense   4,000

Assets	=	Liabilities	+	Shareholders' Equity	(Class.)
+4,000				+4,000	IncSt → RE

To increase the balance in the Prepaid Rent account, reducing the amount in the Rent Expense account.

The Rent Expense account will have a balance at the end of Year 7 before closing entries of $26,000 (= $30,000 – $4,000). This amount comprises $16,000 (= $2,000 × 8) for rent from January through August and $10,000 (= $2,500 × 4) for rent from September through December.

3.37 continued.

c. The Prepaid Rent account on the balance sheet at the end of Year 8 should represent two months of prepayments. The rent per month is $3,000 (= $18,000/6), so the required balance in the Prepaid Rent account is $6,000 (= 2 X $3,000). The balance in that account is $20,000, so the adjusting entry must reduce it by $14,000 (= $20,000 – $6,000).

Rent Expense 14,000
    Prepaid Rent..   14,000

Assets	=	Liabilities	+	Shareholders' Equity	(Class.)
−14,000				−14,000	IncSt → RE

To decrease the balance in the Prepaid Rent account, increasing the amount in the Rent Expense account.

The Rent Expense account will have a balance at the end of Year 8 before closing entries of $32,000 (= $18,000 + $14,000). This amount comprises $20,000 (= $2,500 X 8) for rent from January through August and $12,000 (= $3,000 X 4) for rent from September through December.

d. The Wages Payable account should have a credit balance of $4,000 at the end of April, but it has a balance of $5,000 carried over from the end of March. The adjusting entry must reduce the balance by $1,000, which requires a debit to the Wages Payable account.

Wages Payable... 1,000
    Wage Expense   1,000

Assets	=	Liabilities	+	Shareholders' Equity	(Class.)
		−1,000		+1,000	IncSt → RE

To reduce the balance in the Wages Payable account, reducing the amount in the Wage Expense account.

Wage Expense is $29,000 (= $30,000 – $1,000).

3.37 continued.

e. The Prepaid Insurance account balance of $3,000 represents four months of coverage. Thus, the cost of insurance is $750 (= $3,000/4) per month. The adjusting entry for a single month is as follows:

Insurance Expense 750
    Prepaid Insurance 750

Assets	=	Liabilities	+	Shareholders' Equity	(Class.)
−750				−750	IncSt → RE

To recognize cost of one month's insurance cost as expense of the month.

f. The Advances from Tenants account has a balance of $25,000 carried over from the start of the year. At the end of Year 7, it should have a balance of $30,000. Thus, the adjusting entry must increase the balance by $5,000, which requires a credit to the liability account.

Rent Revenue.. 5,000
    Advance from Tenants 5,000

Assets	=	Liabilities	+	Shareholders' Equity	(Class.)
		+5,000		−5,000	IncSt → RE

To increase the balance in the Advances from Tenants account, reducing the amount in the Rent Revenue account.

Rent Revenue for Year 7 is $245,000 (= $250,000 – $5,000).

g. The Depreciation Expense for the year should be $2,000 (= $10,000/5). The balance in the Accumulated Depreciation account should also be $2,000; thus, the firm must credit Retained Earnings (Depreciation Expense) by $8,000 (= $10,000 – $2,000). The adjusting entry not only reduces recorded depreciation for the period but also sets up the asset account and its accumulated depreciation contra account.

3.37 g. continued.

Equipment 10,000
    Accumulated Depreciation 2,000
    Depreciation Expense 8,000

Assets	=	Liabilities	+	Shareholders' Equity	(Class.)
+10,000				+8,000	IncSt → RE
−2,000					

To reduce the recorded amount in Depreciation Expense from $10,000 to $2,000, setting up the asset and its contra account.

This page is intentionally left blank

CHAPTER 4

BALANCE SHEET: PRESENTING AND ANALYZING RESOURCES AND FINANCING

Questions, Exercises, and Problems: Answers and Solutions

4.1   See the text or the glossary at the end of the book.

4.3   One justification relates to the requirement that an asset or liability be measured with sufficient reliability. When there is an exchange between a firm and some other entity, there is market evidence of the economic effects of the transaction. The independent auditor verifies these economic effects by referring to contracts, canceled checks, and other documents underlying the transaction. If accounting recognized events without such a market exchange (for example, the increase in market value of a firm's assets), increased subjectivity would enter into the preparation of the financial statements.

4.5   The justification relates to the uncertainty as to the ultimate economic effects of the contracts. One party or the other may pull out of the contract. The accountant may not know the benefits and costs of the contract at the time of signing. Until one party or the other begins to perform under the contract, accounting usually gives no recognition. Accountants often disclose significant contracts of this nature in the notes to the financial statements.

4.7   a. The contract between the investors and the construction company as well as canceled checks provide evidence as to the acquisition cost.

        b. Adjusted acquisition cost differs from the amount in Part *a.* by the portion of acquisition cost applicable to the services of the asset consumed during the first five years. There are several generally accepted methods of computing this amount (discussed in **Chapter 10**). A review of the accounting records for the office building should indicate how the firm calculated this amount.

4.7 continued.

c. There are at least two possibilities for ascertaining current replacement cost. One alternative is to consult a construction company to determine the cost of constructing a similar office building (that is, with respect to location, materials, and size). The accountant would then adjust the current cost of constructing a new building downward to reflect the used condition of the five-year-old office building. The current replacement cost amount could be reduced by 12.5% (= 5/40) if the asset's service potential decreases evenly with age. The actual economic decline in the value of the building during the first five years is likely to differ from 12.5% and, therefore, some other rate is probably appropriate. A second alternative for ascertaining current replacement cost is to consult a real estate dealer to determine the cost of acquiring a used office building providing services similar to the building that the investors own. The accountant might encounter difficulties in locating such a similar building.

d. The accountant might consult a local real estate dealer to ascertain the current market price, net of transactions cost, at which the investors might sell the building. There is always the question as to whether an interested buyer could be found at the quoted price. The accountant might also use any recent offers to purchase the building received by the investors.

e. The accountant might use the amount described in Part *d*. but exclude transactions cost when measuring fair value. The accountant might also measure fair value using the present value of the future net cash flows based on estimated rental receipts and operating expenses (excluding depreciation) for the building's remaining 35-year life. These cash flows are then discounted to the present using an appropriate rate of interest. The inputs to the fair value measurement are those that a market participant would use.

4.9   a. Yes; amount of accrued interest payable.

b. Yes. The balance sheet reports a liability in the amount of the cash received.

c. No; accounting does not record executory promises.

4.9 continued.

  d. Yes; at the expected, undiscounted value of future costs arising from sales made prior to the balance sheet date. The income statement includes warranty expense in order to recognize the expenses related to the sale in the same period as the sale. When recognizing the expense, the accountant credits a liability account for the estimated cost to provide warranty services for sales made in the current period.

  e. Depends. If management determined that it was probable the firm would have to pay a reasonably estimable amount in the suit, then it would show an estimated liability.

  f. No; viewed as executory.

  g. Yes, at either the estimated cost to provide future flights or the fair value of the obligation to provide future flights.

4.11 a. In the definitions of assets and liabilities, *probable* is used to capture the idea that in commercial operations nothing can be entirely certain. It is used in its ordinary sense to refer to that which can be reasonably expected.

  b. In the recognition criteria for liabilities with uncertain amount and/or timing, *probable* is used in U.S. GAAP to refer to a relatively high threshold of likelihood—a rule of thumb used in practice is approximately 80%. In IFRS, *probable* as recognition criterion for liabilities with uncertain amount and/or timing means "more likely than not"—approximately 51%.

    Odd-numbered Solutions

4.13   (Delicious Foods Group; balance sheet formats.)

DELICIOUS FOODS GROUP
Balance Sheet
For Fiscal Year 7
(amounts in millions of euros)

Assets

Current Assets:

Cash and Cash Equivalents	€	248.9
Receivables		564.6
Inventories		1,262.0
Other Current Assets		121.5
Total Current Assets	€	2,197.0

Noncurrent Assets:

Property, Plant, and Equipment	€	3,383.1
Intangible Assets		552.1
Goodwill		2,445.7
Other Noncurrent Assets		244.0
Total Noncurrent Assets	€	6,624.9
Total Assets	€	8,821.9

Liabilities and Shareholders' Equity

Current Liabilities:

Accounts Payable	€	1,435.8
Accrued Expenses		375.7
Income Tax Payable		58.7
Short-Term Borrowings		41.5
Long-Term Debt, Current Portion		108.9
Obligations Under Finance Lease, Current Portion		39.0
Provisions		41.8
Other Current Liabilities		119.3
Total Current Liabilities	€	2,220.7

Noncurrent Liabilities:

Long-Term Debt	€	1,911.7
Obligations Under Finance Leases		595.9
Provisions		207.2
Other Noncurrent Liabilities		210.4
Total Noncurrent Liabilities	€	2,925.2
Total Liabilities	€	5,145.9

4.13 continued.

Shareholders' Equity:
Share Capital	€ 50.1
Share Premium	2,698.9
Retained Earnings	2,355.3
Other Reserves and Adjustments	(1,428.3)
Total Shareholders' Equity	€ 3,676.0
Total Liabilities and Shareholders' Equity	€ 8,821.9

4.15   (Jennings Group; balance sheet relations.)

The missing items appear in boldface type (amounts in millions of ringgit [RM]).

	Year 7	Year 6	Year 5	Year 4
Current Assets	RM 10,999.2	RM **9,507.3**	RM **7,202.2**	RM 6,882.6
Noncurrent Assets	**19,179.7**	18,717.4	11,289.1	9,713.9
Total Assets	RM 30,178.9	RM 28,224.7	RM 18,491.3	RM 16,596.5
Current Liabilities	RM **2,919.9**	RM 4,351.3	RM 1,494.2	RM 1,755.2
Noncurrent Liabilities	5,721.7	**7,206.5**	**7,995.1**	3,540.7
Shareholders' Equity	21,537.3	16,666.9	9,002.0	**11,300.6**
Total Liabilities and Shareholders' Equity	RM 30,178.9	RM 28,224.7	RM 18,491.3	RM 16,596.5

4.17   (Finmest Corporation; balance sheet relations.)

The missing items appear in boldface type (amounts in millions of euros).

	Year 11	Year 10	Year 9	Year 8
Current Assets	€ 3,357	€ 2,995	€ **2,477**	€ 2,097
Noncurrent Assets	**1,897**	1,973	**1,427**	**1,473**
Total Assets	€ 5,254	€ 4,968	€ 3,904	€ 3,570
Current Liabilities	€ **2,706**	€ 2,610	€ 1,802	€ 1,466
Noncurrent Liabilities	957	**908**	**810**	1,109
Total Liabilities	€ 3,663	€ 3,518	€ 2,612	€ 2,575
Contributed Capital	€ **681**	€ 711	€ **739**	€ 634
Retained Earnings	910	**739**	553	361
Total Shareholders' Equity	€ 1,591	€ 1,450	€ 1,292	€ 995
Total Liabilities and Shareholders' Equity	€ 5,254	€ 4,968	€ 3,904	€ 3,570

4.19   (Duke University; asset recognition and measurement.)

The expenditures do not qualify as an asset because (1) Duke University cannot point to a specific future economic benefit that it controls (employees can choose to work elsewhere even though doing so sacrifices the tuition benefit), and (2) there is not a reasonably reliable measurement attribute for this benefit.

4.21   (Nordstrom; recognition of a loss contingency.)

a. Nordstrom should recognize the contingency as soon as it is probable that it has incurred a loss and it can reasonably estimate the amount of the loss. Whether the store recognizes a loss at the time of the injury on July 5, 2013, depends on the strength of the case the store feels it has against the customer's claims. If the cause of the accident was an escalator malfunction, then Nordstrom may determine that it is probable that it has incurred a liability. If, on the other hand, the customer fell while running up the clearly identified down side of the escalator, then Nordstrom may determine that it is probable that it has not incurred a liability. Attorneys, not accountants, must make these probability assessments.

    If Nordstrom does not recognize a loss at the time of the injury, the next most likely time is June 15, 2014, when the jury renders its verdict. Unless attorneys for the store conclude that it is probable that the court will reverse the verdict on appeal, Nordstrom should recognize the loss at this time.

    If management in consultation with the firm's attorneys conclude, based on the available information, that the grounds for appeal are strong, then the next most likely time to record the loss is on April 20, 2015, when the jury in the lower court reaches the same verdict as previously. This is the latest time in this case at which the store should recognize the loss. If the store had recognized a loss on June 15, 2014, in the amount of $400,000, it would recognize only the extra damage award of $100,000 on April 20, 2015.

b. Under IFRS, the threshold for recognition is also probable but the meaning differs, such that a lower probability (more than 50%) will result in liability recognition under IFRS than under U.S. GAAP (more than approximately 80%).

4.23   (Ryanair Holdings, Plc.; asset recognition and measurement.)

a.   Under both U.S. GAAP and IFRS, a decision on the part of Ryanair's board of directors does not give rise to an asset.

b.   Under both U.S. GAAP and IFRS, Ryanair's placing of an order does not give rise to an asset.

c.   Under both U.S. GAAP and IFRS, Ryanair's payment gives rise to an asset on their balance sheet, Deposit on Aircraft (noncurrent asset), €60 million.

d.   Under both U.S. GAAP and IFRS, Ryanair's purchase gives rise to an asset, Landing Rights (noncurrent asset), €50 million.

e.   Under both U.S. GAAP and IFRS, Ryanair's purchase gives rise to an asset on their balance sheet, Equipment (noncurrent asset), €77 million. Ryanair would also record a liability, Mortgage Note Payable (noncurrent), €65 million.

f.   Under both U.S. GAAP and IFRS, Ryanair's purchase gives rise to an asset, Equipment (noncurrent asset), €160 million. The carrying, or book, value of the aircraft on the seller's books is not relevant to Ryanair's recording of the purchase.

4.25   (Berlin Philharmonic; liability recognition and measurement.)

a.   Under both U.S. GAAP and IFRS, the Berlin Philharmonic would record Advances from Customers (current liability), €3,040,000.

b.   Under both U.S. GAAP and IFRS, the Berlin Philharmonic does not recognize a liability because it has not yet received benefits obligating it to pay.

c.   Under both U.S. GAAP and IFRS, the Berlin Philharmonic would record Accounts Payable (current liability), €185,000.

d.   Under both U.S. GAAP and IFRS, the Berlin Philharmonic would not normally recognize a liability for an unsettled lawsuit unless payment is probable and the entity can reliably estimate the loss. Because the suit has not yet come to trial, it is unclear whether any liability exists.

4.25 continued.

    e.   Under both U.S. GAAP and IFRS, the Berlin Philharmonic would not recognize a liability for this mutually unexecuted contract.

    f.   Under both U.S. GAAP and IFRS, accounting normally does not recognize a liability for mutually unexecuted contracts. Thus, at the time of contract signing, the Berlin Philharmonic would record no liability. In 2012, however, the firm would record a liability for the portion of the yearly compensation earned by Sir Simon Rattle each month, or Salary Payable (current liability), €0.167 million per month.

4.27   (Magyar Telekom; effect of recording errors on balance sheet equation.) (amounts in millions of Hungarian forints [HUF])

Transaction Number	Assets	=	Liabilities	+	Shareholders' Equity
(1)	No		No		No
(2)	O/S HUF 900		O/S HUF 900		No
(3)	U/S HUF 14,500		U/S HUF 14,500		No
(4)	No[a]		No		No
(5)	U/S HUF 6,000		U/S HUF 6,000		No
(6)	U/S HUF 1,200		No		U/S HUF 1,200
(7)	No		No		No

[a]The value of total assets is correctly stated; the problem is that rather than debiting Property for the insurance payment, the firm should have debited Prepaid Insurance.

4.29 (Hathway Atlantic Airways Limited; balance sheet format, terminology, and accounting methods.) (amounts in millions of Hong Kong dollars [HKD])

a.
HATHWAY ATLANTIC AIRWAYS LIMITED
Balance Sheet, U.S. GAAP
(amounts in millions of HKD)

	December 31,	
	Year 11	**Year 10**
Assets		
Current Assets:		
Cash and Cash Equivalents[a]	HKD 21,649	HKD 15,624
Trade and Other Receivables	11,376	8,735
Inventory[b]	882	789
Assets Pledged Against Current Liabilities[c]	910	1,352
Total Current Assets	34,817	26,500
Noncurrent Assets:		
Investments in Associates	10,054	8,826
Fixed Assets	62,388	57,602
Other Long-Term Receivables and Investments	3,519	3,406
Intangible Assets	7,782	7,749
Assets Pledged Against Noncurrent Liabilities[d]	7,833	8,164
Total Noncurrent Assets	91,576	85,747
Total Assets	HKD 126,393	HKD 112,247

4.29 a. continued.

Liabilities and Shareholders' Equity

Current Liabilities:

Trade and Other Payables	HKD	14,787	HKD	10,999
Current Portion of Long-Term Liabilities		4,788		7,503
Unearned Transportation Revenue		6,254		4,671
Income Taxes Payable[e]		2,475		2,902
Total Current Liabilities		28,304		26,075

Noncurrent Liabilities:

Long-Term Liabilities		40,323		33,956
Retirement Benefit Obligations		268		170
Deferred Tax Liability[f]		6,771		6,508
Total Noncurrent Liabilities		47,362		40,634
Total Liabilities		75,666		66,709
Minority Interests		178		152

Shareholders' Equity:

Share Capital		788		787
Reserves		49,761		44,599
Total Shareholders' Equity		50,549		45,386
Total Liabilities and Shareholders' Equity[g]	HKD	126,393	HKD	112,247

Terminology

[a]Liquid Funds.

[b]Stock.

[c]Related Pledged Security Deposits (Current Portion of Long-Term Debt).

[d]Related Pledged Security Deposits (Noncurrent Portion of Long-Term Debt).

[e]Taxation.

[f]Deferred Taxation.

[g]Funds Attributable to Hathway Shareholders.

4.29 continued.

b.

HATHWAY ATLANTIC AIRWAYS LIMITED
Balance Sheet, IFRS
(amounts in millions of HKD)

	December 31, Year 11	December 31, Year 10
Assets		
Noncurrent Assets:		
Intangible Assets	HKD 7,782	HKD 7,749
Fixed Assets	62,388	57,602
Assets Pledged Against Noncurrent Liabilities[d]	7,833	8,164
Investments in Associates	10,054	8,826
Other Long-Term Receivables and Investments	3,519	3,406
Total Noncurrent Assets	91,576	85,747
Current Assets:		
Inventory[b]	882	789
Assets Pledged Against Current Liabilities[c]	910	1,352
Trade and Other Receivables	11,376	8,735
Cash and Cash Equivalents[a]	21,649	15,624
Total Current Assets	34,817	26,500
Total Assets	HKD 126,393	HKD 112,247

4.29 b. continued.

Liabilities and Shareholders' Equity

Noncurrent Liabilities:

Long-Term Liabilities	HKD	40,323	HKD	33,956
Retirement Benefit Obligations		268		170
Deferred Tax Liability[f]		6,771		6,508
Total Noncurrent Liabilities		47,362		40,634

Current Liabilities:

Income Taxes Payable[e]		2,475		2,902
Trade and Other Payables		14,787		10,999
Current Portion of Long-Term Liabilities		4,788		7,503
Unearned Transportation Revenue		6,254		4,671
Total Current Liabilities		28,304		26,075
Total Liabilities		75,666		66,709

Shareholders' Equity:

Minority Interests		178		152
Share Capital		788		787
Reserves		49,761		44,599
Total Shareholders' Equity		50,727		45,538
Total Liabilities and Shareholders' Equity[g]	HKD	126,393	HKD	112,247

Terminology

[a]Liquid Funds.

[b]Stock.

[c]Related Pledged Security Deposits (Current Portion of Long-Term Debt).

[d]Related Pledged Security Deposits (Noncurrent Portion of Long-Term Debt).

[e]Taxation.

[f]Deferred Taxation.

[g]Funds Attributable to Hathway Shareholders.

4.31 (Svenson; balance sheet format, terminology, and accounting methods.)

SVENSON
U.S. GAAP Balance Sheet
For Fiscal Year 7
(amounts in millions of SEK)

Assets

Current Assets:

Cash and Cash Equivalents	SEK	28,310
Short-Term Investments		29,406
Trade Receivables		60,492
Customer Financing, Current		2,362
Other Current Receivables		15,062
Inventories		22,475
Total Current Assets	SEK	158,107

Noncurrent Assets:

Equity in Joint Ventures	SEK	10,903
Other Investments in Shares		738
Customer Financing, Noncurrent		1,012
Other Financial Assets, Noncurrent		2,918
Deferred Tax Assets		11,690
Property, Plant, and Equipment		8,404
Intellectual Property Rights, Brands		23,958
Goodwill		22,826
Total Noncurrent Assets	SEK	82,449
Total Assets	SEK	240,556

4.31 continued.

Liabilities and Shareholders' Equity

Current Liabilities:

Trade Payables	SEK	17,427
Borrowings, Current		5,896
Provisions, Current		8,858
Other Current Liabilities		44,995
Total Current Liabilities	SEK	77,176

Noncurrent Liabilities:

Provisions, Noncurrent	SEK	368
Borrowings, Noncurrent		21,320
Post-Employment Benefits		6,188
Deferred Tax Liabilities		2,799
Other Noncurrent Liabilities		1,714
Total Noncurrent Liabilities	SEK	32,389
Total Liabilities	SEK	109,565
Minority Interest		940
Shareholders' Equity		130,051
Total Liabilities and Equity	SEK	240,556

Explanation of changes to apply U.S. GAAP

1. U.S. GAAP does not permit the capitalization of development costs. Removal of these costs reduces assets by SEK3,661 million, and reduces shareholders' equity (Retained Earnings) by SEK3,661 million.

2. U.S. GAAP does not permit the upward revaluation of land. In Year 7, this upward revaluation led to land being stated at a value SEK900 million higher on Svenson's balance sheet than would have been permitted under U.S. GAAP. The upward revaluation would also have been included as an unrealized gain, in Svenson's shareholders' equity. To conform to U.S. GAAP, removal of the upward revaluation of the land would therefore reduce assets and shareholders' equity by SEK900 million for Year 7.

3. Both U.S. GAAP and IFRS require assessments for impairment of noncurrent assets. Thus, the write-down of the equipment in Year 7 from SEK2,400 to SEK1,600 would also exist under U.S. GAAP.

4.31 continued.

4. From the information provided, the probability of loss is 60% for the patent infringement lawsuit. Thus, the lawsuit meets the IFRS threshold for recognition; it does not, however, meet the probable standard under U.S. GAAP (80%). Thus, under U.S. GAAP, Svenson would not have recognized a liability for this lawsuit. Under IFRS, Svenson would have recognized the "best" estimate as the amount of the liability. This best estimate was likely SEK500, since this is the amount of expected damages with the largest probability of occurring. Another best estimate that is possible is the expected value of the range of estimates, or SEK994 million. Whatever the best estimate, the amount would need to be removed from current provisions, and added back to shareholders' equity, to derecognize this liability under U.S. GAAP. The balance sheet shown earlier displays a best estimate of SEK500.

Summary Calculations for Shareholders' Equity:

Balance per Svenson Balance Sheet, Year 7 (IFRS) ...	SEK 134,112
Removal of Capitalized Development Costs That Would Be Expensed Under U.S. GAAP	(3,661)
Removal of Upward Revaluation of Land That Would Not Have Been Made Under U.S. GAAP	(900)
Removal of Lawsuit Expense That Would Not Have Met the Standard for Recognition Under U.S. GAAP	500
Balance per Svenson Balance Sheet, Year 7 U.S. GAAP	SEK 130,051

This page is intentionally left blank

CHAPTER 5

INCOME STATEMENT: REPORTING THE RESULTS OF OPERATING ACTIVITIES

Questions, Exercises, and Problems: Answers and Solutions

5.1 See the text or the glossary at the end of the book.

5.3 Cost is the economic sacrifice made to acquire goods or services. When the good or service acquired has reliably measurable future benefits to a firm, the cost is an asset. When the firm consumes the good or service, the cost is an expense.

5.5 The assets and income from operations that a firm has decided to discontinue (and dispose of or abandon) will not be part of that firm's future performance. Thus, separating the two income components allows users to form better predictions of future earnings.

5.7 At the time the firm receives the cash, the firm has not yet earned the revenues because it has not done anything (i.e., it has not yet delivered the merchandise to the customer). Accounting does not permit the firm to recognize revenues until the earnings process is complete, which in this case means when the firm delivers the merchandise.

5.9 It is not straightforward to compare the operating profits of two firms, even two otherwise similar firms, because authoritative guidance does not define the term "operating" or "operating profits." Although it is generally understood that this term refers to revenues less costs related to operations, there are no rules specifying what items comprise operating expenses. Further, there is no requirement that a firm even report a line in its income statement called "operating profit."

Odd-numbered Solutions

5.11   (Neiman Marcus; revenue recognition.) (amounts in US$)

	February	March	April
a.	—	—	$ 800
b.	—	$ 2,160	—
c.	$39,200	—	—
d.	—	$ 59,400	—
e.	—	$ 9,000	$ 9,000
f.	—	$ 9,000	$ 9,000

5.13   (Sun Microsystems; expense recognition.)   (amounts in US$)

	June	July	August
a.	—	$ 15,000	$ 15,000
b.	$ 4,560	—	—
c.	—	$ 5,800	$ 6,300
d.	$ 600	$ 600	$ 600
e.	—	—	—
f.	—	—	$ 4,500
g.	$ 6,600	—	—

5.15   (Bondier Corporation; relating net income to balance sheet changes.) (amounts in millions of US$)

a.   Net Income = [($1,040 – $765) + $30 – $12] = $293 million.

b.   Net Income = [($20,562 – $18,577) – ($17,444 – $15,844) – ($2,078 – $1,968) + $30 – $12] = $293 million.

5.17   (Novo Limited; income statement relations.) (amounts in thousands of US$)

The missing items appear in boldface type below:

	Year 10	Year 9
Sales	$ 16,351,503	$ 13,978,309
Cost of Goods Sold	(13,901,523)	(12,091,433)
Gross Profit	$ 2,449,980	$ 1,886,876
Selling and Administrative Expense	(1,103,713)	(1,033,296)
Advertising Expense	(595,902)	(488,150)
Research and Development Expense	(229,759)	(196,225)
Other Income (Expense)	11,715	18,130
Profit Before Taxes	$ 532,321	$ 187,335
Income Tax Expense	(47,613)	(26,197)
Net Income	$ 484,708	$ 161,138

5.19   (James John Corporation; income and equity relations.) (amounts in millions of US$)

The missing items appear in boldface below:

JAMES JOHN CORPORATION
Comparative Balance Sheets
March 31, Years 12, 11, and 10

	March 31,		
	Year 12	Year 11	Year 10
Common Stock	$ 1.1[a]	$ 1.1[a]	$ 1.1
Accumulated Other Comprehensive Income	40.5	(27.2)	0.0
Retained Earnings	1,742.3	1,379.2[b]	1,090.3
Treasury Stock	(321.5)[c]	(87.1)	(80.0)
Additional Paid-In Capital	872.5	783.6	664.3
Total Shareholders' Equity	$ 2,334.9	$ 2,049.6	$1,675.7

5.19 continued.

Calculations:

[a]No new stock issuance implies same balance in common stock for Year 12 and Year 11 as the balance in this account in Year 10.

[b]Retained Earnings, End of Year 11 = Retained Earnings, End of Year 10 + Net Income, Year 11 – Dividend Declared, Year 11 = $1,090.3 + $308.5 – $19.6 = $1,379.2.

[c]Treasury Shares, Year 12 = Treasury Shares, Year 11 + Repurchases, Year 12 = $(87.1) + $(234.4) = $(321.5).

5.21 (MosTechi Corporation; accumulated other comprehensive income relations.) (amounts in millions of yen)

The missing items appear in boldface below:

MOSTECHI CORPORATION
Comparative Balance Sheets
March 31, Years 8, 7, and 6

	March 31,		
	Year 8	Year 7	Year 6
Common Stock	¥ 626,907	¥ 624,124	¥ 621,709
Accumulated Other Comprehensive Income	(115,493)[b]	(156,437)[a]	(385,675)
Retained Earnings	1,700,133[c]	1,602,654	1,506,082
Treasury Stock	(3,470)	(3,127)	(6,000)
Additional Paid-In Capital	1,143,423	1,136,638	1,134,222
Total Shareholders' Equity	¥3,351,500	¥3,203,852	¥2,870,338

5.21 continued.

Calculations:

[a]Accumulated Other Comprehensive Income, End of Year 7 = Accumulated Other Comprehensive Income, End of Year 6 + Other Comprehensive Income, Year 7 = ¥(385,675) + ¥229,238 = ¥(156,437).

[b]Accumulated Other Comprehensive Income, End of Year 8 = Accumulated Other Comprehensive Income, End of Year 7 + Other Comprehensive Income, Year 8 = ¥(156,437) + ¥40,944 = ¥(115,493).

[c]Retained Earnings, End of Year 8 = Retained Earnings, End of Year 7 + Net Income, Year 8 – Dividends Declared, Year 8 + Adjustment, Year 8 = ¥1,602,654 + ¥126,328 – ¥25,042 – ¥3,807 = ¥1,700,133.

5.23   (PharmaCare; discontinued operations.) (amounts in millions of euros)

a. In Year 7, 51% [= €2,410/(€2,410 + €2,306)] of PharmaCare's income came from discontinued operations, compared to 10% [= €169/(€169 + €1,526)] in Year 6.

b. In Year 7, less than 0.2% (= €84/€51,378) of PharmaCare's total assets were associated with discontinued operations, compared to 5.2% (= €2,925/€55,891) in Year 6.

c. The large decline in PharmaCare's assets held for discontinued operations is due to the fact that PharmaCare disposed of the assets in Year 7. The assets are no longer owned by PharmaCare and, therefore, no longer a part of PharmaCare's balance sheet at the end of Year 7. The income those assets generated during the year prior to disposal is, however, part of PharmaCare's income for Year 7.

5.25 (Cementex Corporation; income statement formats.) (amounts in millions of pesos)

The missing items appear in boldface type below:

CEMENTEX CORPORATION
IFRS Income Statements
December 31, Years 10 and 9

	December 31,	
	Year 10	**Year 9**
Net Sales	$ 236,669	$ 213,767
Cost of Sales	(157,696)	**(136,447)**
Gross Profit	$ **78,973**	$ 77,320
Administrative and Selling Expenses	(33,120)	(28,588)
Distribution Expenses	(13,405)	**(14,227)**
Other Expenses, Net	(3,281)	(580)
Operating Income	$ **29,167**	$ 33,925
Financial Expenses	(8,809)	**(5,785)**
Financial Income	862	536
Income (Expense) from Financial Instruments	2,387	(161)
Other Financial Income (Expense)	6,647	4,905
Equity in Income of Associates	1,487	1,425
Profit Before Income Tax	$ **31,741**	$ 34,845
Income Tax	(4,796)	**(5,697)**
Consolidated Profit	$ **26,945**	$ **29,148**
Portion of Profit Attributable to Minority Interest	$ 837	$ **1,293**
Portion of Profit Attributable to Cementex Shareholders	$ **26,108**	$ 27,855

5.27 (Broyo Corporation; correcting errors in income statement transactions.) (amounts in millions of euros)

a. Broyo should not have recognized revenue on this transaction because it has yet to perform on the contract. Revenues are overstated by €200 and Cost of Goods Sold is overstated by €160, so income is overstated by €40.

b. Broyo should not have recorded the advance from customer as revenues. It is a liability (Advance from Customer). Revenues are, therefore, overstated by €20.

5.27 continued.

c. Broyo should have recorded Revenues of €45, and Cost of Goods Sold of €36, for a gross profit of €9.

d. Because the expenditures do not qualify as capitalized development costs, they should have been expensed not capitalized. Broyo's income in Year 13 is, therefore, overstated by €11.

e. Broyo had performed all of its obligations with the customer, so on December 1, Year 13, it should have recognized Revenues of €266, and Cost of Goods Sold of €250. Because they did not, Revenues are understated by €266, Cost of Goods Sold is understated by €250, and Gross Profit is understated by €16.

f. The sale of a plant is not a recurring part of Broyo's business. Therefore, it should not be included as part of Revenues and Cost of Goods Sold, which pertain to recurring transactions. Revenues are, therefore, overstated by €100, and Cost of Goods Sold is overstated by €80. The sale of the plant generated a gain of €20, which should have been included in Other Operating Income.

5.29 (SeaBreeze, Inc.; classification and interpretation of income statements.) (amounts in millions of yuan)

a. The ¥10,000 in Gains on Sales of Assets should not have been included in Sales Revenues because the gains do not reflect a transaction that the firm is regularly engaged in as part of its business model. The gain should have been recorded below the gross margin line and identified as a non-recurring item. Gross Profit would decline by ¥10,000.

b. Net Financial Income of ¥13,800 should have been reported below the gross profit line, because it is not part of the normal, core part of the firm's operations. Removing Net Financial Income will reduce Gross Profit by ¥13,800.

c. The firm included a ¥6,000 write-down of inventory in Selling, General, and Administrative Expenses. Normally in this industry, such a write-down is included in Cost of Sales. Adding the write-down to Cost of Sales would cause Gross Profit to decrease by ¥6,000.

5.29 continued.

    d. The firm included research and development expenditures of ¥34,000 in Cost of Sales. None of the expenditures related to proven technologies (and so were correctly not capitalized). So, even though the expenditures should be expensed on the income statement, R&D is typically not part of Cost of Sales. Removing the R&D from Cost of Sales would cause Gross Profit to increase by ¥34,000.

    e. The results of discontinued operations should be shown separately on the income statement, below the margin line. Removing discontinued operations will cause Gross Profit to decline by ¥22,000.

Each of the above transactions belongs in the income statement (implying that net income is calculated correctly) but is not correctly displayed in the income statement (implying that gross profit may be calculated incorrectly).

A summary of the effects of reclassifying the items on gross profit and net income is provided below:

	Gross Profit	Net Income
Original Amount	¥ 154,039	¥ 31,921
Effect of (a)	(10,000)	No effect on Net Income
Effect of (b)	(13,800)	No effect on Net Income
Effect of (c)	(6,000)	No effect on Net Income
Effect of (d)	34,000	No effect on Net Income
Effect of (e)	(22,000)	No effect on Net Income
Revised Amount	¥ 136,239	¥ 31,921

5.31   (Calculation of tax rates.) (amounts in millions of US$)

    a. Year 9: $7,712/$87,548 = 8.8%; Year 10: $8,093/$88,396 = 9.2%.

    b. Year 9: $11,757/$87,548 = 13.4%; Year 10: $11,534/$88,396 = 13.0%.

    c. Year 9: $4,045/$11,757 = 34.4%; Year 10: $3,441/$11,534 = 29.8%.

    d. The improved profitability clearly relates to an improved income tax position. The ratio of income before income taxes to revenues computed in Part b. indicates that profitability before taxes decreased between Year 9 and Year 10.

CHAPTER 6

STATEMENT OF CASH FLOWS

Questions, Exercises, and Problems: Answers and Solutions

6.1   See the text or the glossary at the end of the book.

6.3   Accrual accounting provides a measure of operating performance that relates inputs to outputs without regard to when a firm receives or disburses cash. Accrual accounting portrays the resources of a firm and the claims on those resources without regard to whether the firm holds the resource in the form of cash. Although accrual accounting may satisfy user's needs for information about operating performance and financial position, it does not provide sufficient information about the cash flow effects of a firm's operating, investing, and financing activities. The latter is the purpose of the statement of cash flows.

6.5   The indirect method reconciles net income, the primary measure of a firm's profitability, with cash flow from operations. Some argue that the relation between net income and cash flow from operations is less evident when a firm reports using the direct method. More likely, the frequent use of the indirect method prior to the issuance of FASB *Statement No. 95* probably explains its continuing popularity. Why might accountants have preferred the indirect method before FASB *Statement No. 95*? We have heard the following: The direct method's format resembles the income statement. Where the income statement has a line for revenues, the direct method has a line for cash collections from customers. Where the income statement has a line for cost of goods sold, the direct method might have a line for payments to suppliers of income. Where the income statement has a line for income tax expense, the direct method has a line for income tax payments. The resemblance of the two statements, the income statement and the direct method presentation in the statement of cash flows, might cause confusion. Some argue that preparing the direct method costs more. But you can see how easy preparing the direct method's version is; you learn how in this chapter.

6.7 The classification in the statement of cash flows parallels that in the income statement, where interest on debt is an expense but dividends are a distribution of earnings, not an expense. This is, in our opinion, a weak explanation. The overarching rule seems to be that "if it's in the income statement, it's operating." We think that dividends on shares and interest on borrowings are both financing transactions. IFRS permits firms to classify cash interest payments as a financing activity.

6.9 This is an investing and financing transaction whose disclosure helps the statement user understand why property, plant, and equipment and long-term debt changed during the period. Because the transaction does not affect cash directly, firms must distinguish it from investing and financing transactions that do affect cash flow.

6.11 The firm must have increased substantially its investment in accounts receivable or inventories or decreased substantially its current liabilities.

6.13 Direct Method: The accountant classifies the entire cash proceeds from the equipment sale as an investing activity. Indirect Method: As above, the entire cash proceeds appear as an investing activity. Because the calculation of cash flow from operations starts with net income (which includes the gain on sale of equipment), the accountant must subtract the gain to avoid counting cash flow equal to the gain twice, once as an operating activity and once as an investing activity.

6.15 (Electropin Company; derive cost of goods sold from data in the statement of cash flows.) (amounts in millions of US$)

Cash Payments for Inventories for the Year..............................	$ 64,713
Subtract: Increase in Inventories for the Year	(1,753)
Cost of Goods Sold for the Year	$ 62,960

6.17 (Yoshi Group; derive wages and salaries expense from data in the statement of cash flows.) (amounts in millions of yen)

Cash Payments for Wages and Salaries for the Year.................	¥ 8,853
Subtract: Decrease in Wages and Salaries Payable During the Year	(21)
Wages and Salaries Expense for the Year	¥ 8,832

6.19 (Gillette Limited; effect of borrowing and interest on statement of cash flows.) (amounts in millions of pounds sterling)

Cash 250

    Bonds Payable 250

Change in Cash	=	Change in Liabilities	+	Change in Shareholders' Equity	–	Change in Non-cash Assets
+250 Finan		+250				

October 1 bond issue. Refer to Exhibit 6.12. Line (11) increases by £250. Line (8) increases by £250.

Interest Expense 3.75

    Interest Payable [(0.06/12) X £250 X 3 Months] 3.75

Change in Cash	=	Change in Liabilities	+	Change in Shareholders' Equity	–	Change in Non-cash Assets
		+3.75		–3.75		

Refer to Exhibit 6.12. Line (3) decreases by £3.75. Line (4) increases by £3.75.

6.21 (Jennings Company; effect of rent transactions on statement of cash flows.) (amounts in US$)

Rent Expense 1,200

    Prepaid Rent 1,200

Change in Cash	=	Change in Liabilities	+	Change in Shareholders' Equity	–	Change in Non-cash Assets
				–1,200		–1,200

January rent expense.

6.21 continued.

Prepaid Rent.. 18,000
  Cash 18,000

Change in Cash	=	Change in Liabilities	+	Change in Shareholders' Equity	–	Change in Non-cash Assets
–18,000 Opns						+18,000

Payment on February 1.

Rent Expense.. 16,500
  Prepaid Rent.. 16,500

Change in Cash	=	Change in Liabilities	+	Change in Shareholders' Equity	–	Change in Non-cash Assets
				–16,500		–16,500

Rent expense for February through December; $18,000/12 per month = $1,500. 11 X $1,500 = $16,500.

All of these combine in a single journal entry as follows:
Rent Expense.. 17,700
Prepaid Rent.. 300
  Cash 18,000

Change in Cash	=	Change in Liabilities	+	Change in Shareholders' Equity	–	Change in Non-cash Assets
–18,000 Opns				–17,700		+300

All transactions of the year. Refer to Exhibit 6.12. Line (2) increases by $18,000. Line (3) decreases by $17,700. Line (5) increases by $300. Line (11) decreases by $18,000.

6.23 (Infotech Corporation; calculating components of cash outflow from operations.) (amounts in thousands of US$)

  a. Cost of Goods Sold for the Year .... $ 11,596
      Subtract: Increase in Accounts Payable for Inventories..... (90)
      Subtract: Decrease in Inventories for the Year.................. (66)
      Cash Payments for Inventories for the Year........................ $ 11,440

6.23 continued.

b. Other Expenses, Total.. $ 2,276
    Subtract: Decrease in Prepayments for Other Costs .... (102)
    Add: Decrease in Wages and Salaries Payable During the
        Year 240
    Cash Payments to Employees and Suppliers of Other
        Services for the Year .... $ 2,414

6.25 (Dearing Incorporated; working backward from changes in Buildings and Equipment account.) (amounts in millions of US$)

Buildings and Equipment

(Original Cost)		Accumulated Depreciation	
Balance, 1/1	$16,825	Balance, 1/1	$ 4,914
Outlays During Year	1,314	Depreciation During Year.	1,253
	$18,139		$ 6,167
Balance, 12/31	17,369	Balance, 12/31	5,465
Retirements During Year ..	$ 770	Retirements During Year .	$ 702

Proceeds = Book Value at Retirement
         = $770 − $702
         = $68.

6.27 (Bamberger Enterprises; calculating and interpreting cash flow from operations.) (amounts in thousands of US$)

a. Net Income.. $ 290
    Additions:
      Depreciation Expense.. 210
      Decrease in Accounts Receivable 780
      Decrease in Inventories... 80
      Decrease in Prepayments.. 100
      Increase in Accounts Payable 90
    Subtraction:
      Decrease in Other Current Liabilities............................ (240)
    Cash Flow from Operations .... $ 1,310

b. Bamberger Enterprises decreased its non-cash current assets, particularly accounts receivable, generating positive cash flows. Although it repaid other current liabilities, the reduction in accounts receivable dominated and caused cash flow from operations to exceed net income.

6.29 (Market Star; calculating and interpreting cash flows.) (amounts in millions of US$)

a.

MARKET STAR
Comparative Statement of Cash Flows
(amounts in millions of US$)

	2013	2012	2011
Operations			
Net Income	$ 499	$ 363	$ 279
Depreciation and Amortization	226	196	164
(Inc.) Dec. in Accounts Receivable	(514)	(648)	(238)
(Inc.) Dec. in Inventories	(98)	(13)	(35)
(Inc.) Dec. in Prepayments	(125)	10	(64)
Inc. (Dec.) in Accounts Payable	277	786	330
Inc. (Dec.) in Other Current Liabilities	420	278	70
Cash Flow from Operations	$ 685	$ 972	$ 506
Investing			
Acquisition of Property, Plant, and Equipment	$ (150)	$ (130)	$ (115)
Acquisition of Investments in Securities	(885)	(643)	(469)
Cash Flow from Investing	$ (1,035)	$ (773)	$ (584)
Financing			
Long-Term Debt Issued	$ 599	$ 83	$ 208
Common Stock Issued (Reacquired)	(187)	(252)	42
Dividends Paid	(122)	(104)	(88)
Cash Flow from Financing	$ 290	$ (273)	$ 162
Change in Cash	$ (60)	$ (74)	$ 84

6.29 continued.

b. Interpreting cash flow from operations for a marketing services firm requires a comparison of the change in accounts receivable from clients and accounts payable to various media. Marketing services firms act as agents between these two constituents. In Year 2011 and Year 2012, the increase in accounts payable slightly exceeded the increase in accounts receivable, indicating that Market Star used the media to finance its accounts receivable. In Year 2013, however, accounts payable did not increase nearly as much as accounts receivable. It is unclear whether the media demanded earlier payment, whether the media offered incentives to pay more quickly, or some other reason. As a consequence, cash flow from operations decreased in Year 2013. Cash flow from operations continually exceeds expenditures on property, plant, and equipment. This relation is not surprising, given that marketing services firms are not capital intensive. Market Star invested significantly in other entities during the three years. The classification of these investments as noncurrent suggests that they were not made with temporarily excess cash but as a more permanent investment. Cash flow from operations was not sufficient to finance both capital expenditures and these investments, except in Year 2012. The firm relied on long-term debt to finance the difference. Given that marketing services firms are labor intensive, one might question the use of debt instead of equity financing for these investments. In fact, Market Star repurchased shares of its common stock in Year 2012 and Year 2013. Thus, the capital structure of the firm became more risky during the three years.

6.31   (Effect of various transactions on statement of cash flows.) (amounts in US$)

Note: We use this question for in-class discussion. We seldom assign it for actual homework. A favorite form of question for examinations is to present a schematic statement of cash flows and to ask which lines certain transactions affect and how much. When we use this problem in class, we tell students that it makes a good examination question; this serves to strengthen their interest in the discussion.

Odd-numbered Solutions

6.31 continued.

a. Amortization Expense 600
    Patent 600

Change in Cash	=	Change in Liabilities	+	Change in Shareholders' Equity	–	Change in Non-cash Assets
				–600		–600

(3) Decreases by $600; reduces net income through amortization expense.

(4) Increases by $600; amount of expense is added back to net income in deriving cash flow from operations.

No effect on net cash flow from operations or cash.

b. Factory Site 50,000
    Common Stock 50,000

Change in Cash	=	Change in Liabilities	+	Change in Shareholders' Equity	–	Change in Non-cash Assets
				+50,000		+50,000

The transaction does not appear in the statement of cash flows because it does not affect cash. The firm must disclose information about the transaction in a supplemental schedule or note.

c. Inventory 7,500
    Accounts Payable 7,500

Change in Cash	=	Change in Liabilities	+	Change in Shareholders' Equity	–	Change in Non-cash Assets
		+7,500				+7,500

(4) Increases by $7,500; operating increase in cash from increase in Accounts Payable.

6.31 c. continued.

(5) Increases by $7,500; operating decrease in cash for increase in inventory.

The net effect of these two transactions is to leave cash from operations unchanged because the amounts added and subtracted change in such a way as to cancel out each other.

d. Inventory.. 6,000

  Cash.. 6,000

Change in Cash	=	Change in Liabilities	+	Change in Shareholders' Equity	–	Change in Non-cash Assets
–6,000 Opns						+6,000

(2) Increases by $6,000; use of cash in operations.

(5) Increase the subtraction by $6,000; increase in Inventory account, subtracted.

(11) Decreases by $6,000.

The net effect is to reduce cash from operations and cash by $6,000 the cash expenditure for an operating asset, inventory.

e. Fire Loss.. 1,500

  Inventory 1,500

Change in Cash	=	Change in Liabilities	+	Change in Shareholders' Equity	–	Change in Non-cash Assets
				–1,500		–1,500

(3) Decreases by $1,500; net income goes down.

(4) Increases by $1,500; additions go up because inventory, not cash, was destroyed. OK to show as a reduction to a subtraction for Line (5).

No net effect on cash flow including cash flow from operations or cash.

6.31 continued.

    f.   Cash 1,450
         Accounts Receivable...   1,450

Change in Cash	=	Change in Liabilities	+	Change in Shareholders' Equity	−	Change in Non-cash Assets
+1,450 Opns						−1,450

(1) Increases by $1,450 for collection of cash from customers.

(4) Increases by $1,450; operating increase in cash reflected by decrease in the amount of Accounts Receivable. OK to show as a reduction in the subtraction on Line (5).

(11) Increases by $1,450.

Cash flow from operations increases by $1,450, which causes cash to increase by $1,450.

    g.   Cash 10,000
         Bonds Payable..   10,000

Change in Cash	=	Change in Liabilities	+	Change in Shareholders' Equity	−	Change in Non-cash Assets
+10,000 Finan		+10,000				

(8) Increases by $10,000; increase in cash from security issue.

(11) Increases by $10,000.

6.31 continued.

h. Cash 4,500

      Equipment (Net) 4,500

Change in Cash	=	Change in Liabilities	+	Change in Shareholders' Equity	–	Change in Non-cash Assets
+4,500 Invst						–4,500

    (6) Increases by $4,500; increase in cash from sale of noncurrent asset.

    (11) Increases by $4,500.

6.33   (Digit Retail Enterprises, Inc.; inferring cash flows from balance sheet and income statement data.) (amounts in US$)

a. Sales Revenue... $ 270,000
    Less Increase in Accounts Receivable ($38,000 – $23,000)... (15,000)
    Less Decrease in Advances from Customers ($6,100 – $8,500)... (2,400)
    Cash Received from Customers During 2013...................... $ 252,600

b. Cost of Goods Sold .... $ (145,000)
    Less Increase in Merchandise Inventory ($65,000 – $48,000)... (17,000)
    Acquisition Cost of Merchandise Purchased During 2013 .. $ (162,000)

c. Acquisition Cost of Merchandise Purchased During 2013 (from Part b.) .... $ (162,000)
    Plus Increase in Accounts Payable—Merchandise Suppliers ($20,000 – $18,000).. 2,000
    Cash Paid for Acquisitions of Merchandise During 2013.... $ (160,000)

d. Salaries Expense .... $ (68,000)
    Plus Increase in Salaries Payable ($2,800 – $2,100) 700
    Cash Paid to Salaried Employees During 2013 .... $ (67,300)

e. Insurance Expense .... $ (5,000)
    Less Increase in Prepaid Insurance ($12,000 – $9,000) ...... (3,000)
    Cash Paid to Insurance Companies During 2013 .... $ (8,000)

6.33 continued.

f.

Rent Expense	$ (12,000)
Plus Decrease in Prepaid Rent ($0 – $2,000)	2,000
Plus Increase in Rent Payable ($3,000 – $0)	3,000
Cash Paid to Landlords for Rental of Space During 2013	$ (7,000)

g.

Increase in Retained Earnings ($11,800 – $11,500)	$ 300
Less Net Income	(9,600)
Dividend Declared	$ (9,300)
Less Decrease in Dividend Payable ($2,600 – $4,200)	(1,600)
Cash Paid for Dividends During 2013	$ (10,900)

h.

Depreciation Expense		$ (20,000)
Plus Increase in Accumulated Depreciation ($35,000 – $20,000)		15,000
Accumulated Depreciation of Property, Plant, and Equipment Sold		$ (5,000)
Cost of Property, Plant, and Equipment Sold ($100,000 – $90,000)		10,000
Book Value of Property, Plant, and Equipment Sold		$ 5,000
Plus Gain on Sale of Property, Plant, and Equipment		3,200
Cash Received from Sale of Property, Plant, and Equipment		$ 8,200

6.35 (Dickerson Manufacturing Company; preparing and interpreting a statement of cash flows using a T-account work sheet.) (amounts in US$)

a. **DICKERSON MANUFACTURING COMPANY**
Statement of Cash Flows
For the Year

Operations:		
Net Income	$ 568,000	
Additions:		
Depreciation	510,000	
Loss on Sale of Machinery	5,000	
Increase in Accounts Payable	146,000	
Increase in Taxes Payable	16,000	
Increase in Short-Term Payables	138,000	
Subtractions:		
Increase in Accounts Receivable	(106,000)	
Increase in Inventory	(204,000)	
Cash Flow from Operations		$ 1,073,000
Investing:		
Sale of Machinery	$ 25,000	
Acquisition of Land	(36,000)	
Acquisition of Buildings and Machinery	(1,018,000)	
Cash Flow from Investing		(1,029,000)
Financing:		
Issue of Common Stock	$ 32,000	
Dividends Paid	(60,000)	
Bonds Retired	(50,000)	
Cash Flow from Financing		(78,000)
Net Change in Cash		$ (34,000)
Cash, January 1		358,000
Cash, December 31		$ 324,000

6.35 a. continued.

The amounts in the T-account work sheet below are in thousands of U.S. dollars.

Cash

		√	358			

Operations

Net Income	(1)	568		106	(5)	Increase in Accounts Receivable
Depreciation Expense	(3)	510				
Loss on Sale of Equipment	(4)	5		204	(6)	Increase in Inventory
Increase in Accounts Payable	(9)	146				
Increase in Taxes Payable	(10)	16				
Increase in Other Short-Term Payables	(11)	138				

Investing

Sale of Machinery	(4)	25		1,018	(7)	Acquisition of Buildings and Machinery
				36	(8)	Acquisition of Land

Financing

Issue of Common Stock	(13)	32		60	(2)	Dividends
				50	(12)	Retirement of Bonds

		√	324			

Accounts Receivable			Inventory	
√	946		√	1,004
(5)	106		(6)	204
√	1,052		√	1,208

6.35 a. continued.

	Buildings and Machinery				Accumulated Depreciation—Buildings and Machinery			
√	8,678					3,974		√
(7)	1,018	150	(4)	(4)	120	510		(3)
√	9,546					4,364		√

	Land			Accounts Payable		
√	594			412		√
(8)	36			146		(9)
√	630			558		√

	Taxes Payable			Other Short-Term Payables	
	274	√		588	√
	16	(10)		138	(11)
	290	√		726	√

	Bonds Payable			Common Stock	
	1,984	√		1,672	√
(12)	50			32	(13)
	1,934	√		1,704	√

	Retained Earnings		
	2,676		√
(2)	60	568	(1)
	3,184		√

b. Dickerson Manufacturing Company is capital intensive. Its cash flow from operations exceeds net income because of the depreciation expense addback. Cash flow from operations appears substantial, but so are its expenditures for building and equipment. The firm's relatively low dividend payout rate suggests that it expects large capital expenditures to continue.

6.37   (Carter Corporation; interpreting a statement of cash flows based on the direct method for presenting cash flow from operations.)   (amounts in millions of US$)

a.   **2013**
   Net Revenues .... $ 76,329.5
   Less Cash Receipts from Revenues ....   (61,986.3)
   Increase in Accounts Receivable .... $ 14,343.2

b. Cash Paid for Inventory .... $ 45,772.6
    Increase in Accounts Payable for Inventory......................   181.4
    Purchases for Inventory .... $ 45,954.0
    Less Cost of Revenues ....   (60,221.8)
    Change (Decrease) in Inventories for the Year .... $ (14,267.8)

    Beginning Inventory + Purchases − COGS = Ending Inventory
    Purchases − COGS = Ending Inventory − Beginning Inventory
    Change in Inventory = Purchases − COGS

c. Amount Paid for Interest .... $ 468.2
    Interest Expense..   (434.6)
    Payment Exceeded Expenses by .... $ 33.6

d. The company acquired another large company.

6.39   (Quintana Company; working backward through the statement of cash
        flows.) (amounts in thousands of US$)

QUINTANA COMPANY
Condensed Balance Sheet
January 1, 2013
(amounts in thousands of US$)

Assets

Current Assets:		
Cash	$ 20	
Accounts Receivable	190	
Merchandise Inventories	280	
Total Current Assets		$ 490
Land		50
Buildings and Equipment	$ 405	
Less Accumulated Depreciation	(160)	245
Investments		140
Total Assets		$ 925

Liabilities and Shareholders' Equity

Current Liabilities:		
Accounts Payable	$ 255	
Other Current Liabilities	130	
Total Current Liabilities		$ 385
Bonds Payable		60
Common Stock		140
Retained Earnings		340
Total Liabilities and Shareholders' Equity		$ 925

Following are T-accounts for deriving the solution. Entries (1)–(13) are
reconstructed from the statement of cash flows. Changes for the year are
appropriately debited or credited to end-of-year balances to get beginning-
of-year balances. T-account amounts are shown in thousands.

Cash

	20		
(1)	200	30	(4)
(2)	60	40	(5)
(3)	25	45	(6)
(7)	40	130	(10)
(8)	15	200	(13)
(9)	10		
(11)	60		
(12)	40		
√	25		

Accounts Receivable

	190	
(4)	30	
√	220	

Merchandise Inventories

	280	
(5)	40	
√	320	

Land

	50		
		10	(9)
√	40		

Buildings and Equipment

	405		
(10)	130	35	(8)
√	500		

Accumulated Depreciation

		160	
(8)	20	60	(2)
		200	√

Investments

	140	
		40 (7)
√	100	

Accounts Payable

		255	
		25	(3)
		280	√

Other Current Liabilities

		130	
(6)	45		
		85	√

Bonds Payable

	60	
	40	(12)
	100	√

Common Stock

	140	
	60	(11)
	200	√

Retained Earnings

		340	
(13)	200	200	(1)
		340	√

6.41   (Spokane Paper Group; interpreting the statement of cash flows.)

   a.   Forest products companies are capital intensive. Depreciation is therefore a substantial non-cash expense each year. The addback for depreciation converts a net loss each year into positive cash flow from operations. Note that cash flow from operations increased each year as the net loss decreased.

   b.   Spokane Paper Group had substantial changes in its property, plant, and equipment during the three years. It likely built new, more efficient production facilities and sold off older, less efficient facilities.

   c.   For the three years combined, Spokane Paper Group reduced its long-term debt and replaced it with preferred stock. The sales of forest products are cyclical. When the economy is in a recession, as apparently occurred during the three years, the high fixed cost of capital-intensive manufacturing facilities can result in net losses. If Spokane Paper Group is unable to repay debt on schedule during such years, it causes expensive financial distress or even bankruptcy. Firms have more latitude with respect to dividends on preferred stock than interest on debt. Thus, a shift toward preferred stock and away from long-term debt reduces the bankruptcy risk of Spokane Paper Group. Note that Spokane Paper Group continued to pay, and even increase, dividends despite operating at a net loss. Most shareholders prefer less rather than more fluctuation in their dividends over the business cycle.

6.43   (Fierce Fighters Corporation; interpreting direct and indirect methods.)

   a.   We think this is hopeless. We cannot write a coherent explanation of the decline from these data alone, at least not without further analysis.

Odd-numbered Solutions

6.43 continued.

b. Some academics think that even the question is nonsense—that is, trying to explain changes in the data which themselves explain changes in cash. The statement of cash flows explains the change in the cash account from year to year. Consider that the statement of income and retained earnings explains the change in Retained Earnings from year to year. Most analysts think it sensible comparing income statements from one year to the next, to understand the causes of the change in income (which itself explains the causes of part of the changes in Retained Earnings). We think it sensible comparing statements of cash flows from one year to the next to explain the causes of the changes in cash flow from operations (which itself explains the causes of part of the changes in Cash).

In this case, the decline in cash flow from operations appears to result from a decreased margin of collections from customers for sales. The focus must be on what is going on with long-term and other sales contracts. From 2012 to 2013, we see increased payments to suppliers and employees that the analysis should investigate. We cannot be sure what is happening, but we can see where to inquire. Focus on those contracts, not on the changes in balance sheet operating accounts.

c. A reader can more easily interpret the direct method. The fundamental problem with the indirect method is that not a single number is itself a cash flow. So, changes in those numbers from year to year do not illuminate.

CHAPTER 7

INTRODUCTION TO FINANCIAL STATEMENT ANALYSIS

Questions, Exercises, and Problems: Answers and Solutions

7.1 See the text or the glossary at the end of the book.

7.3 The numerator in the ROA formula should reflect the income generated by all assets, irrespective of how those assets are financed. Because net income deducts interest charges on borrowings in arriving at net income, we must add back to net income the interest expense that has been deducted. The adjustment also considers the tax effects of deducting interest expense. The correct adjustment is, therefore, to add back to net income the aftertax cost of interest expense, equal to interest expense times one minus the tax rate.

7.5 For two otherwise identical firms, the firm with preferred stock in its capital structure will have a higher ROE because ROE measures the return to the firm's *common* shareholders. Preferred stock is not included in measuring the common shareholders' equity, the denominator of the ROE ratio. Thus, holding all other factors constant, the firm with preferred stock in its capital structure will have a smaller amount of common equity (a smaller denominator in the ROE ratio), which will cause ROE to be higher.

7.7 Management strives to keep its inventories at a level that is neither too low so that it loses sales nor too high so that it incurs high storage costs. Thus, there is an optimal level of inventory for a particular firm in a particular period and an optimal inventory turnover ratio.

7.9 It would be unusual to have a firm generate superior performance on both the profit margin and asset turnover dimension. The reason is that these two ratios typically reflect tradeoffs that are either imposed on the firm by industry forces (such as barriers to entry) or by the business models that work well in the industry. For example, the oil-refining industry requires a relatively high level of fixed assets. The high fixed assets lead to low asset

Odd-numbered Solutions

7.9 continued.

turnover ratios, but high profit margins. The high profit margins come about because oil-refining firms face less price competition because the high level of fixed assets acts as a barrier to entry to new firms. Grocery stores are the opposite: they require relatively low levels of assets to operate. As a result, (i) barriers to entry are small, leading to price competitiveness and low profit margins, but (ii) asset turnover ratios are high because the asset levels are low. A new firm could conceivably generate both superior profit margin and superior asset turnover performance. However, one would expect that such superior results would immediately attract competition, forcing profit margins to decrease, and possibly volumes to erode as well.

7.11 (Calem and Garter; calculating and disaggregating rate of return on assets.) (amounts in millions of US$)

a. **Calem:** $\dfrac{\$76}{\$1,473} = 5.16\%$.

Garter: $\dfrac{\$2,335}{\$29,183} = 8.00\%$.

b.

Return on Assets	=	Profit Margin	X	Total Assets Turnover Ratio
Calem:				
$\dfrac{\$76}{\$1,473}$	=	$\dfrac{\$76}{\$2,352}$	X	$\dfrac{\$2,352}{\$1,473}$
5.16%	=	3.23%	X	1.6
Garter:				
$\dfrac{\$2,335}{\$29,183}$	=	$\dfrac{\$2,335}{\$22,787}$	X	$\dfrac{\$22,787}{\$29,183}$
8.00%	=	10.24%	X	0.8

7.11 continued.

c.   Garter has a higher ROA, the result of a higher profit offset by a lower total assets turnover. Garter's higher profit margin might result from its larger size, permitting it to benefit from spreading fixed costs over a larger sales base. Garter also generates revenues from franchise fees, which increase net income but not sales revenue. Garter's lower total assets turnover might result from having the land and buildings of some of its franchisees on its balance sheet but not including the sales of these franchisees in its sales.

7.13   (Mobilex; calculating and disaggregating rate of return on common shareholders' equity.) (amounts in millions of US$)

a.

Year	Numerator	Denominator	Return on Equity
2011	$ 36,130	$ 106,471	33.9%
2012	39,500	112,515	35.1%
2013	40,610	117,803	34.5%

b. **Profit Margin**

Year	Numerator	Denominator	Profit Margin
2011	$ 36,130	$ 370,680	9.75%
2012	39,500	377,635	10.46%
2013	40,610	404,552	10.04%

Total Assets Turnover

Year	Numerator	Denominator	Total Assets Turnover
2011	$ 370,680	$ 201,796	1.84
2012	377,635	213,675	1.77
2013	404,552	230,549	1.75

Financial Leverage Ratio

Year	Numerator	Denominator	Financial Leverage Ratio
2011	$ 201,796	$ 106,471	1.90
2012	213,675	112,515	1.90
2013	230,549	117,803	1.96

7.13 continued.

    c. The rate of return on equity was relatively steady during the three years. Between 2011 and 2012, the profit margin and the financial leverage ratio increased but the total assets turnover decreased. Sales increased at a higher rate in 2013 than in 2012 but the profit margin declined. Mobilex might have increased expenditures on exploration or development of petroleum resources in 2013, which lowered net income and thus reduced the profit margin. The higher sales level should have provided Mobilex with benefits of economies of scale, but any such benefits were offset by higher other expenses.

7.15   (Profitability analysis for two companies.) (amounts in millions of US$)

a.

	Return on Assets	=	Profit Margin	X	Total Assets Turnover
Company A:	$\dfrac{\$6,986}{\$52,010}$	=	$\dfrac{\$6,986}{\$38,334}$	X	$\dfrac{\$38,334}{\$52,010}$
	13.4%	=	18.2%	X	0.74
Company B:	$\dfrac{\$6,999}{\$187,882}$	=	$\dfrac{\$6,999}{\$93,469}$	X	$\dfrac{\$93,469}{\$187,882}$
	3.7%	=	7.5%	X	0.50

b.

	Return on Equity	=	Profit Margin	X	Total Assets Turnover	X	Financial Leverage Ratio
Company A:	$\dfrac{\$6,986}{\$39,757}$	=	$\dfrac{\$6,986}{\$38,334}$	X	$\dfrac{\$38,334}{\$52,010}$	X	$\dfrac{\$52,010}{\$39,757}$
	17.5%	=	18.2%	X	0.74	X	1.3
Company B:	$\dfrac{\$6,999}{\$49,558}$	=	$\dfrac{\$6,999}{\$93,469}$	X	$\dfrac{\$93,469}{\$187,882}$	X	$\dfrac{\$187,882}{\$49,558}$
	14.1%	=	7.5%	X	0.50	X	3.8

7.15 continued.

c. Company A is the semiconductor manufacturer and Company B is the telecommunications provider. Both of these firms are fixed-asset intensive, so their total assets turnovers are small. Their ROAs and ROEs differ with respect to profit margin and financial leverage. Semiconductors are technology-intensive products and can command high profit margins if the products are on the technology edge. Telecommunication services, on the other hand, are commodity products and are difficult to differentiate from competitors. The technological intensity of semiconductors leads to short product life cycles. Firms in this industry tend not to take on substantial debt because of the short product life cycles. Telecommunication services are somewhat less technology intensive, at least with respect to the need to create the technologies. Firms in the telecommunications industry have capital-intensive fixed assets that can serve as collateral for borrowing and a somewhat more stable revenue stream, relative to semiconductors.

7.17 (Funtime, Inc.; analyzing inventories over three years.) (amounts in millions of euros)

a.

Year	Numerator	Denominator	Inventory Turnover
2011	€ 2,806	€ 415	6.76
2012	3,038	380	7.99
2013	3,193	406	7.86

b.

Year	Numerator	Denominator	Days Inventory Held
2011	365	6.76	54.0
2012	365	7.99	45.7
2013	365	7.86	46.4

c.

Year	Numerator	Denominator	Cost of Goods Sold Percentage
2011	€ 2,806	€ 5,179	54.2%
2012	3,038	5,650	53.8%
2013	3,193	5,970	53.5%

7.17 continued.

    d. Funtime experienced an increasing inventory turnover and a decreasing cost of goods sold to sales percentage between 2011 and 2012. Toys are trendy products. Funtime's products might have received rapid market acceptance, so that it was able both to move products more quickly and to achieve a higher gross margin on products sold. The faster turnover for trendy products means that Funtime would not need to mark down products in order to sell them or to incur additional storage costs. Funtime's cost of goods sold to sales percentage declined further in 2013 but its inventory turnover declined. Sales increased 9.1% [= (€5,650/€5,179) − 1] between 2011 and 2012 but only 5.7% [= (€5,970/€5,650) − 1] between 2012 and 2013. Perhaps Funtime increased inventory levels in 2013 expecting a larger sales increase than actually occurred. The unsold inventory resulted in a decrease in the inventory turnover rate.

7.19   (FleetSneak; calculating and interpreting short-term liquidity ratios.) (amounts in millions of US$)

    a. **Current Ratio**

Year	Numerator	Denominator	Current Ratio
2010	$ 5,528	$ 2,031	2.72
2011	6,351	1,999	3.18
2012	7,346	2,613	2.81
2013	8,077	2,584	3.13

Quick Ratio

Year	Numerator	Denominator	Quick Ratio
2010	$ 3,349	$ 2,031	1.65
2011	4,087	1,999	2.04
2012	4,686	2,613	1.79
2013	5,342	2,584	2.07

7.19 continued.

b. **Cash Flow from Operations to Current Liabilities Ratio**

Year	Numerator	Denominator	Cash Flow from Operations to Current Liabilities Ratio
2011	$ 1,571	$ 2,015.0[a]	78.0%
2012	1,668	2,306.0[b]	72.3%
2013	1,879	2,598.5[c]	72.3%

[a]$0.5(\$2,031 + \$1,999) = \$2,015.0$.
[b]$0.5(\$1,999 + \$2,613) = \$2,306.0$.
[c]$0.5(\$2,613 + \$2,584) = \$2,598.5$.

Accounts Receivable Turnover Ratio

Year	Numerator	Denominator	Accounts Receivable Turnover Ratio
2011	$13,740	$ 2,191.0[a]	6.27
2012	14,955	2,322.5[b]	6.44
2013	16,326	2,439.0[c]	6.69

[a]$0.5(\$2,120 + \$2,262) = \$2,191.0$.
[b]$0.5(\$2,262 + \$2,383) = \$2,322.5$.
[c]$0.5(\$2,383 + \$2,495) = \$2,439.0$.

Inventory Turnover Ratio

Year	Numerator	Denominator	Inventory Turnover Ratio
2011	$ 7,624	$ 1,730.5[a]	4.41
2012	8,368	1,944.0[b]	4.30
2013	9,165	2,099.5[c]	4.37

[a]$0.5(\$1,650 + \$1,811) = \$1,730.5$.
[b]$0.5(\$1,811 + \$2,077) = \$1,944.0$.
[c]$0.5(\$2,077 + \$2,122) = \$2,099.5$.

7.19 b. continued.

Accounts Payable Turnover Ratio

Year	Numerator	Denominator	Accounts Payable Turnover Ratio
2011	$ 7,785[a]	$ 777.5[d]	10.01
2012	8,634[b]	863.5[e]	10.00
2013	9,210[c]	996.0[f]	9.25

[a]$7,624 + $1,811 − $1,650 = $7,785.   [d]0.5($780 + $775) = $777.5.

[b]$8,368 + $2,077 − $1,811 = $8,634.   [e]0.5($775 + $952) = $863.5.

[c]$9,165 + $2,122 − $2,077 = $9,210.   [f]0.5($952 + $1,040) = $996.0.

c. The short-term liquidity risk of FleetSneak did not change significantly during the three-year period. The current and quick ratios fluctuated but are well above 1.0. Its cash flow from operations to current liabilities ratio declined slightly but is well above the 40% benchmark for a healthy company. FleetSneak increased its accounts receivable turnover each year, providing operating cash flows. Its inventory turnover was relatively stable. Although the accounts payable turnover decreased between 2012 and 2013, providing operating cash flows, it does not appear that the slower rate of paying suppliers is due to a shortage of liquid assets. Another factor affecting the assessment of short-term liquidity risk is the increased profit margin, net income divided by revenues, between 2011 and 2012. The increasing profit margin ultimately provides more cash than if the profit margin had remained stable.

7.21 (Kyoto Electric; calculating and interpreting long-term liquidity ratios.) (amounts in billions of Japanese yen)

a. **Long-Term Debt Ratio**

Year	Numerator	Denominator	Long-Term Debt Ratio
2010	¥7,391	¥11,540 + ¥2,360	53.2%
2011	7,150	11,247 + 2,502	52.0%
2012	6,278	10,814 + 2,780	46.2%
2013	5,871	10,488 + 3,034	43.4%

7.21 a. continued.

Debt-Equity Ratio

Year	Numerator	Denominator	Debt-Equity Ratio
2010	¥7,391	¥2,360	313.2%
2011	7,150	2,502	285.8%
2012	6,278	2,780	225.8%
2013	5,871	3,034	193.5%

b. **Cash Flow from Operations to Total Liabilities Ratio**

Year	Numerator	Denominator	Cash Flow from Operations to Total Liabilities Ratio
2011	¥1,411	0.5(¥11,540 + ¥ 11,247)	12.4%
2012	936	0.5(¥11,247 + ¥ 10,814)	8.5%
2013	1,074	0.5(¥10,814 + ¥ 10,488)	10.1%

Interest Coverage Ratio

Year	Numerator	Denominator	Interest Coverage Ratio Earned
2011	¥538	¥165	3.3
2012	635	161	3.9
2013	651	155	4.2

c. The proportion of long-term debt in the capital structure declined during the three-year period, but still appears to be at a high level. The cash flow from operations to average total liabilities ratio is low, relative to the 20% level commonly found for healthy firms. The interest coverage ratio was low in 2011 but improved by 2013. If this firm were a manufacturer, we would probably conclude that its long-term liquidity risk level is high. However, Kyoto Electric has a monopoly position in its service area. Regulators would not likely allow the firm to experience bankruptcy. Its protected status allows it to carry heavier levels of debt than a nonregulated manufacturing firm.

7.23 (Effect of various transactions on financial statement ratios.)

Transaction	Return on Equity	Current Ratio	Liabilities to Assets Ratio
a.	No Effect	(1)	Increase
b.	Increase	Increase	Decrease
c.	No Effect	No Effect	No Effect
d.	No Effect	(2)	Decrease
e.	No Effect	Increase	No Effect
f.	Increase	Decrease	Increase
g.	Decrease	Increase	Decrease
h.	No Effect	Decrease	Increase

(1) The current ratio remains the same if it was one to one prior to the transaction, decreases if it was greater than one, and increases if it was less than one.

(2) The current ratio remains the same if it was equal to one prior to the transaction, increases if it was greater than one, and decreases if it was less than one.

7.25 (Bullseye Corporation; calculating and interpreting profitability and risk ratios in a time series setting.) (amounts in millions of US$)

a. 1. $\text{Return on Assets} = \dfrac{\$2,849}{0.5(\$38,599 + \$46,373)} = 6.7\%.$

2. $\text{Profit Margin} = \dfrac{\$2,849}{\$61,471} = 4.6\%.$

3. $\text{Total Assets Turnover} = \dfrac{\$61,471}{0.5(\$38,599 + \$46,373)} = 1.4 \text{ times}.$

4. $\text{Other Revenues/Sales} = \dfrac{\$1,918}{\$61,471} = 3.1\%.$

5. $\text{Cost of Goods Sold/Sales} = \dfrac{\$41,895}{\$61,471} = 68.2\%.$

7.25 a. continued.

6. Selling and Administrative Expense/Sales $= \dfrac{\$16,200}{\$61,471} = 26.4\%.$

7. Interest Expense/Sales $= \dfrac{\$669}{\$61,471} = 1.1\%.$

8. Income Tax Expense/Sales $= \dfrac{\$1,776}{\$61,471} = 2.9\%.$

9. Accounts Receivable Turnover Ratio $= \dfrac{\$61,471}{0.5(\$6,194 + \$8,054)} = 8.6 \text{ times.}$

10. Inventory Turnover Ratio $= \dfrac{\$41,895}{0.5(\$6,254 + \$6,780)} = 6.4 \text{ times.}$

11. Fixed Asset Turnover $= \dfrac{\$61,471}{0.5(\$22,681 + \$25,908)} = 2.5 \text{ times.}$

12. Return on Equity $= \dfrac{\$2,849}{0.5(\$15,633 + \$15,307)} = 18.4\%.$

13. Financial Leverage Ratio $= \dfrac{0.5(\$38,599 + \$46,373)}{0.5(\$15,633 + \$15,307)} = 2.7.$

14. Current Ratio $= \dfrac{\$18,906}{\$11,782} = 1.6.$

15. Quick Ratio $= \dfrac{\$2,450 + \$8,054}{\$11,782} = 0.9.$

16. Accounts Payable Turnover Ratio $= \dfrac{(\$41,895 + \$6,780 - \$6,254)}{0.5(\$6,575 + \$6,721)} = 6.4 \text{ times.}$

Odd-numbered Solutions

7.25 a. continued.

17. Cash Flow from Operations to Current Liabilities Ratio $= \dfrac{\$4,125}{0.5(\$11,117 + \$11,782)} = 36.0\%.$

18. Liabilities to Assets Ratio $= \dfrac{\$31,066}{\$46,373} = 67.0\%.$

19. Long-Term Debt Ratio $= \dfrac{\$16,939}{\$46,373} = 36.5\%.$

20. Debt-Equity Ratio $= \dfrac{\$16,939}{\$15,307} = 110.7\%.$

21. Cash Flow from Operations to Total Liabilities Ratio $= \dfrac{\$4,125}{0.5(\$22,966 + \$31,066)} = 15.3\%.$

22. Interest Coverage Ratio $= \dfrac{(\$2,849 + \$1,776 + \$669)}{\$669} = 7.9 \text{ times.}$

b. **Rate on Assets (ROA)**
Bullseye's ROA increased between the fiscal years ended January 31, 2011 and 2012 and then decreased between fiscal years ended January 31, 2012 and 2013. The improved ROA between 2011 and 2012 results from an increased profit margin. The decreased ROA between 2012 and 2013 results from both a decreased profit margin and a decreased total assets turnover.

Profit Margin The changes in the profit margin result primarily from changes in the selling and administrative expense to sales percentage. Sales increased 12.9% between 2011 and 2012 but only 6.2% between 2012 and 2013. Most administrative expenses and some selling expenses are relatively fixed in amount. Variations in sales growth cause this expense percentage to vary as well.

7.25 b. continued.

Total Assets Turnover The total assets turnover declined between 2012 and 2013. Bullseye experienced declines in all three individual asset turnovers. These declines are also likely due to the significant decline in the growth rate in sales in 2013. Customers perhaps purchased more on credit and did not pay as quickly. Bullseye geared its inventory levels expecting a higher growth rate in sales than actually occurred, slowing the inventory turnover. The firm opened new stores expecting a larger growth in sales than occurred, slowing the fixed asset turnover.

c. **Return on Equity**

ROE follows the same path as ROA, increasing between 2011 and 2012 and then decreasing between 2012 and 2013. The total assets turnover declined between 2012 and 2013 for the reasons discussed in Part *b*. above. The financial leverage ratio declined between 2011 and 2012 and increased between 2012 and 2013. The decreased financial leverage ratio between 2011 and 2012 resulted primarily from the retention of earnings. Total liabilities changed only slightly between the end of 2011 and 2012, but shareholders' equity increased because of the retention of earnings. The financial leverage ratio increased between 2012 and 2013 for two principal reasons: an increase in long-term debt and the repurchase of common stock. The increased financial leverage ratio in 2013 moderated the decline in ROA and resulted in a smaller decline in ROE than would have otherwise been the case.

d. **Short-Term Liquidity Risk**

The current and quick ratios of Bullseye vary inversely with changes in the accounts receivable and inventory turnovers. Increased turnovers for these assets between 2011 and 2012 resulted in declines in the current and quick ratios, whereas decreased turnovers for these assets between 2012 and 2013 resulted in increases in the current and quick ratios. When turnovers increase, the firm turns accounts receivable and inventories into cash more quickly, which the firm can use to pay current liabilities, invest in new stores, or pay dividends. When turnovers decrease, the opposite occurs. The levels of the current and quick ratios are not at troublesome levels in any year. The cash flow

7.25 d. continued.

from operations to current liabilities ratio declined between 2012 and 2013 and was less than the 40% benchmark in 2013. The decline below 40% in 2013 occurred because of decreases in the accounts receivable and inventory turnovers and an increase in the accounts payable turnover. Either the sales growth rate will return to more normal levels in 2014 or Bullseye will adjust its accounts receivable and inventory policies for a lower level of sales growth. Thus, Bullseye does not exhibit high short-term liquidity risk.

e. **Long-Term Solvency Risk**

The debt ratios declined between 2011 and 2012 and increased between 2012 and 2013, as Part *b.* discusses. The cash flow from operations to total liabilities declined between 2012 and 2013 for the reasons discussed in Part *d.* Although this ratio is below the 20% benchmark in 2013, it is likely the result of the slower rate of sales growth experienced in that year. The interest coverage ratio declined in all three years but is not at a level in any year that would suggest high long-term liquidity risk. Thus, Bullseye does not exhibit high long-term liquidity risk.

7.27 (Gappo Group and Limito Brands; calculating and interpreting profitability and risk ratios.)

The financial statement ratios on pages 7-31, 7-32, and 7-33 form the basis for the responses to the questions raised.

a. Limito has a higher ROA in the fiscal year ended August 31, 2013, the result of a higher profit margin, offset by a lower total assets turnover. The higher profit margin results from a higher other revenues to sales percentage and a lower selling and administrative expenses to sales percentage. The higher other revenues results primarily from gains on the divestment of stores. The analyst would need to examine previous years to see if Limito regularly sells stores or if the gains in fiscal year 2013 are unusual. The lower selling and administrative expense to sales percentage for Limito is unexpected, given its smaller size and need to emphasize its more fashion-oriented product line. The lower cost of goods sold to sales percentage for Gappo occurs because its clothes are more standardized than those of Limito, perhaps permitting lower manufacturing costs (for example, from quantity discounts on materials, fewer machine setups, less training of employees). Gappo probably also incurs fewer inventory writedowns from obsolescence because its clothing line is less fashion oriented.

7.27 a. continued.

The slower total asset turnover of Limito is not due to either inventories or fixed assets, because Limito has faster turnover ratios for these assets. Accounts receivable comprises such a small proportion of the total assets of Limito that the differences in the accounts receivable turnover ratios exert very little influence on the total assets turnover. The difference in total assets turnover relates to the proportion of Other Noncurrent Assets on the balance sheet of each company. Other Noncurrent Assets averages 4.9% of total assets for Gappo for the two years, whereas it averages 35.2% of total assets for Limito. Other Noncurrent Assets likely relates to goodwill and other intangibles from corporate acquisitions. These items increase total assets and reduce the total assets turnover.

The larger rate of return on assets of Limito carries over to the rate of return on common shareholders' equity. In addition to larger operating profitability, Limito carries substantially more financial leverage, enhancing its profitability advantage over Gappo.

b. The current and quick ratios vary considerably between fiscal 2012 and fiscal 2013, but neither company appears risky by these measures. Limito pays its suppliers more quickly than Gappo. The cash flow from operations to average current liabilities ratios for Gappo and Limito both exceed the 40% benchmark, particularly for Gappo. Although neither company appears to have much short-term liquidity risk, the ratios for Limito are not as strong as those of Gappo.

c. Limito has higher levels of debt than Gappo. Its cash flow from operations to total liabilities ratio is less than the 20% benchmark. Its interest coverage ratio is less than that of Gappo but not at a troublesome level. Thus, Limito has higher long-term liquidity risk.

7.27 continued.

		Gappo Group	Limito Brands
1.	Return on Assets	$= \dfrac{\$867}{0.5(\$7,838 + \$8,544)} = 10.6\%.$	$= \dfrac{\$718}{0.5(\$7,437 + \$7,093)} = 9.9\%.$
2.	Profit Margin	$= \dfrac{\$867}{\$15,763} = 5.5\%.$	$= \dfrac{\$718}{\$10,134} = 7.1\%.$
3.	Total Assets Turnover	$= \dfrac{\$15,763}{0.5(\$7,838 + \$8,544)} = 1.9 \text{ times per year.}$	$= \dfrac{\$10,134}{0.5(\$7,437 + \$7,093)} = 1.4 \text{ times per year.}$
4.	Other Revenues/Sales	$= \dfrac{\$117}{\$15,763} = 0.7\%.$	$= \dfrac{(\$146 + 230)}{\$10,134} = 3.7\%.$
5.	Cost of Goods Sold to Sales	$= \dfrac{\$10,071}{\$15,763} = 63.9\%.$	$= \dfrac{\$6,592}{\$10,134} = 65.0\%.$
6.	Selling and Administration Expenses to Sales	$= \dfrac{\$4,377}{\$15,763} = 27.8\%.$	$= \dfrac{\$2,640}{\$10,134} = 26.1\%.$
7.	Interest Expenses to Sales	$= \dfrac{\$26}{\$15,763} = 0.2\%.$	$= \dfrac{\$149}{\$10,134} = 1.5\%.$
8.	Income Tax Expenses to Sales	$= \dfrac{\$539}{\$15,763} = 3.4\%.$	$= \dfrac{\$411}{\$10,134} = 4.1\%.$
9.	Accounts Receivable Turnover	$= \dfrac{\$15,763}{0.5(\$0 + \$0)} = \text{N/A}$	$= \dfrac{\$10,134}{0.5(\$355 + \$176)} = 38.2 \text{ times per year.}$
10.	Inventory Turnover	$= \dfrac{\$10,071}{0.5(\$1,575 + \$1,796)} = 6.0 \text{ times per year.}$	$= \dfrac{\$6,592}{0.5(\$1,251 + \$1,770)} = 4.4 \text{ times per year.}$

7.27 continued.

11. Fixed Asset Turnover

$$= \frac{\$15,763}{0.5(\$3,267 + \$3,197)} = 4.9 \text{ times per year.}$$

$$= \frac{\$10,134}{0.5(\$1,862 + \$1,862)} = 5.4 \text{ times per year.}$$

12. Return on Equity

$$= \frac{\$867}{0.5(\$4,274 + \$5,174)} = 18.4\%.$$

$$= \frac{\$718}{0.5(\$2,219 + \$2,955)} = 27.8\%.$$

13. Financial Leverage Ratio

$$= \frac{0.5(\$7,838 + \$8,544)}{0.5(\$4,274 + \$5,174)} = 1.7.$$

$$= \frac{0.5(\$7,437 + \$7,093)}{0.5(\$2,219 + \$2,955)} = 2.8.$$

14. Current Ratio:
August 31, 2012

$$= \frac{\$5,029}{\$2,272} = 2.2.$$

$$= \frac{\$2,771}{\$1,709} = 1.6.$$

August 31, 2013

$$= \frac{\$4,086}{\$2,433} = 1.7.$$

$$= \frac{\$2,919}{\$1,374} = 2.1.$$

15. Quick Ratio:
August 31, 2012

$$= \frac{\$2,644}{\$2,272} = 1.2.$$

$$= \frac{(\$500 + \$176)}{\$1,709} = 0.4.$$

August 31, 2013

$$= \frac{\$1,939}{\$2,433} = 0.8.$$

$$= \frac{(\$1,018 + \$355)}{\$1,374} = 1.0.$$

16. Days Accounts Receivable

$$= \frac{365}{0} = \text{N/A.}$$

$$= \frac{365}{38.2} = 9.6.$$

17. Days Inventory

$$= \frac{365}{6.0} = 60.8.$$

$$= \frac{365}{4.4} = 83.0.$$

18. Accounts Payable Turnover

$$= \frac{(\$10,071 + \$1,575 - \$1,796)}{0.5(\$1,006 + \$772)} = 11.1.$$

$$= \frac{(\$6,592 + \$1,251 - \$1,770)}{0.5(\$517 + \$593)} = 10.9.$$

7.27 continued.

19. Days Accounts Payable $= \dfrac{365}{11.1} = 32.9.$ $\dfrac{365}{10.9} = 33.5.$

20. Cash Flow from Operations to Current Liabilities $= \dfrac{\$2,081}{0.5(\$2,433+\$2,272)} = 88.5\%.$ $\dfrac{\$765}{0.5(\$1,374+\$1,709)} = 49.6\%.$

21. Liabilities to Assets Ratio:

August 31, 2012 $= \dfrac{\$3,370}{\$8,544} = 39.4\%.$ $\dfrac{\$4,138}{\$7,093} = 58.3\%.$

August 31, 2013 $= \dfrac{\$3,564}{\$7,838} = 45.5\%.$ $\dfrac{\$5,218}{\$7,437} = 70.2\%.$

22. Long-Term Debt Ratio:

August 31, 2012 $= \dfrac{\$188}{\$8,544} = 2.2\%.$ $\dfrac{\$1,665}{\$7,093} = 23.5\%.$

August 31, 2013 $= \dfrac{\$50}{\$7,838} = 0.6\%.$ $\dfrac{\$2,905}{\$7,437} = 39.1\%.$

23. Debt-Equity Ratio:

August 31, 2012 $= \dfrac{\$188}{\$5,174} = 3.6\%.$ $\dfrac{\$1,665}{\$2,955} = 56.3\%.$

August 31, 2013 $= \dfrac{\$50}{\$4,274} = 1.2\%.$ $\dfrac{\$2,905}{\$2,219} = 130.9\%.$

24. Cash Flow from Operations to Total Liabilities $= \dfrac{\$2,081}{0.5(\$3,564+\$3,370)} = 60.0\%.$ $\dfrac{\$765}{0.5(\$5,218+\$4,138)} = 16.4\%.$

25. Interest Coverage Ratio $= \dfrac{(\$867+\$539+\$26)}{\$26} = 55.1 \text{ times.}$ $\dfrac{(\$718+\$411+\$149)}{\$149} = 8.6 \text{ times.}$

7.29   (Scantania; interpreting profitability and risk ratios.)

a. The increase in the profit margin results from decreases in the cost of goods sold to sales percentage and the selling and administrative expense to sales percentage. Both of these expenses include depreciation and other fixed costs. Scantania experienced rapid sales growth in all three years and likely benefited from economies of scale as it spread these fixed costs over a larger sales base. Investment and net financing income as a percentage of revenues both declined and would not account for the increased profit margin.

b. Economies of scale (see the discussion in Part *a*. above) explains the decreased cost of goods sold to sales percentage but not the increasing inventory turnover. Any benefits from economies of scale affect both the numerator and denominator of the inventory turnover ratio. One possibility is that the firm instituted just-in-time manufacturing, which reduced raw materials and finished goods inventories and lowered inventory-carrying costs. Another possibility is that the sales mix shifted to higher margin, made-to-order vehicles. The high growth rates in sales also suggest that Scantania enjoyed pricing advantages for its products and experienced little difficulty in selling its products quickly.

c. The growth rate in sales in 2013 was higher than in 2011 and 2012. Perhaps Scantania had geared its productive capacity for 2013 for sales growth of approximately 12%. With a 19.4% sales growth in 2013, Scantania had to utilize its plant capacity more intensely, driving up the fixed-asset turnover. Another possibility is that Scantania enjoyed pricing advantages in its markets and was able to increase sales revenue without having to raise production levels.

d. Scantania must have experienced increases in cash, investments, or other assets besides accounts receivable, inventories, or fixed assets. The firm's annual report indicates that other noncurrent assets increased during these years.

e. Cash flow from operations likely increased as a result of the increase in the accounts receivable and inventory turnovers and the decrease in the days accounts payable. The explanation does not appear to be in the denominator of these cash flow ratios because total liabilities to assets did not change significantly and the long-term debt ratio declined.

Odd-numbered Solutions

7.29 continued.

    f.   The increase in the accounts receivable and inventory turnovers moderated the increase in current assets for these two items, thereby affecting the numerator of these ratios. The firm might have sold marketable securities and used the cash proceeds to acquire property, plant and equipment, to pay dividends, or other purposes. Current liabilities likely increased as a percentage of total assets, given that the liabilities to assets ratio increased 2.6 percentage points (= 72.9% − 70.3%), whereas the long-term debt ratio increased only 1.4 percentage points (= 21.7% − 20.3%).

7.31   (Bullseye Corporation; preparing pro forma financial statements.)

    a.   See attached pro forma financial statements and related financial ratios (pages 7-41 to 7-46).

    b.   Bullseye Corporation needs to increase borrowing. Cash flow from operations is positive in each year. Thus, the financing need does not appear to be short term. Although Bullseye Corporation increases long-term debt at the growth rate in property, plant, and equipment, the amount invested in property, plant, and equipment at the end of fiscal 2013 of $25,908 million is larger than long-term debt at the end of fiscal 2013 of $16,939. Growing long-term debt at the same growth rate as property, plant, and equipment does not adequately finance the fixed assets. If we assume that long-term debt increases at 2 times the growth rate in property, plant, and equipment, long-term debt (after reclassifications to current liabilities), grows 20% (= 2 times 10%) annually and provides adequate cash.

    c.   The pro forma financial statement ratios indicate a decreasing ROE. The projected profit margin and total assets turnover ratios are stable. The declining ROE results from a declining capital structure leverage ratio. Even if we grow long-term debt at 2 times the growth rate in property, plant, and equipment (see Part *b.* above), the financial leverage ratio and ROE decline. The reason for the declining

7.31 c. continued.

financial leverage ratio is that retained earnings grows faster than
borrowing. Still further increases in borrowing to stabilize the
financial leverage ratio results in too much cash on the balance sheet.
Bullseye Corporation would then need to increase its dividends or
repurchase common stock with the excess cash. To stabilize the
capital structure leverage ratio, Bullseye Corporation needs to
increase borrowing, increase the growth rate in dividends, or
repurchase common stock.

We used a spreadsheet program that rounds to many decimal places
to generate the following pro forma financial statements. Rounding causes
some of the subtotals and totals to differ from the sum of the amounts
that comprise them.

BULLSEYE CORPORATION
PRO FORMA INCOME STATEMENT
YEAR ENDED DECEMBER 31
(amounts in millions of US$)

	2013	2014	2015	2016	2017	2018
Sales Revenue........	$ 61,471	$ 67,003	$ 73,034	$ 79,607	$ 86,771	$ 94,581
Other Revenues	1,918	2,010	2,191	2,388	2,603	2,837
Total Revenues ..	$ 63,389	$ 69,013	$ 75,225	$ 81,995	$ 89,374	$ 97,418
Expenses:						
Cost of Goods Sold...............	$ 41,895	$ 45,629	$ 49,736	$ 54,212	$ 59,091	$ 64,409
Selling and Administration.	16,200	17,421	18,989	20,698	22,561	24,591
Interest..............	669	934	911	906	894	913
Income Taxes	1,776	1,911	2,124	2,348	2,595	2,852
Total Expenses	$ 60,540	$ 65,895	$ 71,760	$ 78,164	$ 85,141	$ 92,766
Net Income.............	$ 2,849	$ 3,118	$ 3,465	$ 3,831	$ 4,233	$ 4,652
Less Dividends	442	513	595	690	800	928
Increase in Retained Earnings.	$ 2,407	$ 2,606	$ 2,870	$ 3,141	$ 3,433	$ 3,724

(See Following Page for Assumptions)

7.31 c. continued.

Assumptions:

Growth Rate of Sales...	9.0%	
Other Revenues............	3.0%	of sales
Cost of Goods Sold	68.1%	of sales
Selling and Administration Expense.............	26.0%	of sales
Interest Expense	5.0%	on average amount of interest-bearing debt
Income Tax Rate	38.0%	of income before income taxes
Dividends	16.0%	growth rate

7.31 c. continued.

BULLSEYE CORPORATION
PRO FORMA BALANCE SHEET
DECEMBER 31
(amounts in millions of US$)

	2013	2014	2015	2016	2017	2018
Cash	$ 2,450	$ 1,778	$ 768	$ 680	$ (668)	$ 292
Accounts Receivable	8,054	8,779	9,569	10,430	11,369	12,392
Inventories	6,780	7,390	8,055	8,780	9,571	10,432
Prepayments	1,622	1,768	1,927	2,101	2,290	2,496
Total Current Assets	$ 18,906	$ 19,715	$ 20,319	$ 21,991	$ 22,561	$ 25,612
Property, Plant, and Equipment	25,908	28,499	31,349	34,484	37,932	41,725
Other Assets	1,559	1,559	1,559	1,559	1,559	1,559
Total Assets	$ 46,373	$ 49,773	$ 53,227	$ 58,033	$ 62,052	$ 68,896
Accounts Payable	$ 6,721	$ 7,507	$ 8,001	$ 8,902	$ 9,523	$ 10,561
Notes Payable	0	0	0	0	0	0
Current Portion—Long-Term Debt	1,964	1,951	1,251	2,236	107	2,251
Other Current Liabilities	3,097	3,376	3,680	4,011	4,372	4,765
Total Current Liabilities	$ 11,782	$ 12,833	$ 12,932	$ 15,149	$ 14,001	$ 17,577
Long-Term Debt	16,939	16,487	16,759	15,976	17,456	16,725
Other Noncurrent Liabilities	2,345	2,556	2,786	3,037	3,310	3,608
Total Liabilities	$ 31,066	$ 31,876	$ 32,477	$ 34,162	$ 34,767	$ 37,910
Common Stock	$ 68	$ 68	$ 68	$ 68	$ 68	$ 68
Additional Paid-in Capital	2,656	2,656	2,656	2,656	2,656	2,656
Retained Earnings	12,761	15,367	18,237	21,378	24,812	28,536
Accumulated Other Comprehensive Income	(178)	(194)	(211)	(231)	(251)	(274)
Total Shareholders' Equity	$ 15,307	$ 17,897	$ 20,750	$ 23,872	$ 27,284	$ 30,986
Total Liabilities and Shareholders' Equity	$ 46,373	$ 49,773	$ 53,227	$ 58,033	$ 62,052	$ 68,896

(See Following Page for Assumptions)

7.31 c. continued.

(Assumptions for Pro Forma Balance Sheet)

Assumptions:

Cash	PLUG					
Accounts Receivable	Sales Growth Rate					
Inventory.......................	Sales Growth Rate					
Prepayments	Sales Growth Rate					
Property, Plant, and Equipment................	10.0% Growth Rate					
Other Assets	0.0% Growth Rate					
Accounts Payable Turnover	6.4	6.5	6.5	6.5	6.5	6.5
Merchandise Purchases		46,240	50,401	54,937	59,882	65,271
Average Payables.........		7,114	7,754	8,452	9,213	10,042
Notes Payable	No change					
Other Current Liabilities	Sales Growth Rate					
Long-Term Debt	Property, Plant, and Equipment Growth Rate					
Other Noncurrent Liabilities	Sales Growth Rate					
Common Stock, APIC	0.0% Growth Rate					
Accumulated Other Comprehensive Income	Sales Growth Rate					

7.31 c. continued.

BULLSEYE CORPORATION
PRO FORMA STATEMENT OF CASH FLOWS
FOR THE YEAR ENDED DECEMBER 31
(amounts in millions of US$)

Cash Flow Statement	2013	2014	2015	2016	2017	2018
Operations:						
Net Income	$ 2,849	$ 3,118	$ 3,465	$ 3,831	$ 4,233	$ 4,653
Depreciation	1,659	1,825	2,007	2,208	2,429	2,672
Other	485	195	213	232	253	275
(Inc.)/Dec. in Accounts Receivable	(602)	(725)	(790)	(861)	(939)	(1,023)
(Inc.)/Dec. in Inventory	(525)	(610)	(665)	(725)	(790)	(861)
(Inc.)/Dec. in Prepayments	(38)	(146)	(159)	(173)	(189)	(206)
Inc./(Dec.) in Accounts Payable	111	786	495	901	621	1,038
Inc./(Dec.) in Other Current Liabilities	186	279	304	331	361	393
Cash Flow from Operations	$ 4,125	$ 4,722	$ 4,869	$ 5,743	$ 5,979	$ 6,940
Investing:						
Acquisition of Property, Plant, and Equipment	$ (4,369)	$ (4,416)	$ (4,857)	$ (5,343)	$ (5,877)	$ (6,465)
Other Investing	0	0	0	0	0	0
Cash Flow from Investing	$ (4,369)	$ (4,416)	$ (4,857)	$ (5,343)	$ (5,877)	$ (6,465)
Financing:						
Inc./(Dec.) in Short-Term Borrowing	$ 500	$ 0	$ 0	$ 0	$ 0	$ 0
Inc./(Dec.) in Long-Term Borrowing	6,291	(465)	(427)	201	(649)	1,413
Inc./(Dec.) in Common Stock	(2,598)	0	0	0	0	0
Dividends	(442)	(513)	(595)	(690)	(800)	(928)
Other Financing	(44)	0	0	0	0	0
Cash Flow from Financing	$ 3,707	$ (978)	$ (1,022)	$ (489)	$ (1,449)	$ 485
Change in Cash	$ 1,637	$ (672)	$ (1,010)	$ (88)	$ (1,348)	$ 960
Cash, Beginning of Year	813	2,450	1,778	768	680	(668)
Cash, End of Year	$ 2,450	$ 1,778	$ 768	$ 680	$ (668)	$ 292
Cash Balance from Balance Sheet	2,450	1,778	768	680	(668)	292
Difference	$ 0	$ 0	$ 0	$ 0	$ 0	$ 0

7.31 c. continued.

(Assumptions for Pro Forma Statement of Cash Flows)

Assumptions:

Depreciation Growth Rate	Same as Property, Plant, and Equipment
Other Operating Add-backs	Change in Other Noncurrent Liabilities and Change in Accumulated Other Comprehensive Income
Other Investing Cash Flows	Change in Other Noncurrent Assets
Other Financing Cash Flows	Zero

BULLSEYE CORPORATION
PRO FORMA FINANCIAL RATIOS

	2013	2014	2015	2016	2017	2018
Return on Assets	6.7%	6.5%	6.7%	6.9%	7.0%	7.1%
Profit Margin	4.6%	4.7%	4.7%	4.8%	4.9%	4.9%
Total Assets Turnover	1.4	1.4	1.4	1.4	1.4	1.4
Cost of Goods Sold/Sales	68.2%	68.1%	68.1%	68.1%	68.1%	68.1%
Selling and Administrative Expenses/Sales	26.4	26.0	26.0	26.0	26.0	26.0
Interest Expense/Sales	1.1%	1.4%	1.2%	1.1%	1.0%	1.0%
Income Tax Expense/Sales	2.9%	2.9%	2.9%	2.9%	3.0%	3.0%
Accounts Receivable Turnover Ratio	8.6	8.0	8.0	8.0	8.0	8.0
Inventory Turnover Ratio	6.4	6.4	6.4	6.4	6.4	6.4
Fixed-Assets Turnover Ratio	2.5	2.5	2.4	2.4	2.4	2.4
Return on Equity	18.4%	18.8%	17.9%	17.2%	16.6%	16.0%
Financial Leverage Ratio	2.7	2.9	2.7	2.5	2.3	2.2
Current Ratio	1.60	1.54	1.57	1.45	1.61	1.46
Quick Ratio	0.89	0.82	0.80	0.73	0.76	0.72
Cash Flow from Operations/ Current Liabilities	36.0%	38.4%	37.8%	40.9%	41.0%	44.0%
Accounts Payable Turnover Ratio	6.4	6.5	6.5	6.5	6.5	6.5
Liabilities to Assets Ratio	67.0%	64.0%	61.0%	58.9%	56.0%	55.0%
Long-Term Debt Ratio	36.5%	33.1%	31.5%	27.5%	28.1%	24.3%
Debt-Equity Ratio	110.7%	92.1%	80.8%	66.9%	64.0%	54.0%
Cash Flow from Operations/ Total Liabilities	15.3%	15.0%	15.1%	17.2%	17.3%	19.1%
Interest Coverage Ratio	7.9	6.4	7.1	7.8	8.6	9.2

CHAPTER 8

REVENUE RECOGNITION, RECEIVABLES, AND ADVANCES FROM CUSTOMERS

Questions, Exercises, and Problems: Answers and Solutions

8.1   See the text or the glossary at the end of the book.

8.3   Both approaches apply accounting criteria to determine the amount and timing of revenue recognition when an arrangement with a customer (a contract) is not yet complete. The percentage-of-completion method uses the cost of work performed to date as the criterion. The accounting for a multiple-element arrangement first determines the number of separable components (or deliverables) in the contract; the criterion for revenue recognition timing is the performance of a deliverable and the amount is based on the relative selling price of the deliverable, as a portion of the total contract price.

8.5   a.   Most businesses ought not to set credit policies so stringent that they have no uncollectible accounts. To do so would require extremely careful screening of customers, which is costly, and the probable loss of many customers who will take their business elsewhere. So long as the total revenues collected from credit sales, including finance charges and other fees, exceed the sum of both selling costs (including the costs of uncollectible accounts) and the cost of goods sold on credit, the firm should not be concerned if some percentage of its accounts receivable are uncollectible.

       b.   When the larger uncollectible accounts result from a credit-granting policy that increases income overall. A business might liberalize its credit policy by extending credit to a new group of customers with the intent of generating net revenues from the new credit customers that exceed the cost of goods sold to them and the selling expenses of executing the sales, including the expenses of uncollectible accounts. The extension of credit to new customers can increase net income even though it results in more uncollectible accounts.

Odd-numbered Solutions

8.5 continued.

    c. A higher percentage of uncollectible accounts is better when the overall value to the firm of the receipts from selling goods and services to customers exceeds the total costs of those sales, including the costs of uncollectible accounts.

8.7   Manufacturing firms typically do not identify a customer or establish a firm selling price until they sell products. Thus, these firms do not satisfy the criteria for revenue recognition while production is taking place. In contrast, construction companies might identify a customer and establish a contract price before construction begins. In addition, the production process for a manufacturing firm is usually shorter than for a construction firm. The recognition of revenue at the time of production or at the time of sale does not result in a significantly different pattern of income for a manufacturing firm. For a construction company, the pattern of income could differ significantly.

8.9   Application of the installment method requires a reasonably accurate estimate of the total amount of cash the firm expects to receive from customers, but a firm cannot use this method unless cash collections are uncertain. The cost-recovery-first method does not require such an estimate.

8.11   Both customer returns and bad debts ultimately affect the net cash collected from customers. In accounting for estimated sales returns, the firm debits a contra revenue account (thus reducing net revenues), and in accounting for bad debt expense, the firm typically debits an expense account, which does not affect net revenues. The accounting is similar in that income is reduced in the period in which sales occur, not in the period in which the customer returns an item or when a customer's account is determined to be uncollectible.

8.13   (Revenue recognition for various businesses.)

We have found this question to be an excellent one for class discussion because it forces the student to think about both revenue *and* expense timing and measurement questions. It also generates active student interest. Some of the items are relatively obvious, whereas others require more discussion.

    a. Time of sale; there may be an allowance for sales returns.

8.13 continued.

b. Probably as work progresses using the percentage-of-completion method. Students might discuss whether the identity of the customer matters, for example, the U.S. government versus a relatively weak government with lower credit quality. This question gets at the issue of whether the amount of cash the firm will receive is subject to reasonably accurate estimation.

c. Probably as the firm collects cash using the installment method. U.S. GAAP (**Codification Topic 976-605**) provides special guidance for retail land sales that is beyond the scope of this textbook.

d. At the time of sale.

e. At the time the firm picks citrus products and delivers them to customers. We ask students if their response would change if the citrus firm had a five-year contract at a set price to supply a particular quantity of citrus products to a citrus processor. The issue here is whether, given uncertainties about future weather conditions, the citrus grower will be able to make delivery on the contract. Citrus fruit is an example of a biological asset; IFRS but not U.S. GAAP provides special guidance for biological assets that is beyond the scope of this textbook (IAS 41, *Agriculture*, revised 2003).

f. U.S. GAAP (**Codification Topic 926**) but not IFRS provides special guidance for film and similar arrangements. The firm should not recognize revenue until it meets all of the following conditions:

1. The firm knows the sales price.

2. The firm knows the cost of the film or can reasonably estimate the loss.

3. The firm is reasonably assured as to the collectibility of the selling price.

4. A licensee has accepted the film in accordance with the license agreement.

5. The film is available (that is, the licensee can exercise the right to use the film and all conflicting licenses have expired).

Odd-numbered Solutions

8.13 f. continued.

Revenue recognition from the sale of rights to the television network is appropriate as soon as the firm meets these conditions even though the license period is three years. The firm cannot recognize revenues from the sale of subsequent rights to others until the three-year licensing period has expired. An important question in this example is when to recognize the production costs as an expense. Should the firm recognize all of the costs as an expense on the initial sale to the television network? Or, should it treat some portion of the costs as an asset, matched against future sales of license rights? Most accountants would probably match all of the costs against revenue from the television network license agreement, unless the firm has signed other license agreements for periods beginning after the initial three-year period at the same time as the television license agreement.

g. At the time of sale of each house to a specific buyer.

h. At the time of sale to a specific buyer at a set price. This will vary, depending on who owns the whiskey during the aging process. We pose the following situation: Suppose a particular whiskey producer has an on-going supplier relationship with a whiskey distributor. The quantity purchased by the distributor and the price set depend on supply and demand conditions at the time aged whiskey is brought to the market. The supplier always purchases some minimum quantity. When should the firm recognize revenue? This question gets at the issue of measuring revenue in a reasonably reliable manner.

i. After a loan is made, with the passage of time.

j. The alternatives here are (1) as customers make reservations, (2) as customers incur a liability or pay cash, or (3) as the agency receives cash from commissions. The second alternative is probably best. However, past experience may provide sufficient evidence as to the proportion of reservations that customers ultimately confirm to justify earlier recognition.

k. At the completion of the printing activity and delivery of the product to the customer.

8.13 continued.

l. The issue here is whether to recognize revenue when the firm sells coupons to food stores or when customers turn in the coupons for redemption. One might argue for revenue recognition at the time of sale of the coupons, since the seller must have some estimate of the redemption rate in setting the price for the sale of the coupons.

m. At the time the wholesaler delivers food products to stores.

n. The issue here is whether to recognize revenue while the livestock is growing. A grower of timber faces a similar issue. This question is similar to Part *h.* above.

o. One alternative is to apply the percentage-of-completion method. In practice firms use several methods.

8.15 (Meaning of allowance for uncollectible accounts.)

a. This characterization of the allowance account is incorrect. The allowance account normally has a credit balance, and assets have debit balances. Firms do not set aside assets in an amount equal to the credit balance in the allowance account.

b. This characterization of the allowance account is incorrect for the same reasons as in Part *a.* above. Firms do not set aside cash in an amount equal to the balance in the allowance account.

c. This characterization of the allowance account is incorrect. The balance in the allowance accounts is an estimate of the amount from sales on account in all periods, not just the current period, that firms have not yet collected nor expect to collect.

d. This characterization of the allowance account is incorrect. It is a more nearly correct characterization of the allowance for sale returns.

e. This characterization of the allowance account is correct.

f. This characterization of the allowance account is incorrect. The issue with uncollectible accounts is nonpayment of amounts owed, not an obligation to pay cash or transfer assets.

8.15 continued.

g. This characterization is incorrect for the same reasons the characterization in Part *f.* is incorrect.

h. This characterization is incorrect because the Allowance for Uncollectible Accounts accumulates amounts recognized as Bad Debt Expense. A portion of the balance in the allowance account does likely result from recognizing bad debt expense during the current period. However, the balance also includes portions of bad debt expense of earlier periods as well. There is no way to know how much of the balance in the allowance account relates to provisions made during the current period versus earlier periods.

i. Deferred revenues, advances from customers, have credit balances and are liabilities. The firm owes cash to those making advances if the firm does not deliver the goods and services as promised. The firm does not receive cash when it credits the allowance for uncollectibles account, nor does it owe cash to customers.

j. This characterization is incorrect. When firms credit the allowance account, they debit bad debt expense, a part of the retained earnings account. Thus, the allowance account indirectly links with retained earnings but is not an accurate characterization of its nature.

8.17 (Bed, Bath & Beyond; revenue recognition at time of sale and advances from customers.)

Cash..	556.5	
Sales Revenue...		280.0
Advances from Customer (Gift Certificate)...........		250.0
Sales Taxes Payable...		26.5

Assets	=	Liabilities	+	Shareholders' Equity	(Class.)
		+250.0			
+556.5		+26.5		+280.0	IncSt → RE

8.19 (Lentiva Group Limited; revenue recognition at time of sale.) (amounts in US$)

Separate Selling Price of Laptop Component (= $1,500 X
    50,000 Laptops) .... $ 75,000,000
Separate Selling Price of Training Component (= $100 X
    50,000 Laptops) 5,000,000
    Total .... $ 80,000,000

Journal Entries on January 1, 2013
Cash.. 15,000,000
Accounts Receivable.. 60,000,000
    Sales Revenue.. 70,312,500
    Advances from Customer 4,687,500

Assets	=	Liabilities	+	Shareholders' Equity	(Class.)
+15,000,000		+4,687,500		+70,312,500	IncSt → RE
+60,000,000					

To record the sale of the laptops and training services.

The laptop sales meet the criteria for recognizing revenue equaling $70,312,500 [= ($75,000,000/$80,000,000) X $75,000,000]. The training revenue equaling $4,687,500 [= ($5,000,000/$80,000,000) X $75,000,000] is deferred and will be earned as training services are delivered.

Cost of Goods Sold 60,000,000
    Inventory 60,000,000

Assets	=	Liabilities	+	Shareholders' Equity	(Class.)
–60,000,000				–60,000,000	IncSt → RE

To record the cost of the laptop sales.

8.19 continued.

Journal Entries on December 31, 2013

Advances from Customer..	2,343,750	
Cost of Training Services...	1,250,000	
Sales Revenue...		2,343,750
Salaries Payable...		1,250,000

Assets	=	Liabilities	+	Shareholders' Equity	(Class.)
		−2,343,750		+2,343,750	IncSt → RE
		+1,250,000		−1,250,000	IncSt → RE

To record the revenues and expenses for training services provided during 2013. Revenues equal $2,343,750 (= $4,687,500/2 years); Expenses equal $1,250,000 [= ($50 per laptop X 50,000 laptops)/2 years].

Journal Entries on December 31, 2014

Advances from Customer..	2,343,750	
Cost of Training Services...	1,250,000	
Sales Revenue...		2,343,750
Salaries Payable...		1,250,000

Assets	=	Liabilities	+	Shareholders' Equity	(Class.)
		−2,343,750		+2,343,750	IncSt → RE
		+1,250,000		−1,250,000	IncSt → RE

To record the revenues and expenses for training services provided during 2014. Revenues equal $2,343,750 (= $4,687,500/2 years); Expenses equal $1,250,000 [= ($50 per laptop X 50,000 laptops)/2 years].

8.21　(Abson Corporation; journal entries for service contracts.)　(amounts in US$)

a.　**1/31/13–3/31/13**
Cash.. 180,000
　　Service Contract Fees Received in Advance........ 　　　　180,000

Assets	=	Liabilities	+	Shareholders' Equity	(Class.)
+180,000		−180,000			

To record sale of 300 annual contracts.

3/31/13
Service Contract Fees Received in Advance............ 22,500
　　Contract Revenues .... 　　　　22,500

Assets	=	Liabilities	+	Shareholders' Equity	(Class.)
		−22,500		+22,500	IncSt → RE

To recognize revenue on 200 contracts sold during the first quarter; 1.5/12 x $180,000.

1/01/13–3/31/13
Service Expenses 32,000
　　Cash (and Other Assets and Liabilities) .... 　　　　32,000

Assets	=	Liabilities	+	Shareholders' Equity	(Class.)
−32,000				−32,000	IncSt → RE

4/01/13–6/30/13
Cash.. 300,000
　　Service Contract Fees Received in Advance........ 　　　　300,000

Assets	=	Liabilities	+	Shareholders' Equity	(Class.)
+300,000		−300,000			

To record the sale of 500 annual contracts.

8.21 a. continued.

6/30/13

Service Contract Fees Received in Advance............ 82,500

    Contract Revenues 82,500

Assets	=	Liabilities	+	Shareholders' Equity	(Class.)
		−82,500		+82,500	IncSt → RE

To recognize revenue on 500 contracts sold during the second quarter and 300 contracts outstanding from the first quarter:

    First Quarter:

        3/12   X $180,000   = $ 45,000

    Second Quarter:

        1.5/12 X $300,000   =   37,500

                                   $ 82,500

4/01/13–6/30/13

Service Expenses 71,000

    Cash (and Other Assets and Liabilities) 71,000

Assets	=	Liabilities	+	Shareholders' Equity	(Class.)
−71,000				−71,000	IncSt → RE

7/01/13–9/30/13

Cash.. 240,000

    Service Contract Fees Received in Advance........ 240,000

Assets	=	Liabilities	+	Shareholders' Equity	(Class.)
+240,000		−240,000			

To record the sale of 400 annual contracts.

8.21 a. continued.

9/30/13

Service Contract Fees Received in Advance............ 150,000
    Contract Revenues 150,000

Assets	=	Liabilities	+	Shareholders' Equity	(Class.)
		−150,000		+150,000	IncSt → RE

To recognize revenue on 400 contracts sold during the
third quarter and 800 contracts outstanding from sales
in prior quarters:

    First Quarter Sales:
        3/12   x $180,000 = $ 45,000
    Second Quarter Sales:
        3/12   x $300,000 =   75,000
    Third Quarter Sales:
        1.5/12 x $240,000 =   30,000
                               = $ 150,000

7/01/13–9/30/13

Service Expenses 105,000
    Cash (and Other Assets and Liabilities) 105,000

Assets	=	Liabilities	+	Shareholders' Equity	(Class.)
−105,000				−105,000	IncSt → RE

b. Balances in Service Contract Fees Received in Advance Account:

January 1, 2013..	—
Less First Quarter Expirations	$ (22,500)
Plus First Quarter Sales...	180,000
March 31, 2013..	$ 157,500
Less Second Quarter Expirations	(82,500)
Plus Second Quarter Sales	300,000
June 30, 2013	$ 375,000
Less Third Quarter Expirations	(150,000)
Plus Third Quarter Sales..	240,000
September 30, 2013	$ 465,000
Less Fourth Quarter Expirations	(195,000)
Plus Fourth Quarter Sales..	120,000
December 31, 2013...	$ 390,000

8.21 b. continued.

OR

Contracts	X	Balance Remaining	X	$600	=	Amount
300	X	1.5/12	X	$600	=	$ 22,500
500	X	4.5/12	X	$600	=	112,500
400	X	7.5/12	X	$600	=	150,000
200	X	10.5/12	X	$600	=	105,000
						$ 390,000

8.23   (York Company; aging of accounts receivable.) (amounts in US$)

Bad Debt Expense.. 9,050
    Allowance for Uncollectible Accounts 9,050

Assets	=	Liabilities	+	Shareholders' Equity	(Class.)
−9,050				−9,050	IncSt → RE

The Allowance account requires a balance of $25,050 [= (0.005 x $1,200,000) + (0.01 x $255,000) + (0.10 x $75,000) + (0.30 x $30,000)]. The adjusting entry *increases* the Allowance account by $9,050 (= $25,050 − $16,000) and recognizes Bad Debt Expense for the period by the same amount.

8.25   (Hamilia S.A.; aging of accounts receivable.) (amounts in euros)

Allowance for Uncollectible Accounts 21,500
    Bad Debt Expense 21,500

Assets	=	Liabilities	+	Shareholders' Equity	(Class.)
+21,500				+21,500	IncSt → RE

The Allowance account requires a balance of €75,100 [= (0.005 x €980,000) + (0.03 x €130,000) + (0.15 x €102,000) + (0.75 x €68,000)]. The adjusting entry *decreases* the allowance account by €21,500 (= €96,600 − €75,100) and recognizes a credit to Bad Debt Expense by the same amount.

8.27   (Pandora Company; allowance method: reconstructing journal entry from events.) (amounts in US$)

Bad Debt Expense.. 3,700
   Allowance for Uncollectible Accounts 3,700

Assets	=	Liabilities	+	Shareholders' Equity	(Class.)
–3,700				–3,700	IncSt → RE

Write-off of $2,200 + Ending Balance of Allowance of $5,000 – Beginning Balance of $3,500 = $3,700.

8.29   (Reconstructing events from journal entries.) (amounts in US$)

a. Bad debt expense for the period is $2,300 using the allowance method.

b. A firm writes off specific customers' accounts totaling $450 as uncollectible under the allowance method.

c. A firm realizes that its expected uncollectibles in the future are less than the amount already reserved in the allowance for uncollectibles. It records a credit to Bad Debt Expense for $200 to reduce the balance in the Allowance for Uncollectibles to the necessary (lower) amount.

8.31   (Schneider Corporation; journal entries for the allowance method.) (amounts in US$)

a. **2011**
    Bad Debt Expense (0.02 X $750,000)...................... 15,000
       Allowance for Uncollectible Accounts................. 15,000

Assets	=	Liabilities	+	Shareholders' Equity	(Class.)
–15,000				–15,000	IncSt → RE

Allowance for Uncollectible Accounts...................... 1,300
   Accounts Receivable... 1,300

Assets	=	Liabilities	+	Shareholders' Equity	(Class.)
+1,300					
–1,300					

Odd-numbered Solutions

8.31 a. continued.

2012

Bad Debt Expense (0.02 x $1,200,000)................... 24,000
    Allowance for Uncollectible Accounts.................   24,000

Assets	=	Liabilities	+	Shareholders' Equity	(Class.)
−24,000				−24,000	IncSt → RE

Allowance for Uncollectible Accounts..................... 11,200
    Accounts Receivable...   11,200

Assets	=	Liabilities	+	Shareholders' Equity	(Class.)
+11,200					
−11,200					

2013

Bad Debt Expense (0.02 x $2,400,000)................... 48,000
    Allowance for Uncollectible Accounts.................   48,000

Assets	=	Liabilities	+	Shareholders' Equity	(Class.)
−48,000				−48,000	IncSt → RE

Allowance for Uncollectible Accounts..................... 23,600
    Accounts Receivable...   23,600

Assets	=	Liabilities	+	Shareholders' Equity	(Class.)
+23,600					
−23,600					

b. Yes. The actual loss experience is 1.9% (= $82,500/$4,350,000) of sales on account for sales during 2011 through 2013.

8.33   (WollyMartin Limited; effects of transactions involving suppliers and customers on cash flows.) (amounts in euros)

a.   127,450   = 130,000 − (8,600 − 8,000) + (750 − 700) − 2,000
                        = 130,000 − 600 + 50 − 2,000.

8.33 continued.

    b. 84,700   = 85,000 − (7,500 − 7,000) + (11,200 − 11,000)
                          = 85,000 − 500 + 200.

8.35   (Raytheon; percentage-of-completion and completed contract methods of income recognition.) (amounts in millions of US$)

Percentage-of-Completion Method

Year	Degree of Completion	Revenue	Expense	Income
2011	$200/$700 = 28.6%	$ 257.4	$ 200	$ 57.4
2012	$200/$700 = 28.6%	257.4	200	57.4
2013	$300/$700 = 42.8%	385.2	300	85.2
		$ 900.0	$ 700	$ 200.0

Completed Contract Method

Year	Revenue	Expense	Income
2011	—	—	—
2012	—	—	—
2013	$ 900	$ 700	$ 200
	$ 900	$ 700	$ 200

8.37   (Installment and cost recovery methods of income recognition.) (amounts in millions of US$)

Installment Method

Year	Revenue	Expense[b]	Income[a]
		(PLUG)	
2012	$ 24	$ 19	$ 5
2013	24	19	5
2014	24	19	5
	$ 72	$ 57	$ 15

[a]Income = Gross Margin Percentage × Cash Received, or ($15/$72) × $24 = $5 million.

[b]Expense = Revenue − Income = $24 − $5 = $19 million.

    Odd-numbered Solutions

8.37 continued.

Cost-Recovery-First Method

Year	Revenue	Expense	Income
2012	$ 24	$ 24	$ -0-
2013	24	24	-0-
2014	24	9	15
	$ 72	$ 57	$ 15

8.39 (Hilton Garden Inn; revenue recognition at and after time of sale.) (amounts in US$)

a. **February 2, 2013:** Journal entry to record internet special reservation for four nights at $150 per night.

Cash.. 600
   Advances from Customer.................................... 600

Assets	=	Liabilities	+	Shareholders' Equity	(Class.)
+600		+600			

February 20, 2013: Journal entry to record revenue after services supplied.

Advances from Customer.. 600
   Sales Revenue 600

Assets	=	Liabilities	+	Shareholders' Equity	(Class.)
		−600		+600	IncSt → RE

b. **February 2, 2013:** Journal entry to record internet special reservation for four nights at $150 per night.

Cash.. 600
   Advances from Customer.................................... 600

Assets	=	Liabilities	+	Shareholders' Equity	(Class.)
+600		+600			

8.39 b. continued.

February 14, 2013: Journal entry to record revenue after customer cancels the reservation.

Advances from Customers 600
    Sales Revenue 600

Assets	=	Liabilities	+	Shareholders' Equity	(Class.)
		−600		+600	IncSt → RE

c. **February 2, 2013:** Journal entry to record refundable room reservation for four nights at $220 per night.

Cash.. 880
    Advances from Customer................................... 880

Assets	=	Liabilities	+	Shareholders' Equity	(Class.)
+880		+880			

February 20, 2013: Journal entry to record revenue after services supplied.

Advances from Customer....................................... 880
    Sales Revenue 880

Assets	=	Liabilities	+	Shareholders' Equity	(Class.)
		−880		+880	IncSt → RE

d. **February 2, 2013:** Journal entry to record refundable room reservation for four nights at $220 per night.

Cash.. 880
    Advances from Customer................................... 880

Assets	=	Liabilities	+	Shareholders' Equity	(Class.)
+880		+880			

8.39 d. continued.

February 14, 2013: Journal entry to record cancellation of refundable room reservation.

Advances from Customer... 880
  Cash... 880

Assets	=	Liabilities	+	Shareholders' Equity	(Class.)
−880		−880			

e. **February 2, 2013:** Journal entry to record refundable room reservation for four nights at $220 per night.

Cash... 880
  Advances from Customer.................................... 880

Assets	=	Liabilities	+	Shareholders' Equity	(Class.)
+880		+880			

February 16, 2013: Journal entry to record revenue (for one night) after customer cancels the reservation after 3 p.m., and to refund the remaining three nights.

Advances from Customer... 880
  Sales Revenue 220
  Cash... 660

Assets	=	Liabilities	+	Shareholders' Equity	(Class.)
−660		−880		+220	IncSt → RE

8.41   (Kajima Corporation; analyzing changes in accounts receivable.) (amounts in millions of Japanese yen)

a.   **(1) Sales on Account**

	2012	2011	2010
Accounts Receivable ...	1,891,466	1,775,274	1,687,380
Sales Revenue	1,891,466	1,775,274	1,687,380

Assets	=	Liabilities	+	Shareholders' Equity	(Class.)
+1,891,466				+1,891,466	IncSt → RE
+1,775,274				+1,775,274	IncSt → RE
+1,687,380				+1,687,380	IncSt → RE

(2) Provision for Estimated Uncollectible Accounts

	2012	2011	2010
Bad Debt Expense	1,084	3,152	2,999
Allowance for Uncollectible Accounts ...	1,084	3,152	2,999

Assets	=	Liabilities	+	Shareholders' Equity	(Class.)
−1,084				−1,084	IncSt → RE
−3,152				−3,152	IncSt → RE
−2,999				−2,999	IncSt → RE

(3) Write-Off of Actual Bad Debts

	2012	2011	2010
Allowance for Uncollectible Accounts	6,471[a]	820[b]	8,099[c]
Accounts Receivable	6,471	820	8,099

[a] ¥10,673 + ¥1,084 − ¥5,286 = ¥6,471.

[b] ¥8,341 + ¥3,152 − ¥10,673 = ¥820.

[c] ¥13,441 + ¥2,999 − ¥8,341 = ¥8,099.

8.41 a. continued.

Assets	=	Liabilities	+	Shareholders' Equity	(Class.)
+6,471/–6,471					
+820/–820					
+8,099/–8,099					

(4) Collection of Cash from Customers

	2012	2011	2010
Cash	1,723,338[d]	1,761,584[e]	1,606,456[f]
Accounts Receivable	1,723,338	1,761,584	1,606,456

[d]$¥468,387 + ¥1,891,466 – ¥6,471 – ¥630,044 = ¥1,723,338.$

[e]$¥455,517 + ¥1,775,274 – ¥820 – ¥468,387 = ¥1,761,584.$

[f]$¥382,692 + ¥1,687,380 – ¥8,099 – ¥455,517 = ¥1,606,456.$

Assets	=	Liabilities	+	Shareholders' Equity	(Class.)
+1,723,338/ –1,723,338					
+1,761,584 –1,761,584					
+1,606,456/ –1,606,456					

8.41 continued.

b.

	2012	2011	2010

(1) Accounts Receivable Turnover
2012: ¥1,891,466/0.5(¥624,758 + ¥457,714) . 3.49
2011: ¥1,775,274/0.5(¥457,714 + ¥447,176) .   3.92
2010: ¥1,687,380/0.5(¥447,176 + ¥369,251) .   4.13

(2) Bad Debt Expense/Revenues
2012: ¥1,084/¥1,891,466 .... 0.06%
2011: ¥3,152/¥1,775,274 ....   0.18%
2010: ¥2,999/¥1,687,380 ....   0.18%

(3) Allowance for Uncollectible Accounts/ Gross Accounts Receivable at End of Year
2012: ¥5,286/¥630,044 .... 0.84%
2011: ¥10,673/¥468,387 ....   2.28%
2010: ¥8,341/¥455,517 ....   1.83%

(4) Accounts Written Off/Average Gross Accounts Receivable
2012: ¥6,471/0.5(¥630,044 + ¥468,387) 1.18%
2011: ¥820/0.5(¥468,387 + ¥455,517) 0.18%
2010: ¥8,099/0.5(¥455,517 + ¥382,692) 1.93%

c. The accounts receivable turnover ratio decreased during the three-year period from 4.13 (in 2010) to 3.92 (in 2011) to 3.49 (in 2012). The firm decreased the amount of accounts written off between 2010 and 2011, from 1.93% to 0.18%, leading to a decrease in the allowance account relative to the gross accounts receivable. The firm decreased its provision for estimated uncollectible accounts in 2012 (the percentage of bad debt expense to sales declined from 0.18% in 2010 and 2011 to 0.06% in 2012), consistent with the buildup in the allowance account. The accounts written off as a percentage of gross accounts receivable increased in 2012, from 0.18% in 2011 to 1.18% in 2012, perhaps because credit conditions worsened in that year. The latter is consistent with the decrease in the accounts receivable turnover ratio, from 3.92 in 2011 to 3.49 in 2012.

8.43   (Aracruz Celulose; analyzing disclosures of accounts receivable.) (amounts in thousands of US$)

    a. Carrying Value = Accounts Receivable, Net.
        For 2012: $361,603 (= $365,921 – $4,318).
        For 2011: $285,795 (= $290,429 – $4,634).

    b. Total Amount Customers Owe = Accounts Receivable, Gross.
        For 2012: $365,921.
        For 2011: $290,429.

    c. Journal Entries for Bad Debt Expense:

2012

Bad Debt Expense	117	
Allowance for Uncollectible Accounts		117

Assets	=	Liabilities	+	Shareholders' Equity	(Class.)
–117				–117	IncSt → RE

Bad Debt Expense equals $117 (= $4,318 + $433 – $4,634).

2011

Bad Debt Expense	592	
Allowance for Uncollectible Accounts		592

Assets	=	Liabilities	+	Shareholders' Equity	(Class.)
–592				–592	IncSt → RE

Bad Debt Expense equals $592 (= $4,634 + $25 – $4,067).

8.45   (Pins Company; reconstructing transactions affecting accounts receivable and uncollectible accounts.) (amounts in US$)

    a. $192,000 Dr. = $700,000 – $500,000 – $8,000.

    b. $6,000 Cr. = (0.02 × $700,000) – $8,000.

    c. $21,000 = $10,000 + $11,000.

8.45 continued.

    d. $16,000 = $6,000 + $10,000.

    e. $676,000 = $192,000 + $800,000 − $16,000 − $300,000.

    f. $289,000 = $300,000 − $11,000.

8.47   (Areva Group: income recognition for a nuclear generator manufacturer.) (amounts in millions of US$)

a.1. **Percentage-of-Completion Method**

Year	Incremental Percentage Complete	Revenue Recognized	Expenses Recognized	Income
2013	340/1,700 (0.20)	$ 400	$ 340	$ 60
2014	238/1,700 (0.14)	280	238	42
2015	238/1,700 (0.14)	280	238	42
2016	238/1,700 (0.14)	280	238	42
2017	238/1,700 (0.14)	280	238	42
2018	238/1,700 (0.14)	280	238	42
2019	170/1,700 (0.10)	200	170	30
Total.....	120/120 (1.00)	$ 2,000	$ 1,700	$ 300

2. **Completed Contract Method**

Year	Revenue Recognized	Expenses Recognized	Income
2013	-0-	-0-	-0-
2014	-0-	-0-	-0-
2015	-0-	-0-	-0-
2016	-0-	-0-	-0-
2017	-0-	-0-	-0-
2018	-0-	-0-	-0-
2019	$ 2,000	$ 1,700	$ 300
Total....	$ 2,000	$ 1,700	$ 300

8.47 continued.

b. **Journal Entries:**

1. **Percentage-of-Completion Method**

2012
December 20, 2012: At time of contract signing.
Cash.. 20
   Advances from Customer............................... 20

Assets	=	Liabilities	+	Shareholders' Equity	(Class.)
+20		+20			

2013
Construction in Process 340
   Cash... 340

Assets	=	Liabilities	+	Shareholders' Equity	(Class.)
+340					
−340					

Cash.. 100
Advances from Customer...................................... 20
Receivable from Customer..................................... 280
   Sales Revenue 400

Assets	=	Liabilities	+	Shareholders' Equity	(Class.)
+100		−20		+400	IncSt → RE
+280					

Cost of Sales... 340
   Construction in Process 340

Assets	=	Liabilities	+	Shareholders' Equity	(Class.)
−340				−340	IncSt → RE

8.47 b. continued.

2014–2018

| Construction in Process | 238 | |
| Cash | | 238 |

Assets	=	Liabilities	+	Shareholders' Equity	(Class.)
+238					
−238					

Cash	100	
Receivable from Customer	180	
Sales Revenue		280

Assets	=	Liabilities	+	Shareholders' Equity	(Class.)
+100				+280	IncSt → RE
+180					

| Cost of Sales | 238 | |
| Construction in Process | | 238 |

Assets	=	Liabilities	+	Shareholders' Equity	(Class.)
−238				−238	IncSt → RE

2019

| Construction in Process | 170 | |
| Cash | | 170 |

Assets	=	Liabilities	+	Shareholders' Equity	(Class.)
+170					
−170					

Cash	1,380	
Receivable from Customer		1,180
Sales Revenue		200

Assets	=	Liabilities	+	Shareholders' Equity	(Class.)
+1,380				+200	IncSt → RE
−1,180					

8.47 b. continued.

Cost of Sales.. 170
    Construction in Process 170

Assets	=	Liabilities	+	Shareholders' Equity	(Class.)
−170				−170	IncSt → RE

2. Completed Contract Method

2012
December 20, 2012: At time of contract signing.
Cash.. 20
    Advances from Customer... 20

Assets	=	Liabilities	+	Shareholders' Equity	(Class.)
+20		+20			

2013
Construction in Process 340
    Cash.. 340

Assets	=	Liabilities	+	Shareholders' Equity	(Class.)
+340					
−340					

Cash.. 100
    Advances from Customer... 100

Assets	=	Liabilities	+	Shareholders' Equity	(Class.)
+100		+100			

2014–2018
Construction in Process 238
    Cash.. 238

Assets	=	Liabilities	+	Shareholders' Equity	(Class.)
+238					
−238					

8.47 b. continued.

Cash... 100
   Advances from Customer.................................. 100

Assets	=	Liabilities	+	Shareholders' Equity	(Class.)
+100		+100			

2019
Construction in Process 170
   Cash.. 170

Assets	=	Liabilities	+	Shareholders' Equity	(Class.)
+170					
−170					

Cash... 1,380
Advances from Customer....................................... 620
   Sales Revenue 2,000

Assets	=	Liabilities	+	Shareholders' Equity	(Class.)
+1,380		−620		+2,000	IncSt → RE

Cost of Sales.. 1,700
   Construction in Process 1,700

Assets	=	Liabilities	+	Shareholders' Equity	(Class.)
−1,700				−1,700	IncSt → RE

8.49   (Furniture Retailers; income recognition when collection from the customer is uncertain.) (amounts in US$)

a.   **Installment Method**

(1) **January 2013**

Accounts Receivable.. 8,400
   Inventory.. 6,800
   Deferred Gross Margin... 1,600

Assets	=	Liabilities	+	Shareholders' Equity	(Class.)
+8,400					
−6,800		+1,600			

(2) **When Furniture Retailer Receives Each Payment**

The customer will make 21 payments of $400 each. The gross margin percentage is 19% (= $1,600/$8,400). When each monthly payment is received, Furniture Retailers will recognize $400 of revenues and $76 (= 0.19 × $400) of Deferred Gross Margin.

Cash... 400
Deferred Gross Margin... 76
Cost of Goods Sold (Plug).. 324
   Sales Revenue 400
   Accounts Receivable... 400

Assets	=	Liabilities	+	Shareholders' Equity	(Class.)
+400		−76		−324	IncSt → RE
−400				+400	IncSt → RE

8.49 continued.

b. **Cost Recovery Method**

(1) January 2013

Accounts Receivable...	8,400	
Inventory..		6,800
Deferred Gross Margin..		1,600

Assets	=	Liabilities	+	Shareholders' Equity	(Class.)
+8,400		+1,600			
−6,800					

(2) When Each Payment Is Received

The customer will make 21 payments of $400 each. Furniture Retailers will recover the $6,800 cost of furniture after the customer has made seventeen payments (= $6,800/$400). To record the first seventeen payments, Furniture Retailers makes the following journal entry:

Cash...	400	
Cost of Goods Sold...................................	400	
Sales Revenue		400
Accounts Receivable...............................		400

Assets	=	Liabilities	+	Shareholders' Equity	(Class.)
+400				+400	IncSt → RE
−400				−400	IncSt → RE

8.49 b. continued.

To record the last four payments, Furniture Retailers makes the following journal entry:

Cash 400
Deferred Gross Margin 400
    Sales Revenue 400
    Accounts Receivable 400

Assets	=	Liabilities	+	Shareholders' Equity	(Class.)
+400		−400		+400	IncSt → RE
−400					

8.51   (J. C. Spangle; point-of-sale versus installment method of income recognition.) (amounts in US$)

a.

	2013	2012
Sales	$ 300,000	$ 200,000
Expenses:		
Cost of Goods Sold*	$ 186,000	$ 120,000
All Other Expenses	44,000	32,000
Total Expenses	$ 230,000	$ 152,000
Net Income	$ 70,000	$ 48,000

*Calculation	2013	2012
Beginning Inventory	$ 60,000	$ 0
Purchases	240,000	180,000
Goods Available	$ 300,000	$ 180,000
Ending Inventory	(114,000)	(60,000)
Cost of Goods Sold	$ 186,000	$ 120,000

Cost of Goods Sold/Sales:
    2012—$120,000/$200,000 = 60%.
    2013—$186,000/$300,000 = 62%.

8.51 continued.

b.

	2013	2012
Collections from Customers	$230,000	$ 90,000
Expenses:		
Merchandise Cost of Collections*	$140,400	$ 54,000
All Other Expenses	44,000	32,000
Total Expenses	$184,400	$ 86,000
Net Income	$ 45,600	$ 4,000

*Calculation	2013	2012
Merchandise Cost of Collections:		
Of Goods Sold:		
In 2012, 60% of $90,000		$ 54,000
In 2013, 60% of $110,000	$ 66,000	
Of Goods Sold in 2013:		
62% of $120,000	74,400	
	$140,400	$ 54,000

An Alternative Presentation Would Be:	2013	2012
Realized Gross Margin	$ 89,600	$ 36,000
All Other Expenses	44,000	32,000
Net Income	$ 45,600	$ 4,000

8.53   (Income recognition for various types of businesses.)

a. **Amgen**—The principal income recognition issue for Amgen is the significant lag between the incurrence of research and development expenditures and the realization of sales from any resulting products. Research and development expenditures represent a significant percentage of revenues. Established pharmaceutical firms have established products as well as products in the pipeline and, therefore, research and development expenditures represent both a smaller and a more stable percentage of revenues. U.S. GAAP requires firms to expense research and development expenditures in the year incurred; as discussed in later chapters, IFRS specifies a different treatment for development expenditures.

8.53 a. continued.

Brown-Forman—The principal revenue recognition issue for Brown-Forman is whether it should recognize the increase in value of hard liquors while they are aging (that is, revalue the liquors to market value each year) or wait until the liquors are sold at the end of the aging process. Most accountants would argue that the market values of aging liquors are too uncertain prior to sale to justify periodic revaluations and revenue recognition. Brown-Forman should include in the cost of the liquor inventory not only the initial production costs but also the cost incurred during the aging process. In this way, the firm can match total incurred costs with revenues generated at the time of sale.

Deere—Deere faces issues of revenue recognition with respect to both the sale of farm equipment to dealers and the provision of financing services. The concern with respect to the sale of farm equipment to dealers is the right of dealers to return any unsold equipment. If dealers have no right of return, then recognition of revenue at the time of sale is appropriate. If dealers can return any equipment discovered to be faulty prior to sale and the amount of such returns is reasonably predictable, then Deere can reduce the amount of revenue recognized each year for estimated returns. If dealers can return any unsold equipment, then delaying recognition of revenue until the dealer sells the equipment is appropriate. Deere should match the cost of manufacturing the equipment against the sales revenue. Deere reports research and development expense in its income statement; it is not clear what proportions of these expenditures Deere makes to enhance existing products versus to develop new products. U.S. GAAP does not permit firms to capitalize and amortize research and development costs.

Deere should accrue revenue from financing (interest) and insurance (premiums) services over time. To achieve matching, Deere should capitalize and amortize any initial administrative costs to check customer credit quality and prepare legal documents.

8.53 a. continued.

Fluor—The appropriate timing of revenue recognition for Fluor depends on the basis for pricing its services. If the fee is fixed for a particular construction project, then Fluor should recognize the fee in relation to the degree of completion of the construction project. If the fee is a percentage of total construction costs incurred on the project, then Fluor should recognize revenue in relation to costs incurred. If the fee is a percentage of the costs incurred by Fluor (for example, salaries of their employees working on the project), then it should recognize revenue in relation to the incurrence of these costs. It seems clear that the percentage-of-completion method of revenue recognition is more appropriate than the completed contract method.

Golden West—Golden West should recognize interest revenue from home mortgage loans as time passes. It should provide for estimated uncollectible accounts each year. The uncollectible amount should reflect the resale value of homes repossessed. The more difficult question relates to recognition of revenue from points. One possibility is to recognize the full amount in the initial year of the loan, based on the reasoning that the points cover the cost of originating the loan. Both the points and the administrative costs would be recognized in full in the initial year of the loan. An alternative view is that the points effectively reduce the amount lent by the savings and loan company and increase its yield beyond the stated interest rate. This view suggests that Golden West should amortize the points over the term of the loan and match against this revenue amortization of the initial administrative costs to set up the loan. Golden West should recognize interest expense on deposits as time passes. There is no direct relation between interest expense on deposits and interest revenue from loans so Golden West matches interest expense to the period it is incurred.

Merrill Lynch—The principal income recognition issue for Merrill Lynch is whether it should report financial instruments held as assets and liabilities at their acquisition cost or their fair value. These assets and liabilities generally have easily measured fair values and may be held for short periods (days or weeks). Thus, one can argue that use of current fair values is appropriate. However, we are still left with the question as to whether the unrealized gain or loss should

Odd-numbered Solutions

8.53 a. continued.

flow through to the income statement immediately or wait until realization at the time of sale. The argument for immediate recognition is that Merrill Lynch takes short-term financing and investing positions for short-term returns. Its income statement should reflect its operating performance during this period. The case for not recognizing the unrealized gains and losses is that they could reverse prior to realization and, in any case, will be realized very soon. Merrill Lynch should recognize revenue from fee-based services as it provides the services.

Rockwell Collins—The absence of research and development expense from the income statement suggests that Rockwell Collins charges all such costs to specific contracts. These costs become expenses as Rockwell Collins recognizes revenue from the contracts. The multi-year nature of its contracts and the credit quality of the U.S. government suggest use of the percentage-of-completion method of income recognition. One difficulty encountered in applying the percentage-of-completion method is that Rockwell Collins's contracts for some projects are continually renewed. This procedure makes it difficult to identify a single contract price and accumulate costs for a single contract, which the percentage-of-completion method envisions.

b. **Amgen**—Amgen realized the highest profit margin of the seven companies. Its biotechnology products are protected by patents. It therefore maintains a monopoly position. Note that the cost of manufacturing its products is a small percent of revenues. Amgen's major cost is for research and development. Sales of its existing products are not only sufficient to cover its high, on-going research work but to provide a substantial profit margin as well. Its relatively low revenue to assets percentage is somewhat unexpected, given that its major "assets" are patents and research scientists. The reason for this low percentage (reason not provided in the case) is that cash and marketable securities comprise approximately 25% of its assets. These assets generated a return of approximately 3% during the year. This rate of return decreased the overall ratio of revenues to assets for Amgen.

8.53 b. continued.

Brown-Forman—Brown-Forman realized the third highest profit margin among the seven companies. If one views the excise taxes as a reduction in revenues rather than as an expense, its profit margin is 10.4% [= 8.8%/(100.0% − 15.4%)]. Concerns about excess alcoholic drinking in recent years have resulted in some exodus of companies from the industry, leaving the remaining companies with a larger share of a smaller market. The products of Brown-Forman carry brand name recognition, permitting the firm to obtain attractive prices.

Deere—Deere's relatively low profit margin reflects (1) weaknesses in the farming industry in recent years, which puts downward pressure on margins, and (2) decreased interest rates, which lowers profit margins. The revenue-to-assets percentage of Deere reflects its capital-intensive manufacturing operations and the low interest rate on outstanding loans to dealers and customers.

Fluor—The low profit margin of Fluor reflects the relatively low value added of construction services. It may also reflect recessionary conditions when construction activity is weak and profit margins are thin.

Golden West—The 12% profit margin (ignoring an addback for interest expense, which is common for financial services firms) seems high, relative to interest rates in recent years. Recall though that Golden West pays short-term interest rates on its deposits but obtains long-term interest rates on its loans. An upward-sloping yield curve provides a positive differential. Also, the existence of shareholders' equity funds in the capital structure means that Golden West has assets earning returns for which it recognizes no expense in its income statement (that is, firms do not recognize an expense for the implicit cost of shareholders' funds). Note also that the ratio of revenue to assets is only 0.1. Thus, the assets of Golden West earned a return of only 1.2% (= 12.0% X 0.1) during the year.

Merrill Lynch—The lower profit margin for Merrill Lynch relative to Golden West reflects in part the fact that both the investments and financing of Merrill Lynch are short term. Merrill Lynch, however, realizes revenue from fee-based services. Firms like Merrill Lynch can differentiate these services somewhat and realize attractive profit margins. However, such services have been quickly copied by competitors in recent years, reducing the profit margins accordingly.

Odd-numbered Solutions

8.53 b. continued.

Rockwell Collins—This profit margin is in the middle of the seven companies. Factors arguing for a high profit margin include Rockwell-Collins's technological know-how and its role in long-term contracts with the U.S. government. Factors arguing for a lower profit margin include cutbacks in defense expenditures and excess capacity in the aerospace industry.

CHAPTER 9

WORKING CAPITAL

Questions, Exercises, and Problems: Answers and Solutions

9.1 See the text or the glossary at the end of the book.

9.3 The underlying principle is that acquisition cost includes all costs required to prepare an asset for its intended use. Assets provide future services. Costs that a firm must incur to obtain those expected services are, therefore, included in the acquisition cost valuation of the asset. In the case of merchandise inventory, this includes the costs associated with obtaining the goods (purchase price, transportation costs, insurance costs). For manufactured inventory, acquisition costs include direct labor, direct materials, and manufacturing overhead.

9.5 Both the Merchandise Inventory and Finished Goods Inventory accounts include the cost of completed units ready for sale. A merchandising firm acquires the units in finished form and debits Merchandise Inventory for their acquisition cost. A manufacturing firm incurs direct material, direct labor, and manufacturing overhead costs in transforming the units to a finished, salable condition. The Raw Materials Inventory and Work-in-Process Inventory accounts include such costs until the completion of manufacturing operations. Thus, the accountant debits the Finished Goods Inventory account for the cost of producing completed units. The accountant credits both the Merchandise Inventory and Finished Goods Inventory accounts for the cost of units sold and reports the inventory accounts as current assets on the balance sheet.

9.7 Rising Purchase Prices
Higher Inventory Amount: FIFO
Lower Inventory Amount: LIFO
Higher Cost of Goods
Sold Amount: LIFO
Lower Cost of Goods
Sold Amount: FIFO

9.9 The Parker School should accrue the salary in ten monthly installments of $360,000 each at the end of each month, September through June. It will have paid $300,000 at the end of each of these months, so that by the end of the reporting year, it reports a current liability of $600,000 [= $3,600,000 – (10 X $300,000)].

9.11 **Similarities:** The accountant makes estimates of future events in both cases. The accountant charges the cost of estimated uncollectibles or warranties to income in the period of sale, not in the later period when specific items become uncollectible or break down. The income statement reports the charge against income as an expense in both cases, although some accountants report the charge for estimated uncollectibles as a revenue contra.

Differences: The balance sheet account showing the expected costs of future uncollectibles reduces an asset account, whereas that for estimated warranties appears as a liability.

9.13 (Accounting for prepayments.) (amounts in millions of euros)

a. Journal entry to record insurance premium payments in 2012, 2011, and 2010:

Prepayments	50.0	
Cash		50.0

b. Adjusting journal entries required each year.

2011:

Insurance Expense	66.3	
Prepayments		66.3

To adjust Prepayments for the amount consumed during 2011, of €66.3 million (= €42.1 + €50.0 – €25.8).

2012:

Insurance Expense	45.1	
Prepayments		45.1

To adjust Prepayments for the amount consumed during 2012, of €45.1 million (= €25.8 + €50.0 – €30.7).

9.15   (Ringgold Winery; identifying inventory cost inclusions.) (amounts in US$)

Ringgold should include the costs to acquire the grapes, process them into wine, and mature the wine, but not the expenditures on advertising or research and development. Thus, the cost of the wine inventory (prior to its sale) is $3,673,000 (= $2,200,000 + $50,000 + $145,000 + $100,000 + $250,000 + $600,000 + $120,000 + $180,000 + $28,000).

9.17   (ResellFast; effect of inventory valuation on the balance sheet and net income.) (amounts in millions of US$)

	Carrying Value	Effect on Income
Q1	$ 20.0	$ 0.0
Q2	16.5	(3.5)
Q3	16.5	0.0
Q4	0.0	11.0

9.19   (Tesco Plc.; inventory and accounts payable journal entries.) (amounts in millions of pounds sterling)

a. Trade Payables 43,558

     Cash 43,558

b. Beginning Balance in Trade Payables + Purchases of Merchandise Inventory = Payments to Venders + Ending Balance in Trade Payables.

£3,317 + Purchases of Merchandise Inventory = £43,558 (from Part a.) + £3,936.

Purchases of Merchandise Inventory = £44,177.

Merchandise Inventory 44,177

    Accounts Payable 44,177

9.19 continued.

    c.   Beginning Balance in Merchandise Inventory + Purchases of Inventory = Amount Sold (Cost of Goods Sold) + Ending Balance in Merchandise Inventory.

£1,911 + £44,177 (from Part *b.*) = Cost of Goods Sold + £2,420.
Cost of Goods Sold = £43,668.

Cost of Goods Sold	43,668	
Merchandise Inventory		43,668

9.21   (GenMet; income computation for a manufacturing firm.)   (amounts in millions of US$)

Sales	$ 6,700.2
Less Cost of Goods Sold	(2,697.6)
Less Selling and Administrative Expenses	(2,903.7)
Less Interest Expense	(151.9)
Income Before Income Taxes	$ 947.0
Income Tax Expense at 35%	(331.5)
Net Income	$ 615.5
Work-in-Process Inventory, October 31, 2012	$ 100.8
Plus Manufacturing Costs Incurred During Fiscal Year 2013....	2,752.0
Less Work-in-Process Inventory, October 31, 2013	(119.1)
Cost of Goods Completed During Fiscal Year 2013	$ 2,733.7
Plus Finished Goods Inventory, October 31, 2012	286.2
Less Finished Goods Inventory, October 31, 2013	(322.3)
Cost of Goods Sold	$ 2,697.6

9.23   (Warren Company; effect of inventory errors.)

a.	NO/None.	f.	US/Understatement by $1,000.
b.	NO/None.	g.	US/Understatement by $1,000.
c.	US/Understatement by $1,000.	h.	NO/None.
d.	OS/Overstatement by $1,000.	i.	NO/None.
e.	OS/Overstatement by $1,000.		

9.25   (Ericsson; lower of cost or market for inventory.) (amounts in millions of Swedish kronor [SEK])

a.   SEK22,475 million (= SEK25,227 – SEK2,752).

b.   Journal entry to record impairment charge for inventory during the year:

Impairment Loss on Inventory	1,276	
Allowance for Impairment		1,276

The carrying value of the inventory is now SEK2,224 (= SEK3,500 – SEK1,276).

c.   January: Journal entry to record a reversal of a portion of the impairment charge for inventory taken in the preceding year:

Allowance for Impairment	576	
Reversal of Impairment Loss on Inventory		576

To reverse a portion of the impairment loss; SEK576 = SEK2,800 – SEK2,224.

d.   U.S. GAAP would not permit Ericsson to reverse a previous impairment of inventory.

9.27   (Arnold Company; computations involving different cost-flow assumptions.) (amounts in US$)

	Pounds	a. FIFO	b. Weighted Average	c. LIFO
Raw Materials Available for Use	10,700	$24,384	$24,384	$ 24,384
Less Ending Inventory	(3,500)	(8,110)[a]	(7,976)[c]	(7,818)[e]
Raw Materials Issued to Production	7,200	$16,274[b]	$16,408[d]	$ 16,566[f]

[a] $(3,000 \times \$2.32) + (500 \times \$2.30) = \$8,110.$

[b] $(1,200 \times \$2.20) + (2,200 \times \$2.25) + (2,800 \times \$2.28) + (1,000 \times \$2.30) = \$16,274.$

[c] $(\$24,384/10,700) \times 3,500 = \$7,976.$

[d] $(\$24,384/10,700) \times 7,200 = \$16,408.$

[e] $(1,200 \times \$2.20) + (2,200 \times \$2.25) + (100 \times \$2.28) = \$7,818.$

[f] $(3,000 \times \$2.32) + (1,500 \times \$2.30) + (2,700 \times \$2.28) = \$16,566.$

Odd-numbered Solutions

9.29   (EKG Company; LIFO provides opportunity for income manipulation.)
        (amounts in US$)

   a.   Largest cost of goods sold results from producing 70,000 (or more)
        additional units at a cost of $22 each, giving cost of goods sold of
        $1,540,000.

   b.   Smallest cost of goods sold results from producing no additional units,
        giving cost of goods sold of $980,000 [= ($8 x 10,000) + ($15 x 60,000)].

   c.

	Income Reported	
	Minimum	**Maximum**
Revenues ($30 x 70,000)	$2,100,000	$2,100,000
Less Cost of Goods Sold	(1,540,000)	(980,000)
Gross Margin	$ 560,000	$1,120,000

9.31   (Falcon Motor Company; analysis of LIFO and FIFO disclosures.) (amounts
        in millions of US$)

   a.   Falcon Motor Company uses LIFO, so the carrying value of its
        inventories would be $10,121 million as of December 31, 2013, and
        $10,017 as of December 31, 2012.

   b.

	LIFO	**Difference**	**FIFO**
Beginning Inventory	$ 10,017	$ 1,015	$ 11,032
Production Costs (Plug)	142,691	—	142,691
Goods Available for Sale (Plug)	$152,708	$ 1,015	$ 153,723
Less Ending Inventory	(10,121)	(1,100)	(11,221)
Cost of Goods Sold	$142,587	$ (85)	$ 142,502

9.33   (Hurley Corporation; accounting for uncollectible accounts and warranties.)
        (amounts in US$)

   a.   **Allowance for Uncollectible Accounts**

Balance, December 31, 2011	$ 355
Plus Bad Debt Expense for 2012: 0.02 x $18,000	360
Less Accounts Written Off (Plug)	(310)
Balance, December 31, 2012	$ 405
Plus Bad Debt Expense for 2013: 0.02 x $16,000	320
Less Accounts Written Off (Plug)	(480)
Balance, December 31, 2013	$ 245

9.33 continued.

 b. **Estimated Warranty Liability**

Balance, December 31, 2011..	$ 1,325
Plus Warranty Expense for 2012: 0.06 × $18,000.............	1,080
Less Actual Warranty Costs (Plug)...................................	(870)
Balance, December 31, 2012..	$ 1,535
Plus Warranty Expense for 2013: 0.06 × $16,000.............	960
Less Actual Warranty Costs (Plug)...................................	(775)
Balance, December 31, 2013..	$ 1,720

9.35 (Kingspeed Bikes; journal entries for warranty liabilities and subsequent expenditures.) (amounts in US$)

 a. **2011**

Cash	800,000	
Sales Revenue...................................		800,000
Warranty Liability	22,000	
Cash		13,200
Parts Inventory		8,800
Warranty Expense	48,000	
Warranty Liability		48,000

0.06 × $800,000 = $48,000.

2012

Cash	1,200,000	
Sales Revenue...................................		1,200,000
Warranty Liability	55,000	
Cash		33,000
Parts Inventory		22,000
Warranty Expense	72,000	
Warranty Liability		72,000

0.06 × $1,200,000 = $72,000.

9.35 a. continued.

2013

Cash	900,000	
Sales Revenue..		900,000

Warranty Liability	52,000	
Cash		31,200
Parts Inventory		20,800

Warranty Expense	54,000	
Warranty Liability		54,000

0.06 x $900,000 = $54,000.

b. $48,000 – $22,000 + $72,000 – $55,000 + $54,000 – $52,000 = $45,000.

9.37 (Delchamps Group; journal entries for restructuring liabilities and subsequent expenditures.) (amounts in millions of euros)

a. **Journal entries for 2012**

Restructuring Expense	14.2	
Restructuring Provision......................................		14.2

To record new restructuring charges made during 2012.

Restructuring Provision...	7.3	
Restructuring Expense		7.3

To record the reversal of prior period restructuring charges.

Restructuring Provision...	40.0	
Cash		40.0

To record cash expenditures to settle restructuring Provisions; 40.0 = [(84.0 + 14.2) – (7.3 + 50.9)].

b. Delchamps will report a total restructuring provision of €50.9, classified as follows on its balance sheet:

Current Portion of Restructuring Provision...................	€12.5 million
Noncurrent Portion of Restructuring Provision..............	€38.4 million

9.37 continued.

    c.   Delchamps's income in 2012 is lower by €6.9 million (= €14.2 million − €7.3 million). The net change in income of €6.9 million is added to income as a noncash expense to calculate cash flow from operations in the statement of cash flows:

9.39   (Lord Cromptom Plc.; flow of manufacturing costs through the accounts.) (amounts in pounds sterling)

    a.

Beginning Raw Materials Inventory	£ 46,900
Raw Materials Purchased	429,000
Raw Materials Available for Use	£ 475,900
Subtract Ending Raw Materials Inventory	(43,600)
Cost of Raw Materials Used	£ 432,300
Beginning Factory Supplies Inventory	£ 7,600
Factory Supplies Purchased	22,300
Factory Supplies Available for Use	£ 29,900
Subtract Ending Factory Supplies Inventory	(7,700)
Cost of Factory Supplies Used	£ 22,200

    b.

Beginning Work-in-Process Inventory	£ 110,900
Cost of Raw Materials Used (from Part a.)	432,300
Cost of Factory Supplies Used (from Part a.)	22,200
Direct Labor Costs Incurred	362,100
Heat, Light, and Power Costs	10,300
Insurance	4,200
Depreciation of Factory Equipment	36,900
Prepaid Rent Expired	3,600
Total Beginning Work-in-Process and Manufacturing Costs Incurred	£ 982,500
Subtract Ending Work-in-Process Inventory	(115,200)
Cost of Units Completed and Transferred to Finished Goods Storeroom	£ 867,300

    c.

Beginning Finished Goods Inventory	£ 76,700
Cost of Units Completed and Transferred to Finished Goods Storeroom (from Part b.)	867,300
Subtract Ending Finished Goods Inventory	(71,400)
Cost of Goods Sold	£ 872,600

9.39 continued.

    d.   Net Income is £110,040 [= (1 – 0.40)(£1,350,000 – £872,600 – £246,900 – £47,100)].

9.41   (Minevik Group; flow of manufacturing costs.)   (amounts in millions of Swedish kronor [SEK])

    a.   Ending Balance of Total Inventory = Ending Balance of Raw Materials Inventory + Ending Balance of Work-in-Process Inventory + Ending Balance of Finished Goods Inventory.

        Ending Balance of Total Inventory = SEK6,964 + SEK5,157 + SEK13,180 = SEK25,301 million.

    b.   Loss on Impairment of Inventory 281
          Finished Goods Inventory   281

    c.   Cost of Sales, after Write-down = Cost of Sales, before Write-down + Write-down.

        SEK57,222 = (Cost of Sales, before Write-down) + SEK281.
        Cost of Sales, before Write-down = SEK56,941 million.

    d.   Beginning Finished Goods Inventory + Cost of Units Completed = Cost of Sales + Write-downs + Ending Finished Goods Inventory.

        SEK8,955 + Cost of Units Completed = SEK56,941 + SEK281 + SEK13,180.

        Cost of Units Completed = SEK61,447 million.

    e.   Beginning Balance in Work-in-Process Inventory + Direct Materials + Direct Labor + Overhead = Cost of Units Completed + Ending Balance in Work-in-Process Inventory.

        SEK4,093 + Direct Material Costs + 3 X Direct Material Costs = SEK61,447 (from Part d.) + SEK5,157.

        Direct Material Costs = SEK62,511/4 = SEK15,628 million.

        Work-in-Process Inventory.. 15,628
          Raw Materials Inventory.....................................   15,628

9.41 continued.

    f. Beginning Balance in Raw Materials Inventory + Raw Materials Purchases = Raw Materials Used in Production + Ending Balance of Raw Materials Inventory.

        SEK5,690 + Raw Material Purchases = SEK15,628 (from Part *e.*) + SEK6,964.

        Raw Materials Purchases = SEK16,902 million.

9.43   (Burton Corporation; detailed comparison of various choices for inventory accounting.) (amounts in US$)

	FIFO	LIFO	Weighted Average
Inventory, 1/1/2011	$ 0	$ 0	$ 0
Purchases During 2011	14,400	14,400	14,400
Goods Available for Sale During 2011	$14,400	$14,400	$ 14,400
Less Inventory, 12/31/2011	(3,000)[1]	(2,000)[2]	(2,400)[3]
Cost of Goods Sold for 2011	$11,400	$12,400	$ 12,000
Inventory, 1/1/2012	$ 3,000 [1]	$ 2,000 [2]	$ 2,400 [3]
Purchases During 2012	21,000	21,000	21,000
Goods Available for Sale During 2012	$24,000	$23,000	$ 23,400
Less Inventory, 12/31/2012	(5,000)[4]	(6,200)[5]	(5,850)[6]
Cost of Goods Sold for 2012	$19,000	$16,800	$ 17,550

[1] $200 \times \$15 = \$3,000$.

[2] $200 \times \$10 = \$2,000$.

[3] $(\$14,400/1,200) \times 200 = \$2,400$.

[4] $500 \times \$10 = \$5,000$.

[5] $(200 \times \$10) + (300 \times \$14) = \$6,200$.

[6] $(\$23,400/2,000) \times 500 = \$5,850$.

    a. $11,400.   d. $19,000.

    b. $12,400.   e. $16,800.

    c. $12,000.   f. $17,550.

        Odd-numbered Solutions

9.43 continued.

g. FIFO results in higher net income for 2011. Purchase prices for inventory items increased during 2011. FIFO uses older, lower purchase prices to measure cost of goods sold, whereas LIFO uses more recent, higher prices.

h. LIFO results in higher net income for 2012. Purchase prices for inventory items decreased during 2012. LIFO uses more recent, lower prices to measure cost of goods sold, whereas FIFO uses older, higher prices.

9.45 (Burch Corporation; reconstructing underlying events from ending inventory amounts [adapted from CPA examination].) (amounts in US$)

a. Down. Notice that lower of cost or market is lower than acquisition cost (FIFO); current market price is less than cost.

b. Up. FIFO means last-in, still-here. The last purchases (FIFO = LISH) cost $44,000 and the earlier purchases (LIFO = FISH) cost $41,800. Also, lower-of-cost-or-market basis shows acquisition costs, which are greater than or equal to current cost.

c. LIFO Cost. Other things being equal, the largest income results from the method that shows the largest *increase* in inventory during the year.

Margin = Revenues – Cost of Goods Sold
        = Revenues – Beginning Inventory – Purchases + Ending Inventory
        = Revenues – Purchases + Increase in Inventory.

Because the beginning inventory in 2010 is zero, the method with the largest closing inventory amount implies the largest increase and hence the largest income.

d. Lower of Cost or Market. The method with the "largest increase in inventory" during the year in this case is the method with the smallest decrease, because all methods show declines in inventory during 2011. Lower of cost or market shows a decrease in inventory of only $3,000 during 2011—the other methods show larger decreases ($3,800; $4,000).

e. Lower of Cost or Market. The method with the largest increase in inventory: $10,000. LIFO shows a $5,400 increase, whereas FIFO shows $8,000.

9.45 continued.

    f.   LIFO Cost. The lower income for all three years results from the method that shows the smallest increase in inventory over the three years. Because all beginning inventories were zero under all methods, we need merely find the method with the smallest ending inventory at 2012 year-end.

    g.   FIFO lower by $2,000. Under FIFO, inventories increased $8,000 during 2012. Under lower of cost or market, inventories increased $10,000 during 2012. Lower of cost or market has a bigger increase—$2,000— and therefore lower of cost or market shows a $2,000 larger income than FIFO for 2012.

9.47   (Sedan Corporation; interpreting inventory disclosures.) (amounts in millions of Japanese yen)

    a. **March 31, 2013:**

If Sedan had used FIFO, inventory values would have been ¥13,780 less than LIFO amounts.

Ending Balance of Total Inventory (FIFO) = (¥374,210 + ¥239,937 + ¥1,211,569) − ¥13,780 = ¥1,825,716 − ¥13,780 = ¥1,811,936 million.

March 31, 2012:

If Sedan had used FIFO, inventory values would have been ¥30,360 less than LIFO amounts.

Ending Balance of Total Inventory (FIFO) = (¥362,686 + ¥236,749 + ¥1,204,521) − ¥30,360 = ¥1,803,956 − ¥30,360 = ¥1,773,596 million.

    b.   Beginning Balance in Finished Goods (FIFO) + Cost of Units Completed = Cost of Products Sold (FIFO) + Ending Balance in Finished Goods (FIFO).

Beginning Balance of Finished Goods Inventory (FIFO) = ¥1,204,521 − ¥30,360 = ¥1,174,161 million.

9.47 b. continued.

Ending Balance of Finished Goods Inventory (FIFO) = ¥1,211,569 – ¥13,780 = ¥1,197,789 million.

¥1,174,161 + ¥20,459,386 (from Problem 9.40, Part *b*.) = Cost of Products Sold (FIFO) + ¥1,197,789.

Cost of Goods Sold (FIFO) = ¥20,435,758 million.

Also, could calculate as follows:

Cost of Goods Sold (LIFO)	¥ 20,452,338
Change in LIFO reserve (¥30,360 – ¥13,780)	(16,580)
Cost of Goods Sold (FIFO)	¥20,435,758

9.49 (Bayer Group; interpreting restructuring disclosures.) (amounts in millions of euros)

a.

Restructuring Provision	134	
Cash		134

To record utilizations.

Restructuring Provision	31	
Reversal of Restructuring Expense		31

To record reversal.

b. Journal entry to record additions to Restructuring Provision during the year:

Restructuring Expense	128	
Restructuring Provision		128

To record €128 million of restructuring charges made during the year.

Beginning Balance of Restructuring Provision + Additions = Utilizations + Net Other Effects + Reversals + Ending Balance of Restructuring Provision €196 + Additions = €134 + €5 + €31 + €154.

Additions = €128 million.

CHAPTER 10

LONG-LIVED TANGIBLE AND INTANGIBLE ASSETS

Questions, Exercises, and Problems: Answers and Solutions

10.1   See the text or the glossary at the end of the book.

10.3   The central concept underlying U.S. GAAP for these three items is the ability to identify and reliably measure expected future benefits. Expenditures to research new drugs may give rise to future benefits, but identifying the existence of those future benefits while research progresses is problematic. Thus, U.S. GAAP requires immediate expensing of research and development expenditures. The external market transaction for a patent on a new drug validates both the existence and fair value of the patent. U.S. GAAP, therefore, recognizes the patent as an asset. In-process R&D has characteristics of the previous two cases. Whether the in-process project will yield future benefits is uncertain, suggesting that firms should expense such expenditures at the time of acquisition. An external market transaction between independent parties suggests the existence of future benefits, supporting recognition of an asset until such time as the status of the research project becomes more certain. FASB *Statement No. 141 (Revised)* requires firms to recognize as an asset the fair value of in-process R&D acquired in a corporate acquisition, placing greater weight on the evidence provided by the external market transaction than on the uncertainty of future benefits.

10.5   A long-lived asset with a finite life is expected to provide benefits for a limited amount of time. Benefits will eventually decline to zero, either because of physical use, obsolescence, or disposal. Firms depreciate or amortize assets with finite lives. Note that firms must estimate the finite life in most cases. U.S. GAAP and IFRS treat assets that have an extended life, but for which the length of that life is highly uncertain, as having an indefinite life. U.S. GAAP and IFRS do not require firms to depreciate or amortize assets with an indefinite life. U.S. GAAP and IFRS require that these assets—in fact, all long-lived assets—be tested annually for possible asset impairment.

10.7 The treatment of this change in depreciable life would depend on the reason for and the materiality of the change. The change in this case appears prompted by new governmental regulations imposed on the airline industry. If the change in expected life is material, the firm can make a case for recognizing an asset impairment loss and revising its depreciation going forward. If the impact is not material, the airline might treat the change in depreciable life as a change in an estimate and spread the effect of the change over the current and future years. The purpose of this question is to demonstrate that judgments are often required in applying authoritative guidance.

10.9 U.S. GAAP compares the undiscounted cash flows from an asset to its carrying value to determine if an impairment loss has occurred. The rationale is that an impairment loss has not occurred if a firm will receive cash flows in the future at least equal to the carrying value of the asset. Receiving such cash flows will permit the firm to recover the carrying value. This criterion ignores the time value of money. Cash received earlier has more economic value than cash received later, but this criterion ignores such differences.

10.11 An asset impairment loss that arises during a period results from a decline in fair value due to some external event. Fair values are based on discounted cash flows, not undiscounted cash flows. Therefore, using undiscounted cash flows to signal an impairment loss ignores the actual decline in fair value that occurred. Firms will not recognize the asset impairment loss as long as the undiscounted cash flows exceed the carrying value of the asset.

10.13   (Outback Steakhouse; calculating acquisition costs of long-lived assets.)
(amounts in US$)

The relative market values of the land and building are 20%
(= $52,000/$260,000) for the land and 80% (= $208,000/$260,000) for the
building. We use these percentages to allocate the combined $260,000 cost
of the land and building.

	Land	Building
Purchase Price of Land and Building.......	$ 52,000	$ 208,000
Legal Costs Split 20% and 80%...............	2,520	10,080
Renovation Costs.....................................	—	35,900
Property and Liability Insurance Costs During Renovation Split 20% and 80%..	800	3,200
Property Taxes During Renovation Split 20% and 80%......................................	1,000	4,000
Total...	$ 56,320	$ 261,180

Note: One might argue that the split of the insurance and property taxes
should recognize the increase in market value of the building as a
result of the renovation and use some other percentages besides 20%
and 80%. Note also that the insurance and property taxes for the
period after opening are expenses of the first year of operation.

10.15   (Bolton Company; cost of self-constructed assets.) (amounts in US$)

Land: $70,000 + $2,000 (14) = $72,000.

Factory Building: $200,000 (1) + $12,000 (2) + $140,000 (3) + $6,000 (5) −
$7,000 (7) + $10,000 (8) + $8,000 (9) + $3,000[a] (10) + $8,000 (11) + $4,000
(13) + $1,000[a] (15) = $385,000.

Office Building: $20,000 + $13,000 (4) = $33,000.

Site Improvements: $5,000 (12).

[a]The firm might expense these items. It depends on the rationality of
the firm's "self-insurance" policy.

Item (6) is omitted because firms may not recognize opportunity costs in
financial reports.

Odd-numbered Solutions

10.15 continued.

Item (16) is omitted because no arm's length transaction occurred in which the firm earned a profit.

10.17   (Bulls Eye Stores; calculating interest capitalized during construction.) (amounts in US$)

Capitalized Interest on Borrowing Directly Related to
    Construction: 0.06 X $2,000,000.. $ 120,000
Capitalized Interest of Other Borrowing: 0.07 X $1,400,000.....   98,000
    Total Interest Capitalized .... $ 218,000

10.19   (Carlton, Inc.; calculations for various depreciation methods.) (amounts in US$)

		2013	2014	2015
a.	Straight-Line (Time) Method	$14,000	$14,000	$14,000
	($88,800 − $4,800)/6 = $14,000.			
b.	Straight-Line (Use) Method	$12,600	$14,000	$15,400
	$84,000/30,000 = $2.80 per hour.			

10.21   (Thom Corporation; change in depreciable life and salvage value.) (amounts in US$)

Carrying Value on January 1, 2013: $10,000,000 − {2 × [($10,000,000 − $1,000,000)/6]} = $7,000,000. Depreciation expense for 2013 based on the new depreciable life and salvage value is $3,200,000 [= ($7,000,000 − $600,000)/2].

10.23   (Disney World; distinguishing repairs versus improvements.) (amounts in US$)

Repair: (1.00/1.20 X $30,200) + $86,100 + (1.00/1.25 X $26,900) + $12,600 = $145,387.

Improvement: (0.20/1.20 X $30,200) + (0.25/1.25 X $26,900) = $10,413.

10.25 (Kieran Corporation; computing the amount of impairment loss.) (amounts in US$)

	Carrying Value	Undis- counted Cash Flows	Impair- ment Loss Recog- nized	Fair Value	Amount of Loss
Land....................	$ 550,000	$ 575,000	No	$ 550,000	$ 0
Buildings	580,000	600,000	No	580,000	0
Equipment..........	1,200,000	950,000	Yes	800,000	400,000
Goodwill..............	500,000[a]	—	Yes	270,000	230,000
Total	$ 2,830,000			$2,200,000	$ 630,000

[a]$500,000 = $2,400,000 − $400,000 − $600,000 − $900,000.

After recognizing the impairment losses on the property, plant, and equipment, the carrying value of Kieran Corporation is $2,430,000 (= $550,000 for land + $580,000 for buildings + $800,000 for equipment + $500,000 for goodwill). The carrying value of $2,430,000 exceeds the fair value of the entity of $2,200,000, so a goodwill impairment loss may have occurred. The fair value column above shows the allocation of the $2,200,000 fair value to identifiable assets, with the residual of $270,000 attributed to goodwill. The carrying value of the goodwill of $500,000 exceeds its implied fair value of $270,000, so Kieran Corporation recognizes an impairment loss on the goodwill of $230,000.

10.27 (Wilcox Corporation; working backward to derive proceeds from disposition of plant assets.) (amounts in US$)

Cost of Equipment Sold: $400,000 + $230,000 − $550,000 = $80,000.

Accumulated Depreciation on Equipment Sold: $180,000 + $50,000 − $160,000 = $70,000.

Carrying Value of Equipment Sold: $80,000 − $70,000 = $10,000.

Proceeds of Sale: $10,000 + $4,000 = $14,000.

10.29 (Moon Macrosystems; recording transactions involving tangible and intangible assets.) (amounts in US$)

a. Office Equipment.. 400,000
Computer Software 40,000
    Cash... 440,000

10.29 continued.

b.

Office Equipment	20,000	
Computer Software	10,000	
Cash		30,000

c. **2011 and 2012**

Depreciation Expense [($400,000 + $20,000 − $40,000)/10]	38,000	
Amortization Expense [($40,000 + $10,000)/4]	12,500	
Accumulated Depreciation		38,000
Computer Software		12,500

d.

Impairment Loss of Computer Software ($40,000 + $10,000 − $12,500 − $12,500)	25,000	
Computer Software		25,000

e.

Depreciation Expense [($400,000 + $20,000 − $38,000 − $38,000 − $56,000)/12]	24,000	
Accumulated Depreciation		24,000

f.

Depreciation Expense	24,000	
Accumulated Depreciation		24,000

Cash	260,000	
Accumulated Depreciation ($38,000 + $38,000 + $24,000 + $24,000)	124,000	
Loss on Sale of Office Equipment	36,000	
Office Equipment		420,000

10.31 (Recognizing and measuring impairment losses.) (amounts in US$)

a. The loss occurs because of an adverse action by a governmental entity. The undiscounted cash flows of $50 million are less than the carrying value of the building of $60 million. An impairment loss has therefore occurred. The fair value of the building of $32 million is less than the carrying value of $60 million. Thus, the amount of the impairment loss is $28 million (= $60 million − $32 million). The journal entry to record the impairment loss is (in millions):

Loss from Impairment	28	
Accumulated Depreciation	20	
Building		48

10.31 a. continued.

This entry records the impairment loss, eliminates the accumulated depreciation, and writes down the building to its fair value of $32 million (= $80 – $48).

b. The undiscounted cash flows of $70 million exceed the carrying value of the building of $60 million. Thus, no impairment loss occurs according to the definition in U.S. GAAP. An *economic* loss occurred but U.S. GAAP does not recognize it.

c. The loss arises because the accumulated costs significantly exceed the amount originally anticipated. The carrying value of the building of $25 million exceeds the undiscounted future cash flows of $22 million. Thus, an impairment loss has occurred. The impairment loss recognized equals $9 million (= $25 million – $16 million). The journal entry is (in millions):

Loss from Impairment 9
    Construction in Process 9

d. The loss occurs because of a significant decline in the fair value of the patent. U.S. GAAP requires calculation of the impairment loss on the patent before computing the impairment loss on goodwill. The undiscounted future cash flows of $18 million are less than the carrying value of the patent of $20 million. Thus, an impairment loss occurred. The amount of the loss is $8 million (= $20 million – $12 million). The journal entry to record the loss is (in millions):

Loss from Impairment 8
    Patent 8

The second step is to determine if an impairment loss on the goodwill occurred. The fair value of the entity is $25 million. The carrying value after writing down the patent is $27 million (= $12 million for patent and $15 million for goodwill). Thus, a goodwill impairment loss occurred. If the fair value of the patent is $12 million, the market value of the goodwill is $13 million. The impairment loss on goodwill is therefore $2 million (= $15 million – $13 million). The journal entry is (in millions):

Loss from Impairment 2
    Goodwill 2

10.31 continued.

e. The loss occurs because of a significant change in the business climate for Chicken Franchisees. One might question whether this loss is temporary or permanent. U.S. GAAP discusses but rejects the use of a permanency criterion in identifying impairment losses. Thus, an impairment loss occurs in this case because the future undiscounted cash flows of $6 million from the franchise rights are less than the carrying value of the franchise rights of $10 million. The amount of the impairment loss is $7 million (= $10 million – $3 million). The journal entry is (in millions):

Impairment Loss 7
    Franchise Rights 7

This entry assumes that Chicken Franchisees does not use an Accumulated Amortization account.

10.33 (Comerica Mills; interpreting disclosures regarding long-lived assets.) (amounts in millions of US$)

a. Comerica Mills purchased software for its internal use from a software developer. Comerica Mills expects to receive future benefits from using the software and the acquisition cost provides evidence of the amount of expected future benefits.

b. Yes. The computer software has a finite life because of technological obsolescence and would be depreciated.

c. Average Total Life: 0.5($5,806 – $54 – $252 + $6,096 – $61 – $276)/$421 = 13.4 years.

Average Age: 0.5($2,809 + $3,082)/$421 = 7.0 years.

d. Yes. The accumulated depreciation account increased by $273 (= $3,082 – $2,809). Depreciation expense increased accumulated depreciation by $421. Thus, the accumulated depreciation on assets sold or abandoned was $148 (= $273 – $421).

10.33 continued.

e. Comerica Mills has grown heavily by corporate acquisitions. Intangibles comprise 57.9% (= $10,529/$18,184) of total assets. Because GAAP does not require firms to recognize internally developed intangibles, these intangibles arise from corporate acquisitions.

f. Yes. The amount for brands and goodwill increased. Because firms cannot write up assets for increases in fair value, the increased amounts suggest a small acquisition during the year.

g. Patents have a specified legal life. Trademarks are subject to renewal at the end of their legal life as long as a firm continues to use them. Comerica Mills must intend not to renew these trademarks.

h. Comerica Mills must expect the brand names to have an indefinite life. The firm would need to provide evidence based on past experience for its brand names and from industry experience to convince its independent accountants that the timing of any cessation of benefits is highly uncertain.

i. Comerica Mills shows amounts in its Construction in Progress account. Thus, Comerica Mills must capitalize a portion of interest expense. The reported amount is the net of total interest cost minus the amount capitalized in Construction in Progress.

10.35 (HP3; interpreting disclosures regarding long-lived assets.) (amounts in millions of US$)

a. Average Total Life: $0.5(\$15,024 - \$534 + \$16,411 - \$464)/\$1,922 = 7.9$ years.

Average Age: $0.5(\$8,161 + \$8,613)/\$1,922 = 4.4$ years.

b. Yes. The Accumulated Depreciation account increased $452 (= $8,613 − $8,161). Depreciation increased the Accumulated Depreciation account by $1,922. Thus, the accumulated depreciation on assets sold or abandoned was $1,470 (= $452 − $1,922).

10.35 continued.

c. Customer Contracts have a specific term and, therefore, have a finite life. Core Technology likely involves technologies related to the design of computer hardware and software in general and is not product specific. Given the pace of change in the computer industry, even core technologies change over time. HP3 would likely encounter difficulties in convincing its independent accountants that core technologies do not have a finite, albeit uncertain, life. Patents have a 20-year life, although the technological life in the computer industry is much shorter. Trademarks are renewable as long as a firm continues to use them. HP3 must expect to discontinue using the trademarks.

d. Average Remaining Total Life: $0.5(\$4,612 + \$6,122)/\$783 = 6.9$ years.

    Average Age: $0.5(\$2,682 + \$3,465)/\$783 = 3.9$ years.

e. At the time of the acquisition, the Casio name was highly recognizable. HP3 likely had no difficulty convincing its independent accountants that the brand name had an indefinite life. Given the elapsed time since the acquisition and the merging of Casio products into HP3's line of offerings, one wonders whether HP3 will write off the brand name at some point.

f. Yes. The amount of each intangible, except the Casio brand name, increased during 2013. HP3 allocated a portion of the purchase price to these intangibles, with most of the increase involving goodwill.

CHAPTER 11

NOTES, BONDS, AND LEASES

Questions, Exercises, and Problems: Answers and Solutions

11.1   See the text or the glossary at the end of the book.

11.3   Applying the effective interest method using the historical market interest rate gives a constant amount of interest expense only if a firm initially issued bonds at face value. If a firm issued bonds at a discount or a premium to face value, then the amount of interest expense will change each period. A statement that applies to all bonds, whether issued at face value, a discount, or a premium, is that using the historical market interest rate in applying the effective interest method gives a constant rate of interest expense as a percentage of the liability at the beginning of the period. That constant rate is the historical market interest rate.

11.5   The initial issue prices will differ. Although the present value of the $1,000,000 face amount of these bonds will be the same for the two issues, the present value of the coupon payments will differ because the 9% coupon bonds require larger cash outflows each year than the 7% coupon bonds.

11.7   The statement is still correct. Instead of repaying the bonds at maturity, the firm repurchases them in the market. The amount paid to repurchase the bonds depends on market interest rates at the time, but that amount is independent of whether the firm used the historical market interest rate or the current market interest rate to account for the bonds while they were outstanding.

11.9   Old/current rules: The retailer will likely treat it as an operating lease. The minimum contractual lease payments do not include the rental based on sales. If sales are zero, the lease payment will be zero. Thus, the "minimum" payment is zero. The present value of the "small fixed amount" will not likely exceed 90% of the fair market value of the property. The 10-year lease is also likely less than 75% of the useful life of the building.

Odd-numbered Solutions

11.11   Under the current rules, the distinction depends upon which criteria of the lease made it a capital lease. The major difference is that at the end of a lease term the asset reverts to the lessor in a capital lease, whereas at the end of the installment payments, the asset belongs to the purchaser. The criteria for capitalizing a lease are such that the expected value of the asset when it reverts to the lessor is small. In most other respects, capital leases and installment purchases are similar in economic substance.

Under the new/proposed rules, the contractual payments under a lease and the contractual payments under an installment purchase are the same. At the end of the contractual term, the lessee may return the property to the lessor when the property has substantial potential value in use, so that the lessor bears risks and enjoys potential rewards of ownership that would have been the lessee's if the lease had no operating components

11.13   Using the operating lease method for financial reporting permits the lessee to keep the lease liability off the balance sheet and report less cumulative expenses than the capital lease method. The lessee prefers the capital lease for income tax reporting because it reports more cumulative expenses than the operating lease method and therefore minimizes the present value of income tax payments.

11.15   (Hagar Company; amortization schedule for note where stated interest rate differs from historical market rate of interest.) (amounts in US$)

a.   **Amortization Schedule for a Three-Year Note with a Maturity
Value of $40,000, Calling for 6% Annual
Interest Payments, Yield of 8% per Year**

Year (1)	Carrying Value Start of Year (2)	Interest Expense for Period (3)[a]	Payment (4)	Interest Added to Carrying Value (5)	Carrying Value End of Year (6)
1	$37,938	$ 3,035	$ 2,400	$ 635	$38,573
2	38,573	3,086	2,400	686	39,259
3	39,259	3,141	2,400	741	40,000

[a](3) = (2) × 0.08.

11.15 continued.

b. Computer... 37,938

    Note Payable 37,938

To record purchase of computer.

Annual Journal Entry for Interest and Principal

Interest Expense............ Amount in Col. (3)

    Cash .... Amount in Col. (4)*

    Note Payable .... Amount in Col. (5)*

*In third year, the firm also debits Note Payable and credits Cash for $40,000.

11.17 (Computing the issue price of bonds.) (amounts in US$)

a. $1,000,000 x 0.14205[a] .... $ 142,050

[a]Present value of $1 for 40 periods at 5%.

b. $50,000 x 23.11477[a] .... $ 1,155,739

[a]Present value of annuity for 40 periods at 3%.

c. $50,000 x 19.79277[a] .... $ 989,639

$1,000,000 x 0.20829[b] 208,290

$ 1,197,929

[a]Present value of annuity for 40 periods at 4%.

[b]Present value of $1 for 40 periods at 4%.

d. $30,000 x 12.46221[a] .... $ 373,866

$40,000 x 12.46221[a] x 0.37689[b] 187,875

$1,000,000 x 0.14205[c] 142,050

$ 703,791

[a]Present value of annuity for 20 periods at 5%.

[b]Present value of $1 for 20 periods at 5%.

[c]Present value of $1 for 40 periods at 5%.

11.19   (Seward Corporation; amortization schedule for bonds.) (amounts in US$)

a. $100,000 X 0.74622[a] .... $ 74,622

    $4,000 X 5.07569[b]   20,303

    Issue Price .... $ 94,925

[a]Table 2, 5% column and 6-period row.

[b]Table 4, 5% column and 6-period row.

b.

Six-Month Period	Liability at Start of Period	Interest at 5% for Period	Cash Payment	Increase in Carrying Value of Liability	Liability at End of Period
1	$94,925	$ 4,746	$ 4,000	$ 746	$ 95,671
2	95,671	4,784	4,000	784	96,455
3	96,455	4,823	4,000	823	97,278
4	97,278	4,864	4,000	864	98,142
5	98,142	4,907	4,000	907	99,049
6	99,049	4,951[a]	4,000	951	100,000
Total..................		$ 29,075	$ 24,000	$ 5,075	

[a]Does not equal 0.05 X $99,049 due to rounding.

c.   **January 2, 2012**

Cash...	94,925	
Bonds Payable		94,925

To record issue of bonds.

June 30, 2012

Interest Expense..	4,746	
Cash Payable		4,000
Bonds Payable		746

To record interest expense for first six months, the cash payment, and the increase in the liability for the difference.

11.19 c. continued.

December 31, 2012

Interest Expense.. 4,784

    Cash 4,000

    Bonds Payable 784

To record interest expense for the second six
months, the cash payment, and the increase in
the liability for the difference.

d. Bonds Payable (= 0.20 X $98,142) 19,628

    Loss on Retirement of Bonds................................... 772

    Cash 20,400

11.21 (Robinson Company; accounting for bonds using amortized cost
measurement based on the historical market interest rate.) (amounts in
US$)

a. $5,000,000 X 0.37689[a] .... $ 1,884,450

    $200,000 X 12.46221[b] 2,492,442

    Issue Price .... $ 4,376,892

[a]Table 2, 5% column and 20-period row.
[b]Table 4, 5% column and 20-period row.

b. 0.05 X $4,376,892 = $218,845.

c. 0.05($4,376,892 + $218,845 – $200,000) = $219,787.

d. $4,376,892 + $218,845 – $200,000 + $219,787 – $200,000 =
$4,415,524.

e. $5,000,000 X 0.41552[a] .... $ 2,077,600

    $200,000 X 11.68959[b] 2,337,918

    Present Value... $ 4,415,518

[a]Table 2, 5% column and 18-period row.
[b]Table 4, 5% column and 18-period row.

The difference between the carrying value in Part *d.* and the present
value in Part *e.* results from rounding present value factors.

11.23   (Stroud Corporation; accounting for bonds using the fair value option based on the current market interest rate.) (amounts in US$)

a.   **January 1, 2013:** The carrying value of these bonds is $10,000,000, their issue price. The issue price equals the face value because the coupon rate and the required market yield both equal 6%.

   June 30, 2013:

   $10,000,000 × 0.5598676[a]... $ 5,598,676

   $300,000 × 14.197818[b]...   4,259,346

   $ 9,858,022

   [a]Present value of $1 for 19 periods at 3.1%.

   [b]Present value of an annuity for 19 periods at 3.1%.

   December 31, 2013:

   $10,000,000 × 0.557435[a]... $ 5,574,350

   $300,000 × 13.411061[b]...   4,023,318

   $ 9,597,668

   [a]Present value of $1 for 18 periods at 3.3%.

   [b]Present value of an annuity for 18 periods at 3.3%.

b.   **First Six Months of 2013**

   Debt Service Payment: 0.03 × $10,000,000 = $300,000.

   Unrealized Gain: $141,978 (= $10,000,000 − $9,858,022).

   Total interest expense plus holding gain for the first six months is −$158,022 = (−$300,000 + $141,978). That is, the firm has a net borrowing cost of $158,022. The debt service payment was partially offset by a holding gain on the bond, which resulted from an increase in market rates.

11.23 continued.

    c. **Second Six Months of 2013**

        Debt Service Payment:
        Interest Expense: $0.03 \times \$10,000,000 = \$300,000$.

        The fair value of the bonds at the end of the first six months was $9,858,022 and at the end of the second six months has declined to $9,597,668. This implies a holding gain of $260,354 (= $9,858,022 – $9,597,668).

        The total of interest expense and holding gain for the six months' period is $39,646 = ($300,000 – $260,354).

11.25   (Boeing and United Airlines; applying the capital lease criteria under the current/old rules.) (amounts in US$)

    a. This lease is a capital lease because the lease period of 20 years exceeds 75% of the expected life of the aircraft. The lease does not meet any other capital lease criteria. The aircraft reverts to Boeing at the end of 20 years. The present value of the lease payments when discounted at 10% is $51.1 million (= $6 million X 8.51356), which is less than $54 million (= 90% of the fair value of $60 million).

    b. This lease is a capital lease because the present value of the lease payments of $54.8 million (= $7.2 million X 7.60608) exceeds 90% of the $60 million fair value of the aircraft.

    c. The lease is not a capital lease. The present value of the required lease payments of $36.9 million (= $5.5 million X 6.71008) is less than $54 million (= 90% of the fair value of the aircraft). The life of the lease is less than 75% of the expected useful life of the aircraft. The purchase option price coupled with the rental payments provides Boeing with a present value of all cash flows exceeding $62.4 million [= ($5.5 million X 6.71008) + ($55 million X 0.46319)]. This amount exceeds the usual sales price of $60 million, so there does not appear to be a bargain purchase option.

                Odd-numbered Solutions

11.25 continued.

    d. This lease is not a capital lease. The present value of the minimum required lease payments is $50.9 million (= $6.2 million X 8.20141). The fee contingent on usage could be zero, so the calculations exclude it. The life of the lease is less than 75% of the useful life of the aircraft. The aircraft reverts to Boeing at the end of the lease period.

11.27   (Sun Microsystems; preparing lessor's journal entries for an operating lease and a capital lease.) (amounts in US$)

    a. This lease is a capital lease under the current/old rules. The life of the lease equals the expected useful life of the property. The present value of the lease payments of $12,000 [= $4,386.70 + ($4,386.70 X 1.73554)] equals the fair value of the leased asset.

    b. **Beginning of Each Year**

Cash..	4,386.70	
Rental Fees Received in Advance........................		4,386.70

To record cash received in advance from lessee.

End of Each Year

Rental Fees Received in Advance............................	4,386.70	
Rent Revenue		4,386.70

To record rent revenue for each year.

Depreciation Expense..	2,400.00	
Accumulated Depreciation.................................		2,400.00

To record annual depreciation (= $7,200/3).

    c. **January 1, 2013**

Cash..	4,386.70	
Lease Receivable (= $4,386.70 X 1.73554)	7,613.30	
Sales Revenue		12,000.00

To record "sale" of workstation.

Cost of Goods Sold	7,200.00	
Inventory...		7,200.00

To record cost of workstation "sold."

11.27 c. continued.

December 31, 2013

Lease Receivable (= 0.10 X $7,613.30)	761.33	
Interest Revenue		761.33

To record interest revenue for 2013.

January 1, 2014

Cash..	4,386.70	
Lease Receivable..		4,386.70

To record cash received at the beginning of 2014.
The carrying value of the receivable is now
$3,987.93 (= $7,613.30 + $761.33 − $4,386.70).

December 31, 2014

Lease Receivable (= 0.10 X $3,987.93)	398.77	
Interest Revenue		398.77

To record interest revenue for 2014. Interest
revenue is slightly less than 0.10 X $3,987.93
due to rounding of present value factors. The
carrying value of the receivable is now $4,386.70
(= $3,987.93 + $398.77).

January 1, 2015

Cash..	4,386.70	
Lease Receivable..		4,386.70

To record cash received for 2015.

11.29   (Aggarwal Corporation; accounting for long-term bonds.) (amounts in US$)

a. **Interest Expense**
First Six Months: 0.05 X $301,512 = $15,076.
Second Six Months: 0.05($301,512 + $15,076) = $15,829.
Carrying value of bonds on December 31, 2013: $301,512 + $15,076 +
$15,829 = $332,417.

11.29 continued.

   b. **Carrying Value of Bonds on December 31, 2012**
      Interest:
        $35,000 × 8.11090 = $ 283,882   (Table 4, 10 periods and 4%)
      Principal:
       $1,000,000 × 0.67556 = 675,560   (Table 2, 10 periods and 4%)
        Total .... $ 959,442

     Carrying Value of Bonds, December 31, 2012 .... $ 959,442
     Add Interest Expense for 2013 x
     Subtract Coupon Payments during 2013 .... (70,000)
     Carrying Value of Bonds, December 31, 2013 .... $ 966,336

     Interest expense for 2013 is $76,894.

   c. **Carrying Value of Bonds on July 1, 2013**
     Carrying Value of Bonds, December 31, 2012 .... $ 1,305,832
     Plus Interest Expense for First Six Months of 2013:
       0.03 × $1,305,832 39,175
     Subtract Coupon Payment during First Six Months of
       2013 .... (45,000)
     Carrying Value of Bonds, July 1, 2013............................. $ 1,300,007
     Carrying Value of One-Half of Bonds................................ $ 650,004

     July 1, 2013
     Bonds Payable... 650,004
       Cash... 526,720
       Gain on Bonds Retirement 123,284

   d. **Interest Expense for Second Six Months**
     0.03 × $650,004 = $19,500.

11.31   (Understanding and using bond tables.)

   a. The coupon rate on these bonds of 8% compounded semiannually equals the historical market interest rate of 8% compounded semiannually. The initial issue price therefore equals the face value. The carrying value increases each period for interest expense equal to 4% of the carrying value of the liability at the beginning of the period and decreases for 4% of the face value of the liability. Because the carrying value equals the face value throughout the life of the bonds, the carrying value remains at face value.

11.31 continued.

b. The coupon rate on these bonds is 8% compounded semiannually. When the historical market interest rate exceeds the coupon rate, the bonds will have a carrying value greater than face value. When the historical market interest rate is less than the coupon rate, the bonds will have a carrying value less than face value.

c. Firms amortize any initial issue premium as a reduction in interest expense and a reduction in the bond liability over the life of the bonds. Firms amortize any initial issue discount as an increase in interest expense and an increase in the bond liability over the life of the bonds.

d. $1,000,000 X 111.7278% = $1,117,278. Note that the rows indicate *years* to maturity, not the total number of periods.

e. $1,000,000 X 110.6775% = $1,106,775.

f.
Cash Payment for Debt Service	$ 80,000
Decrease in Carrying Value of Liability during 2013:	
$1,000,000 X (110.6775% – 110.4205%)	(2,570)
Interest Expense	$ 77,430

Interest Expense, First Six Months: 0.035 X ($1,000,000 X 110.6775%)	$ 38,737
Interest Expense, Second Six Months: 0.035 X ($1,000,000 X 110.5512%)	38,693
Interest Expense	$ 77,430

11.33 (IBM and Adair Corporation; accounting for lease by lessor and lessee.) (amounts in US$)

a. **January 1, 2013**
Cash	10,000	
Note Payable		10,000
Computer	10,000	
Cash		10,000

11.33 a. continued.

December 31, 2013

Depreciation Expense...	3,333	
Accumulated Depreciation...................................		3,333

Interest Expense (= 0.08 × $10,000)	800	
Note Payable (Plug)	3,080	
Cash (= $10,000/2.57710)..................................		3,880

December 31, 2014

Depreciation Expense...	3,333	
Accumulated Depreciation...................................		3,333

Interest Expense [= 0.08 × ($10,000 − $3,080)].......	554	
Note Payable (Plug)	3,326	
Cash...		3,880

b. **January 1, 2013**
No entry.

December 31, 2013

Rent Expense..	3,810	
Cash..		3,810

December 31, 2014

Rent Expense..	3,810	
Cash..		3,810

c. **January 1, 2013**

Leased Asset...	10,000	
Lease Liability...		10,000

December 31, 2013

Depreciation Expense...	3,333	
Accumulated Depreciation...................................		3,333

Interest Expense (= 0.07 × $10,000)	700	
Lease Liability (Plug)	3,110	
Cash (= $10,000/2.62432)..................................		3,810

11.33 c. continued.

December 31, 2014

Depreciation Expense... 3,333
    Accumulated Depreciation..................................   3,333

Interest Expense [= 0.07 × ($10,000 − $3,110)]....... 482
Lease Liability (Plug) 3,328
    Cash..   3,810

d. **January 1, 2013**

Cash.. 10,000
    Sales Revenue   10,000

Cost of Goods Sold 6,000
    Inventory...   6,000

December 31, 2013 and 2014
No entries necessary.

e. **January 1, 2013**

Computer Equipment 6,000
    Inventory...   6,000

December 31, 2013

Depreciation Expense... 2,000
    Accumulated Depreciation..................................   2,000

Cash... 3,810
    Rent Revenue   3,810

December 31, 2014

Depreciation Expense... 2,000
    Accumulated Depreciation..................................   2,000

Cash... 3,810
    Rent Revenue   3,810

11.33 continued.

f. **January 1, 2013**

Lease Receivable	10,000	
Sales Revenue		10,000

Cost of Goods Sold	6,000	
Inventory		6,000

December 31, 2013

Cash	3,810	
Interest Revenue (see Part *c.*)		700
Lease Receivable		3,110

December 31, 2014

Cash	3,810	
Interest Revenue (see Part *c.*)		482
Lease Receivable		3,328

g.
Lessee	2013	2014	2015	Total
Borrow and Purchase				
Depreciation Expense....	$ 3,333	$ 3,333	$ 3,334	$ 10,000
Interest Expense	800	554	286	1,640
	$ 4,133	$ 3,887	$ 3,620	$ 11,640
Operating Lease				
Rent Expense	$ 3,810	$ 3,810	$ 3,810	$ 11,430
Capital Lease				
Depreciation Expense....	$ 3,333	$ 3,333	$ 3,334	$ 10,000
Interest Expense	700	482	248	1,430
	$ 4,033	$ 3,815	$ 3,582	$ 11,430

11.33 continued.

h.

Lessor	2013	2014	2015	Total
Sale				
Sales Revenue..............	$10,000	$ —	$ —	$ 10,000
Cost of Goods Sold.........	(6,000)	—	—	(6,000)
	$ 4,000	$ —	$ —	$ 4,000
Operating Lease				
Rent Revenue................	$ 3,810	$ 3,810	$ 3,810	$ 11,430
Depreciation Expense....	(2,000)	(2,000)	(2,000)	(6,000)
	$ 1,810	$ 1,810	$ 1,810	$ 5,430
Capital Lease				
Sales Revenue................	$10,000	$ —	$ —	$ 10,000
Cost of Goods Sold.........	(6,000)	—	—	(6,000)
Interest Revenue...........	700	482	248	1,430
	$ 4,700	$ 482	$ 248	$ 5,430

11.35   (Northern Airlines; financial statement effects of capital and operating leases.) (amounts in millions of US$)

a.

Capital Lease Liability, December 31, 2012	$ 1,088
Plus Interest Expense (Plug)...	102
Plus New Capital Leases Signed[a]	0
Less Cash Payment on Capital Leases	(263)
Capital Lease Liability, December 31, 2013	$ 927

[a]A comparison of the commitments under capital leases on December 31, 2012 and December 31, 2013 indicates that Northern Airlines did not sign any new capital leases during 2013.

b. $102/$1,088 = 9.375%.

11.35 continued.

c.

Capitalized Leased Asset, December 31, 2012	$	1,019
Plus New Capital Leases Signed[a]		0
Less Depreciation on Capital Leases (Plug).......................		(154)
Capital Leased Asset, December 31, 2013	$	865

[a]See Footnote a to Part *a*. above.

d. **December 31, 2013**

Interest Expense..	102	
Lease Liability	161	
Cash		263

To record interest expense on capital leases, the cash payment, and decrease in the capital lease liability for the difference.

December 31, 2013

Depreciation Expense...	154	
Accumulated Depreciation		154

To recognize depreciation expense on capitalized leased asset for 2013.

e. **December 31, 2013**

Rent Expense..	1,065	
Cash		1,065

To recognize rent expense on operating leases for 2013.

11.35 continued.

f.
Present Value of Operating Lease Commitment on
December 31, 2012

Year	Payments	Present Value Factor at 10.0%	Present Value
2013	$ 1,065	0.90909	$ 968
2014	1,039	0.82645	859
2015	973	0.75131	731
2016	872	0.68301	596
2017	815	0.62092	506
After 2017	7,453[a]	5.81723[b] x 0.62092[c]	2,944
Total...			$ 6,604

[a]Assume that the firm pays the $7,453 at the rate of $815 a year for 9.145 (= $7,453/$815) periods at 10%.

[b]Factor for the present value of an annuity of $815 million for 9.145 periods at 10%.

[c]Factor for the present value of $1 for five periods at 10%.

11.35 f. continued.

Present Value of Operating Lease Commitment on December 31, 2013

Year	Payments	Present Value Factor at 10.0%	Present Value
2014	$ 1,098	0.90909	$ 998
2015	1,032	0.82645	853
2016	929	0.75131	698
2017	860	0.68301	587
2018	855	0.62092	531
After 2018	6,710[a]	5.26685[b] x 0.62092[c]	2,796
Total..			$ 6,463

[a]Assume that the firm pays the $6,710 at the rate of $855 a period for 7.848 (= $6,710/$855) periods.

[b]Factor for the present value of an annuity of $855 million for 7.848 periods at 10%.

[c]Factor for the present value of $1 for five periods at 10%.

g. **Long-Term Debt Ratio Based on Reported Amounts:**
December 31, 2012: $13,456/$29,495 = 45.6%
December 31, 2013: $12,041/$29,145 = 41.3%

h. **Long-Term Debt Ratio Including Capitalization of Operating Leases:**
December 31, 2012: ($13,456 + $6,604 – $968)/($29,495 + $6,604) = 52.9%
December 31, 2013: ($12,041 + $6,463 – $998)/($29,145 + $6,463) = 49.2%

i. Lessees prefer the operating lease treatment because the capital lease treatment leads the lessee to show more debt on its balance sheet and higher debt-equity ratios.

CHAPTER 12

LIABILITIES: OFF-BALANCE-SHEET FINANCING, RETIREMENT BENEFITS, AND INCOME TAXES

Questions, Exercises, and Problems: Answers and Solutions

12.1 See the text or the glossary at the end of the book.

12.3 Executory contracts carry varying amounts of risk. For example, a firm might back out of a purchase commitment more easily than an employment contract or lease contract. Furthermore, the expected benefits might carry different degrees of risk. An employee might back out of an employment contract more easily than a lessor could demand return of a leased asset prior to the end of the lease. Users of the financial statements might assume that all rights and obligations under executory contracts are equally certain. A contrary view argues that assets and liabilities recognized on the balance sheet (for example, cash, inventory, equipment, goodwill) carry different degrees of uncertainty with respect to expected benefits and risks. Recognizing the benefits and obligations related to executory contracts provides information that firms disclose only in the notes to the financial statements. Recording them in the balance sheet increases their visibility.

12.5 Accrual accounting recognizes a cost as an expense in the period when a firm uses, or consumes, goods and services. Employees provide labor services each period in return for both current compensation (for example, salary) and deferred compensation (for example, pensions, postretirement health care benefits). The absence of deferred compensation arrangements would presumably lead employees to demand higher current compensation to permit them to fund their own retirement plans. Thus, firms must recognize an expense during the current period for both compensation paid and the present value of deferred compensation.

12.7   The amounts that pension plans pay to retirees are based on the employer's contributions plus earnings from investments. Earnings from pension investments appear on the books of the pension plan. In theory, those earnings fund the increase in the pension obligation that results from the passage of time. Although expected earnings from investments and the interest cost on the pension obligation flow through net pension expense on the employer's books, in theory these amounts should perfectly offset—in which case pension expense will equal the employer's cash contribution to the pension plan.

12.9   U.S. GAAP allows firms to defer and amortize changes in prior service costs and actuarial gains and losses that occur during a period. The rationale is that a firm should take a long-term view of its pension plan. This long-term view permits firms to average out short-term changes in prior service costs and actuarial gains and losses over longer periods. These items affect other comprehensive income in the period when they originate. When firms amortize these items and include the amortization as an element of net pension expense, the firms remove the amount originally recognized in other comprehensive income and include it in net income.

12.11   Subtracting the expected return instead of the actual return on investments smoothes out variations between expected and actual rates of return and also enhances a long-term viewpoint appropriate for pension benefits.

12.13   This statement is incorrect. In order for deferred taxes to be a loan, there must be a receipt of cash or other goods or services at the inception of the loan and a disbursement of cash or other goods or services at the maturity date. The entries for a deferred tax liability are as follows:

When Timing Differences Originate:

Income Tax Expense...   X
    Deferred Tax Liability...   X

Assets	=	Liabilities	+	Shareholders' Equity	(Class.)
		+X		−X	IncSt → RE

12.13 continued.

When Timing Differences Reverse:

Deferred Tax Liability   X

     Income Tax Expense   X

Assets	=	Liabilities	+	Shareholders' Equity	(Class.)
		−X		+X	IncSt → RE

There are no cash or other asset flows involved and, therefore, no loan.

Another approach is to raise the question: How would cash flows have differed if a firm used the same methods of accounting for book as it used for tax? The response is that cash flows would have been the same even though there would be no deferred income taxes. Thus, recognizing or not recognizing deferred taxes has no incremental effect on cash or other asset flows and, therefore, cannot represent a loan.

12.15   When firms choose accounting methods that result in recognizing income earlier for book purposes than for tax purposes, they delay the payment of taxes. Income tax expense does not reflect the benefit of these delayed cash payments in that period because firms must include the delayed payment amount in both income tax expense and a deferred income tax liability. In the later period when taxable income exceeds book income, firms reduce income tax expense and the deferred income tax liability for the additional taxes paid. When firms recognize income earlier for tax purposes than for book purposes, they accelerate the payment of taxes. Income tax expense does not reflect the cost of the accelerated cash payment in that period because firms must include the accelerated payment amount as a reduction in income tax expense and a deferred income tax asset. In the later period when book income exceeds taxable income, firms increase income tax expense and reduce the deferred income tax asset for the taxes paid previously.

12.17   Information on individual deferred tax assets and deferred tax liabilities provides information about a firm's operating, investing, and financing activities related to those individual items. For example, a continual increase in deferred tax liabilities for depreciation timing differences suggests a continuing increase in expenditures on depreciable assets. A decrease in deferred tax assets for warranties might suggest a reduction in sales of warranted products.

12.19 (Lorimar Company; using inventory to achieve off-balance-sheet financing.) (amounts in US$)

a. (i) **January 2, 2013**

Cash.. 300,000

    Bank Loan Payable.. 300,000

Assets	=	Liabilities	+	Shareholders' Equity	(Class.)
+300,000		+300,000			

To record bank loan.

December 31, 2013

Interest Expense (= 0.1 x $300,000) 30,000

    Bank Loan Payable.. 30,000

Assets	=	Liabilities	+	Shareholders' Equity	(Class.)
		+30,000		−30,000	IncSt → RE

To record interest expense for 2013.

December 31, 2014

Cash.. 363,000

    Sales Revenue 363,000

Assets	=	Liabilities	+	Shareholders' Equity	(Class.)
+363,000				+363,000	IncSt → RE

To record sale of tobacco inventory.

Cost of Goods Sold 200,000

    Inventory.. 200,000

Assets	=	Liabilities	+	Shareholders' Equity	(Class.)
−200,000				−200,000	IncSt → RE

To record cost of tobacco inventory sold.

12.19 a. continued.

Interest Expense (= 0.10 X $330,000) 33,000
Bank Loan Payable... 330,000
Cash..   363,000

Assets	=	Liabilities	+	Shareholders' Equity	(Class.)
−363,000		−330,000		−33,000	IncSt → RE

To record interest expense for 2014 and repayment of loan.

(ii) **January 2, 2013**

Cash.. 300,000
Sales Revenue   300,000

Assets	=	Liabilities	+	Shareholders' Equity	(Class.)
+300,000				+300,000	IncSt → RE

To record "sale" of tobacco to bank.

Cost of Goods Sold 200,000
Inventory..   200,000

Assets	=	Liabilities	+	Shareholders' Equity	(Class.)
−200,000				−200,000	IncSt → RE

To record cost of tobacco "sold."

b. Both transactions result in a total of $100,000 income for the two years combined. The collateralized loan shows $163,000 gross profit from the sale in 2014 and interest expense of $30,000 in 2013 and $33,000 in 2014. The "sale" results in $100,000 gross profit in 2013. Cash increases by $300,000 in both transactions. Liabilities increase for the collateralized loan, whereas an asset decreases for the "sale."

12.19 continued.

c.   For the transaction to qualify as a sale for accounting purposes, Lorimar Company must shift the risk of changes in storage costs for 2013 and 2014 and the risk of changes in the selling price for the tobacco at the end of 2014 to the bank. Lorimar should not guarantee a price or agree to cover insurance and other storage costs. The bank will require different terms for the loan depending on the risk it incurs.

12.21   (Tasty Dish, Inc.; preparing a summary journal entry for a defined benefit plan.) (amounts in millions of US$)

2013

Pension Expense..	340	
Pension Liability [($5,947 – $5,385) – ($5,771 – $5,086)]	123	
Cash		19
Other Comprehensive Income (Actuarial Gains and Losses: $155 gain + $167 amortization)....		322
Other Comprehensive Income (Excess of Actual Return over Expected Return on Investments: $513 – $391)		122

Assets	=	Liabilities	+	Shareholders' Equity	(Class.)
–19		–123		–340	IncSt → RE
				+322	OCI → AOCI
				+122	OCI → AOCI

To record pension expense, pension funding, the increase in net pension liabilities, and other comprehensive income related to the change in actuarial and performance gains and losses.

12.23 (Fleet Sneaks; preparing journal entries for income tax expense.) (amounts in millions of US$)

a. **2011**

Income Tax Expense	504.4	
Income Tax Payable		495.4
Deferred Tax Liability		9.0

Assets	=	Liabilities	+	Shareholders' Equity	(Class.)
		+495.4		−504.4	IncSt → RE
		+9.0			

To record income tax expense, income tax payable, and the change in deferred taxes for 2011.

2012

Income Tax Expense	648.2	
Income Tax Payable		622.8
Deferred Tax Liability		25.4

Assets	=	Liabilities	+	Shareholders' Equity	(Class.)
		+622.8		−648.2	IncSt → RE
		+25.4			

To record income tax expense, income tax payable, and the change in deferred taxes for 2012.

2013

Income Tax Expense	749.6	
Deferred Tax Liability	26.0	
Income Tax Payable		775.6

Assets	=	Liabilities	+	Shareholders' Equity	(Class.)
		−26.0		−749.6	IncSt → RE
		+775.6			

To record income tax expense, income tax payable, and the change in deferred taxes for 2013.

12.23 continued.

b. Fleet Sneaks has overfunded retirement benefit plans, suggesting that it has contributed more cash to the pension plan and, thereby, received a tax deduction that it has expensed for financial reporting. Fleet Sneaks recognized a deferred tax liability for this temporary difference. The deferred tax liability increased in 2012 due to increased overfunding. The deferred tax liability decreased in 2013 due to a decrease in the extent of overfunding.

12.25 (Pownall Company; deriving permanent and temporary differences from financial statement disclosures.) (amounts in US$)

a.

Income Tax Expense	=	Income Taxes Currently Payable	+	Change in Deferred Tax Liability
$156,000	=	$48,000	+	x
x	=	$108,000		

Temporary Differences	=	Changes in Deferred Tax Liability/0.40
	=	$108,000/0.40
	=	$270,000

b. Because income tax expense exceeds income taxes payable, book income exceeded taxable income.

Taxable Income: $48,000/0.40	$ 120,000
Temporary Differences	270,000
Book Income Before Taxes Excluding Permanent Differences	$ 390,000
Permanent Differences (Plug)	72,000
Book Income Before Taxes (Given)	$ 318,000

12.27 (Woodward Corporation; effect of temporary differences on income taxes.) (amounts in US$)

a.

	2013	2014	2015	2016
Other Pre-Tax Income	$35,000	$35,000	$35,000	$35,000
Income Before Depreciation from Machine	25,000	25,000	25,000	25,000
Depreciation Deduction:				
0.33 x $50,000	(16,500)			
0.44 x $50,000		(22,000)		
0.15 x $50,000			(7,500)	
0.08 x $50,000				(4,000)
Taxable Income	$43,500	$38,000	$52,500	$56,000
Tax Rate	0.40	0.40	0.40	0.40
Income Taxes Payable	$17,400	$15,200	$21,000	$22,400

b.

Financial Reporting	2013	2014	2015	2016
Carrying Value, January 1	$50,000	$37,500	$25,000	$ 12,500
Depreciation Expense	(12,500)	(12,500)	(12,500)	(12,500)
Carrying Value, December 31	$37,500	$25,000	$12,500	$ —
Tax Reporting				
Tax Basis, January 1	$50,000	$33,500	$11,500	$ 4,000
Depreciation Deduction	(16,500)	(22,000)	(7,500)	(4,000)
Tax Basis, December 31	$33,500	$11,500	$ 4,000	$ —

c.

Financial Reporting	2013	2014	2015	2016
Income Before Depreciation	$60,000	$60,000	$60,000	$ 60,000
Depreciation Expense ($50,000/4)	(12,500)	(12,500)	(12,500)	(12,500)
Pretax Income	$47,500	$47,500	$47,500	$ 47,500
Income Tax Expense at 0.40	$19,000	$19,000	$19,000	$ 19,000

d.

	2013	2014	2015	2016
Income Tax Payable (from Part a.)—Cr.	$17,400	$ 15,200	$ 21,000	$22,400
Change in Deferred Tax Liability (Plug): Cr. if Positive, Dr. if Negative	1,600	3,800	(2,000)	(3,400)
Income Tax Expense—Dr.	$19,000	$ 19,000	$ 19,000	$19,000

12.27 d. continued.

2013

Income Tax Expense	19,000
Cash or Income Tax Payable...............................	17,400
Deferred Tax Liability...	1,600

Assets	=	Liabilities	+	Shareholders' Equity	(Class.)
−17,400		+1,600		−19,000	IncSt → RE

2014

Income Tax Expense	19,000
Cash or Income Tax Payable...............................	15,200
Deferred Tax Liability...	3,800

Assets	=	Liabilities	+	Shareholders' Equity	(Class.)
−15,200		+3,800		−19,000	IncSt → RE

2015

Income Tax Expense	19,000
Deferred Tax Liability...	2,000
Cash or Income Tax Payable...............................	21,000

Assets	=	Liabilities	+	Shareholders' Equity	(Class.)
−21,000		−2,000		−19,000	IncSt → RE

2016

Income Tax Expense	19,000
Deferred Tax Liability...	3,400
Cash or Income Tax Payable...............................	22,400

Assets	=	Liabilities	+	Shareholders' Equity	(Class.)
−22,400		−3,400		−19,000	IncSt → RE

12.29   (Lewis Corporation; interpreting note on off-balance-sheet financing.)

1. The receivables are in the possession and ownership of the special purpose entity (SPE). Lewis has no control over the actions of the SPE. Neither Lewis nor its creditors have access to the assets of the SPE and creditors of the SPE have no access to Lewis' assets.

2. Lewis has not placed restrictions on the receivables that constrain the SPE from doing what it pleases with the receivables.

3. The SPE incurs interest rate risk and credit.

12.31   (Treadaway, Inc.; interpreting retirement plan disclosures.) (amounts in millions of US$)

a. Pension plans measure the amount of interest cost using the present value of the pension obligation and the related discount rate. Pension plans measure the amount of the expected return on plan assets using the fair value of the pension assets and the assumed rate of return on investments. For Treadaway, the expected rate of return on investments exceeds the discount rate but the pension obligation exceeds pension assets. The amounts for interest cost and expected return on investments are a mixture of these four factors. The higher pension obligation exceeds the lower discount rate for 2011 and 2012 and results in interest cost exceeding the expected return on investments. The net effect of these four factors results in equal amounts for interest cost and expected return on investments for 2013, and is simply a coincidence.

b. The decline in net health care expense results from a decline in interest cost, likely the result of decreases in the health care obligation that more than offset the effects of increases in the discount rate.

c. Treadaway contributes sufficient cash each year to fund current benefits but no excess contributions to invest in assets.

d. Treadaway increased the discount rate it uses to compute the pension obligation and health care obligation from 5.5% in 2012 to 5.75% in 2013. The increased discount rate reduces the obligations and results in an actuarial gain. In addition, Treadaway decreased the initial health care cost trend rate from 11.5% in 2012 to 11.2% in 2013, which reduces the health care obligation and results in an actuarial gain.

12.31 continued.

e. Prior Service Cost, End of 2012 .... $ 314
Plus Increase in Prior Service Cost During 2013 from Plan
    Amendments 111
Less Amortization of Prior Service Cost During 2013.............. (59)
Prior Service Cost, End of 2013 .... $ 366

f. Net Actuarial Loss, End of 2012 .... $ 1,646
Less Decrease in Actuarial Loss During 2013 from Actuarial
    Gain in Pension Obligation... (120)
Less Amortization of Actuarial Loss During 2013 .... (91)
Less Excess of Actual Return over Expected Return on
    Pension Investments ($478 – $295) .... (183)
Net Actuarial Loss, End of 2013 .... $ 1,252

g. Prior Service Cost, End of 2012 .... $ 339
Plus Increase in Prior Service Cost During 2013 from Plan
    Amendments 1
Less Amortization of Prior Service Cost During 2013.............. (41)
Prior Service Cost, End of 2013 .... $ 299

h. Net Actuarial Loss, End of 2012 .... $ 340
Less Decrease in Actuarial Loss During 2013 from Actuarial
    Gain in Health Care Obligation .... (110)
Less Amortization of Actuarial Loss During 2013 .... (9)
Net Actuarial Loss, End of 2013 .... $ 221

i. **2013**
Pension Expense... 253
Pension Liability (Noncurrent Liabilities: $736 –
    $19) 717
Other Comprehensive Income (Prior Service Cost:
    $366 – $314).. 52
Other... 20
    Cash.. 567
    Pension Liability (Noncurrent Liabilities:
        $1,348 – $1,267)... 81
    Other Comprehensive Income (Actuarial Loss:
        $1,646 – $1,252)... 394

12.31 i. continued.

Assets	=	Liabilities	+	Shareholders' Equity	(Class.)
+20		−717		−253	IncSt → RE
−567		+81		−52	OCI → AOCI
				+394	OCI → AOCI

To record pension expense, pension funding, and the change in balance sheet accounts relating to the pension plan for 2013.

j. **2013**

Health Care Expense	210
Health Care Liability (Current Liabilities: $254 − $231)	23
Health Care Liability (Noncurrent Liabilities: $2,375 − $2,243)	132
Other	27
Cash	233
Other Comprehensive Income (Prior Service Cost: $339 − $299)	40
Other Comprehensive Income (Actuarial Loss: $340 − $221)	119

Assets	=	Liabilities	+	Shareholders' Equity	(Class.)
+27		−23		−210	IncSt → RE
−233		−132		+40	OCI → AOCI
				+119	OCI → AOCI

To record health care expense, health care funding, and the change in balance sheet accounts relating to the health care plan for 2013.

12.33 (E-Drive; interpreting income tax disclosures.) (amounts in millions of euros)

a. **2012**

Income Tax Expense	4,232	
Income Tax Payable		2,047
Deferred Income Taxes		2,185

Assets	=	Liabilities	+	Shareholders' Equity	(Class.)
		+2,047		−4,232	IncSt → RE
−2,185	or	+2,185			

To record income tax expense, income tax payable, and the change in deferred income taxes for 2012.

b. **2013**

Income Tax Expense	3,901	
Income Tax Payable		2,177
Deferred Income Taxes		1,724

Assets	=	Liabilities	+	Shareholders' Equity	(Class.)
		+2,177		−3,901	IncSt → RE
−1,724	or	+1,724			

To record income tax expense, income tax payable, and the change in deferred income taxes for 2013.

c. The deferred tax amounts in Exhibit 12.23 relate not only to amounts affecting income tax expense of the current period but also to tax effects of items included in other balance sheet items. For example, when firms debit or credit other comprehensive income when initially recognizing or subsequently amortizing prior service costs and actuarial gains and losses of pension and health care plans, the firms must credit or debit other comprehensive income for the income tax effects of these items. The deferred tax amounts in Exhibit 12.23 include the tax effects of all temporary differences, not just those affecting income tax expense of the current period.

12.33 continued.

d. The first line of the tax reconciliation assumes that governmental entities tax income before income taxes at 35%, which is only the federal tax rate. Local taxes (net of any tax savings from subtracting local taxes in computing the relevant federal taxable income) increase the effective tax rate above 35%.

e. E-Drive recognizes a deferred tax asset for underfunded retirement plans and a deferred tax liability for overfunded retirement plans. IFRS requires firms to report underfunded retirement plans as liabilities and overfunded retirement plans as assets and not to net them. Similarly, IFRS requires firms to report the deferred tax assets and deferred tax liabilities related to these plans separately and not to net them.

f. A deferred tax asset for expenses suggests that E-Drive recognizes expenses earlier for financial reporting than for tax reporting. IFRS requires firms to recognize expenses for bad debts and warranties in the period of sale, whereas the income tax law does not permit a deduction for such items until actual uncollectible accounts receivable materialize and firms make warranty expenditures.

g. E-Drive is the lessor. The reporting of a deferred tax liability indicates that cumulative book income exceeds cumulative taxable income. E-Drive likely accounts for these leases as capital leases for financial reporting and operating leases for tax reporting. The capital lease method results in the lessor reporting a gain in the year the parties sign the lease, whereas the operating lease method spreads the income over the term of the lease.

h. A deferred tax liability for development costs suggests that E-Drive recognizes expenses earlier for tax reporting than for financial reporting. IFRS requires firms to capitalize as assets and subsequently amortize development costs incurred after the development project reaches the point of technological feasibility and the firm has the ability and intent to complete the project. For tax purposes, firms can deduct expenditures on development costs.

12.35 (Equilibrium Company; behavior of deferred income tax account when a firm acquires new assets every year.) (amounts in euros)

TAX DEPRECIATION (MACRS)

	Units Acquired	Year 1	Year 2	Year 3	Year 4	Year 5	Year 6	Year 7
Year 1	1	€2,400	€3,840	€2,280	€1,440	€1,320	€ 720	€ 0
2	1		2,400	3,840	2,280	1,440	1,320	720
3	1			2,400	3,840	2,280	1,440	1,320
4	1				2,400	3,840	2,280	1,440
5	1					2,400	3,840	2,280
6	1						2,400	3,840
7	1							2,400
a. Annual Depreciation		€2,400	€6,240	€8,520	€9,960	€11,280	€12,000	€12,000
b. Straight-Line Depreciation = €2,000 per Machine per Year		2,000	4,000	6,000	8,000	10,000	12,000	12,000
c. Difference		€ 400	€2,240	€2,520	€1,960	€ 1,280	€ 0	€ 0
d. Increase in Deferred Tax (40%)		€ 160	€ 896	€1,008	€ 784	€ 512	€ 0	€ 0
e. Balance of Deferred Income Taxes		€ 160	€1,056	€2,064	€2,848	€ 3,360	€ 3,360	€ 3,360

f. The Deferred Income Taxes account balance will remain constant at €3,360 so long as the firm continues this replacement policy. If asset prices increase or physical assets increase, or both, the Deferred Tax Liability will continue to grow.

CHAPTER 13

MARKETABLE SECURITIES AND DERIVATIVES

Questions, Exercises, and Problems: Answers and Solutions

13.1 See the text or the glossary at the end of the book.

13.3 Firms acquire trading securities primarily for their short-term profit potential. Including the unrealized gain or loss in income provides the financial statement user with relevant information for assessing the performance of the trading activity. Firms acquire available-for-sale securities to support an operating activity (for example, investment of temporarily excess cash) rather than primarily for the profit potential of these securities. Deferring recognition in income of gains and losses until sale treats available-for-sale securities the same as inventories, equipment, and other assets. Excluding the unrealized gain or loss from earnings also reduces earnings volatility.

13.5 A derivative is an accounting hedge when the firm bears a risk (a variability in outcomes) such that the change in the value of the derivative offsets the change in the value of the hedged item as time passes. A derivative designated as an accounting hedge is required to be "highly effective" in offsetting the hedged risk. When the firm acquires a derivative that is ineffective as a hedge, for example, its changes in fair value are uncorrelated with changes in the value of the hedged item, the derivative would not qualify as an accounting hedge.

Under this interpretation, a derivative is not a hedge when changes in the fair value of the derivative do not at least partially offset changes in the fair value of a hedged item occurring at the same time.

If the firm chooses not to use hedge accounting when it could, the fluctuations in the fair value of the derivative appear in income. That is, they are not offset by the changes in fair value of the hedged item.

Odd-numbered Solutions

13.7   Firms do not recognize the fair value of the commitment except to the extent that they recognize the fair value of the derivative that is hedging that commitment. Thus, firms recognize a portion of the commitment relating to the hedging activity but not the full fair value of that commitment. Firms also do not recognize the asset that the firm will receive when it satisfies the commitment.

13.9   To qualify for hedge accounting, there must be an expectation that the derivative will be effective in hedging a particular risk. Obtaining a derivative that will be highly effective in hedging a particular risk may be costly or impracticable. A firm might be satisfied with obtaining a derivative that will hedge a portion of the risk, accepting the likelihood that the derivative will not be highly effective and will not qualify for hedge accounting treatment. Another explanation is that the firm wishes to speculate on movements in interest rates, foreign exchange rates, or commodity prices. That is, firms acquire certain derivatives for trading gains and not to hedge a business risk.

13.11   (Classifying securities.)

        a.   Available-for-sale securities; current asset.

        b.   Held-to-maturity debt security; noncurrent asset.

        c.   Available-for-sale securities; current asset.

        d.   Available-for-sale securities; noncurrent asset.

        e.   Trading securities; current asset.

        f.   Available-for-sale securities; noncurrent asset (although a portion of these bonds might appear as a current asset).

13.13   (Murray Company; accounting for bonds held to maturity.) (amounts in US$)

        a.   Present Value of Periodic Payments: $3,000 × 6.73274[a] = $ 20,198
             Present Value of Maturity Amount: $100,000 × 0.73069[b] =   73,069
             Total.. $ 93,267

        [a]Present value of an annuity for eight periods at 4%.
        [b]Present value of $1 for eight periods at 4%.

13.13 continued.

b. See Schedule 13.1 below.

**Schedule 13.1
Amortization Table for $100,000 Bonds with Interest
Paid Semiannually at 6% and Priced to Yield 8%
Compounded Semiannually
(Exercise 13)**

Period	Balance at Beginning of Period	Interest Revenue for Period	Cash Received	Portion of Payment Increasing Carrying Value	Balance at End of Period
1	$93,267	$3,731	$3,000	$731	$ 93,998
2	$93,998	$3,760	$3,000	$760	$ 94,758
3	$94,758	$3,790	$3,000	$790	$ 95,548
4	$95,548	$3,822	$3,000	$822	$ 96,370
5	$96,370	$3,855	$3,000	$855	$ 97,225
6	$97,225	$3,889	$3,000	$889	$ 98,114
7	$98,114	$3,925	$3,000	$925	$ 99,039
8	$99,039	$3,961	$3,000	$961	$100,000

c. **January 1, 2013**

Marketable Debt Securities	93,267	
Cash..		93,267

June 30, 2013

Cash..	3,000	
Marketable Debt Securities	731	
Interest Revenue...		3,731

December 31, 2013

Cash..	3,000	
Marketable Debt Securities	760	
Interest Revenue...		3,760

Odd-numbered Solutions

13.13 continued.

    d. **December 31, 2016**

Cash...	3,000	
Marketable Debt Securities	962	
Interest Revenue...		3,962

December 31, 2016

Cash...	100,000	
Marketable Debt Securities		100,000

13.15   (Elston Corporation; accounting for available-for-sale securities.) (amounts in US$)

10/15/2013

Marketable Securities (Security A).............................	28,000	
Cash		28,000
To record acquisition of Security A.		

11/02/2013

Marketable Securities (Security B).............................	49,000	
Cash		49,000
To record acquisition of Security B.		

12/31/2013

Cash...	1,000	
Dividend Revenue		1,000
To record dividend received from Security B.		

12/31/2013

Unrealized Loss on Security A (Other Comprehensive Income)	3,000	
Marketable Securities (Security A)		3,000
To record unrealized loss on Security A.		

12/31/2013

Marketable Securities (Security B).............................	6,000	
Unrealized Gain on Security B (Other Comprehensive Income)		6,000
To record unrealized gain on Security B.		

13.15 continued.

2/10/2014

Cash..	24,000	
Realized Loss on Sale of Available-for-Sale		
Securities (= $24,000 – $28,000)	4,000	
Marketable Securities (Security A)...................		25,000
Unrealized Loss on Security A (Accumulated		
Other Comprehensive Income).......................		3,000

To record sale of Security A including reclassifying
the unrealized loss from Accumulated Other
Comprehensive Income

12/31/2014

Cash..	1,200	
Dividend Revenue...		1,200

To record dividend received from Security B.

12/31/2014

Unrealized Gain on Security B (Other Comprehensive		
Income)..	2,000	
Marketable Securities (Security B) (= $53,000		
– $55,000)..		2,000

To remeasure Security B to fair value.

7/15/2015

Cash..	57,000	
Unrealized Gain on Security B (= $6,000 – $2,000)		
(Accumulated Other Comprehensive Income)	4,000	
Marketable Securities (Security B)		53,000
Realized Gain on Sale of Available-for-Sale		
Securities (= $57,000 – $49,000).....................		8,000

To record sale of Security B including reclassifying
the unrealized gain from Accumulated Other
Comprehensive Income.

13.17 (Fischer/Black Company; working backward from data on marketable securities transaction.) (amounts in US$)

a. $21,000 = $18,000 + $3,000.

13-5

13.17 continued.

b. $18,000, the amount credited to Marketable Securities in the journal entry which the student might think of as $21,000 acquisition cost, derived above, less $3,000 of Unrealized Loss.

c. $5,000 loss from the debit for Realized Loss.

13.19 (Reconstructing events from journal entries.) (amounts in US$)

a. The fair value of a marketable security classified as available for sale is $4,000 less than its carrying value and the firm increases the Unrealized Loss account on the balance sheet.

b. A firm sells marketable securities classified as either trading securities or as available-for-sale securities in the same period as it purchased the securities for an amount that is $200 (= $1,100 – $1,300) less than was originally paid for them.

c. The fair value of marketable securities classified as available for sale is $750 more than its carrying value and the firm increases the Unrealized Gain account on the balance sheet.

d. A firm sells marketable securities classified as either trading securities or available-for-sale securities in the same period that it purchased the securities for an amount that is $100 (= $1,800 – $1,700) more than was originally paid for them.

13.21 (Turner Corporation; accounting for forward currency contract as a fair value hedge.) (amounts in US$)

a. The amount that Turner Corporation would receive if the contract were settled on December 31, 2013, is $1,020 (= $52,000 – $50,980). The present value of $1,020 discounted for six months at 8% per year is $981 (= $1,020 x 0.96154). Turner Corporation would report this amount as an asset.

b. Turner Corporation would also report a commitment to purchase the equipment for $981. The firm would not report a liability for the full purchase price. The commitment is an executory contract. It recognizes the commitment only to the extent of the derivative on the asset side of the balance sheet.

13.21 continued.

c. The fair value of the forward currency contract on June 30, 2014, just before settlement, is the amount of cash Turner Corporation will receive from the counterparty, which is $3,757 (= $54,737 – $50,980).

d. **June 30, 2014**

Equipment	50,980	
Commitment to Purchase Equipment	3,757	
Cash		54,737

e. **June 30, 2014**

Cash	3,757	
Forward Contract		3,757

13.23 (Dostal Corporation; journal entries and financial statement presentation of short-term available-for-sale securities.) (amounts in US$)

a. **2/05/2013**

Marketable Securities (Security A)	60,000	
Cash		60,000

8/12/2013

Marketable Securities (Security B)	25,000	
Cash		25,000

12/31/2013

Marketable Securities (Security A) (= $66,000 – $60,000)	6,000	
Unrealized Gain on Security A (Other Comprehensive Income)		6,000

Unrealized Loss on Security B (Other Comprehensive Income)	5,000	
Marketable Securities (Security B) (= $20,000 – $25,000)		5,000

1/22/2014

Marketable Securities (Security C)	82,000	
Cash		82,000

13-7

13.23 a. continued.

2/25/2014

Marketable Securities (Security D)	42,000	
Cash		42,000

3/25/2014

Marketable Securities (Security E)	75,000	
Cash		75,000

6/05/2014

Cash	72,000	
Unrealized Gain on Security A (Accumulated Other Comprehensive Income)	6,000	
Marketable Securities (Security A)		66,000
Realized Gain on Sale of Available-for-Sale Securities		12,000

6/05/2014

Cash	39,000	
Realized Loss on Sale of Available-for-Sale Securities	3,000	
Marketable Securities (Security D)		42,000

12/31/2014

Unrealized Loss on Security C (Other Comprehensive Income)	3,000	
Marketable Securities (Security C) (= $79,000 – $82,000)		3,000

12/31/2014

Marketable Securities (Security E) (= $80,000 – $75,000)	5,000	
Unrealized Gain on Security E (Other Comprehensive Income)		5,000

13.23 continued.

   b. **Balance Sheet on December 31, 2013**

Marketable Securities at Fair Value.................................. $ 86,000
Net Unrealized Gain on Available- for-Sale Securities
    ($6,000 – $5,000).. $ 1,000

Note

Marketable Securities on December 31, 2013, had an acquisition cost of $85,000 and a fair value of $86,000. Gross unrealized gains total $6,000 and gross unrealized losses total $5,000.

   c. **Balance Sheet on December 31, 2014**

Marketable Securities at Fair Value.................................. $ 179,000
Net Unrealized Loss on Available-for-Sale Securities........ $ (3,000)

Note

Marketable Securities on December 31, 2014, had an acquisition cost of $182,000 and a fair value of $179,000. Gross unrealized gains total $5,000, and gross unrealized losses total $8,000. Proceeds from sales of marketable securities totaled $111,000 during 2014. These sales resulted in gross realized gains of $12,000 and gross realized losses of $3,000. The net unrealized loss on securities available for sale changed as follows during 2014:

Balance, December 31, 2013... $ 1,000 Cr.
Accumulated Other Comprehensive Income
   (Unrealized Gain on Securities Sold) .... (6,000) Dr.
Change in Net Unrealized Loss on Securities Held at
   Year End ($5,000 – $3,000).. 2,000 Cr.
Balance, December 31, 2014... $ (3,000) Dr.

13.25   (Moonlight Mining Company; analysis of financial statement disclosures for available-for-sale securities.) (amounts in thousands of US$)

   a. $10,267 loss = $11,418 – $21,685.

   b. $2,649 gain = $8,807 – $6,158.

   c. $12,459 = $21,685 – $6,158 – $3,068.

13.25 continued.

    d. None. The unrealized loss on current marketable securities of $2,466 (= $4,601 – $7,067) and the unrealized gain on noncurrent marketable securities of $2,649 (= $8,807 – $6,158) appear in Other Comprehensive Income, closed to the Accumulated Other Comprehensive Income account on the balance sheet.

13.27   (Analysis of financial statement disclosures related to marketable securities and quality of earnings.) (amounts in millions of US$)

    a.

Cash...	37,600	
Realized Loss on Sale of Available-for-Sale Securities..	113	
Realized Gain on Available-for-Sale Securities...		443
Marketable Securities		37,270[a]

    [a]$14,075 + $37,163 – $13,968 = $37,270.

Marketable Securities	262	
Unrealized Loss on Available-for-Sale Securities (= $37,270 – $37,008) (Other Comprehensive Income)		262

    b.

Balance, December 31, 2013 (= $957 – $510)	$	447 Cr.
Net Unrealized Loss on Securities Sold (from Part a.)...		262 Cr.
Increase in Net Unrealized Gain on Securities Held on December 31, 2014 (Plug)		518 Cr.
Balance, December 31, 2014 (= $1,445 – $218)	$	1,227 Cr.

    c.

Interest and Dividend Revenue	$ 1,081
Net Realized Gain on Securities Sold from Market Price Changes Occurring during 2014: (= $37,600 – $37,008)...	592
Net Unrealized Gain on Securities Held on December 31, 2014 (from Part b.)..	518
Total Income	$ 2,191

13.27 continued.

d. The bank sold marketable securities during 2014, which had net unrealized losses of $262 million as of December 31, 2014. The sale of these securities at a gain suggests that the securities' market prices increased substantially ($592 million) during 2014. The substantial increase in the net unrealized gain of $518 lends support to this conclusion about market price increases. The bank could have increased its income still further by selecting securities for sale that had unrealized *gains* as of December 31, 2013. If prices continued to increase on such securities during 2014 prior to sale, the realized gain would have been even larger than the reported net realized gain of $330 million (= $443 − $113). Firms with available-for-sale securities with unrealized gains can manage net income, but not comprehensive income, by choosing which items to sell.

13.29 (Owens Corporation; accounting for forward currency contract as a fair value hedge and a cash flow hedge.) (amounts in US$)

a. **July 1, 2013:** The purchase commitment and the forward foreign exchange contract are mutually unexecuted contracts as of July 1, 2013. U.S. GAAP and IFRS do not require firms to recognize mutually unexecuted contracts in the accounts.

December 31, 2013: The change in the value of the undiscounted cash flows related to the purchase commitment and the forward contract is $1,800 [= (60,000 × $1.35) − (60,000 × $1.32)]. The present value of $1,800 discounted at 8% for six months is $1,731 (= $1,800 × 0.96154).

December 31, 2013

Loss on Firm Commitment......................................	1,731	
Commitment to Purchase Equipment.................		1,731

To record a loss in net income on a previously unrecognized firm commitment because the U.S. dollar decreased in value relative to the euro.

December 31, 2013

Forward Contract	1,731	
Gain on Forward Contract		1,731

To measure the forward contract at fair value and recognize a gain in net income.

13.29 a. continued.

June 30, 2014

Interest Expense	69	
Commitment to Purchase Equipment		69

To recognize interest on the commitment because
of the passage of time: $69 = 0.04 \times \$1,731$.

June 30, 2014

Forward Contract	69	
Interest Revenue		69

To record interest on the forward contract because
of the passage of time: $69 = 0.04 \times \$1,731$.

The change in the value of the purchase commitment and the forward contract due to exchange rate changes between December 31, 2013, and June 30, 2014, is $3,000 [= (60,000 \times \$1.40) - (60,000 \times \$1.35)]$.

June 30, 2014

Loss on Firm Commitment	3,000	
Commitment to Purchase Equipment		3,000

To record a loss on the purchase commitment because the value of the U.S. dollar declined relative to the euro.

June 30, 2014

Forward Contract	3,000	
Gain on Forward Contract		3,000

To record the increase in the fair value of the forward contract because the U.S. dollar declined in value relative to the euro.

June 30, 2014

Equipment	79,200	
Commitment to Purchase Equipment	4,800	
Cash		84,000

To record the amount paid in U.S. dollars
[$\$84,000 = (\$60,000 \times \$1.4)$], to eliminate the balance in the Commitment to Purchase Equipment account of $4,800 (= \$1,731 + \$69 + \$3,000)$, and to record the acquisition cost of the equipment for $79,200.

13.29 a. continued.

June 30, 2014

Cash...	4,800	
Forward Contract..		4,800

To record cash received from the counterparty and
eliminate the balance in the Forward Contract
account of $4,800 (= $1,731 + $69 + $3,000).

b. Owens Corporation would not recognize changes in the value of the
purchase commitment. The entries for changes in the fair value of the
forward contract would affect other comprehensive income each period
instead of net income. On June 30, 2014, Accumulated Other
Comprehensive Income would have a balance of $4,800 (= $1,731 + $69
+ $3,000). The entry on this date to purchase the equipment would
involve a debit to Accumulated Other Comprehensive Income instead of
the Commitment to Purchase Equipment account as shown in Part *a.*
above.

c. To treat this hedge as a fair value hedge, Owens Corporation must
intend to protect the value of the equipment. Perhaps Owens
Corporation has committed to resell the equipment to a customer on
June 30, 2014, for a fixed price in U.S. dollars and wants to protect its
expected profit margin from the sale. To treat this hedge as a cash flow
hedge, Owens Corporation must intend to protect the amount of cash it
pays to the European supplier.

13.31 (Avery Corporation; accounting for an interest rate swap as a cash flow
hedge.) (amounts in US$)

January 1, 2013

Equipment..	50,000	
Note Payable..		50,000

To record the acquisition of equipment by giving a
$50,000 note payable with a variable interest rate of
6%.

December 31, 2013

Interest Expense..	3,000	
Cash		3,000

To recognize interest expense and cash payment at
the variable interest rate of 6%: $3,000 = 0.06 X
$50,000.

13.31 continued.

The fair value of the swap agreement on December 31, 2013, after the counterparty resets the interest rate to 8% is $1,783 (= $1,000 x 1.78326). This amount is the present value of the $1,000 that the counterparty will pay Avery Corporation on December 31 of 2014 and December 31 of 2015 if the interest rate remains at 8%.

December 31, 2013

Swap Contract...	1,783	
Gain on Revaluation of Swap Contract..................		1,783

To measure the swap contract at fair value and recognize an asset on the balance sheet and a gain in other comprehensive income.

December 31, 2014

Interest Expense...	4,000	
Cash		4,000

To recognize interest expense and cash payment at the variable interest rate: $4,000 = 0.08 \times $50,000$.

Avery Corporation must also recognize interest on the swap contract because of the passage of time.

December 31, 2014

Swap Contract...	143	
Interest on Swap Contract		143

To record interest for the increase in the carrying value of the swap contract for the passage of time: $143 = 0.08 \times $1,783$.

Avery Corporation receives from the counterparty the $1,000 [= $50,000 x (0.08 − 0.06)] required by the swap contract. The entry is:

December 31, 2014

Cash...	1,000	
Swap Contract		1,000

To record cash received from the counterparty because the interest rate increased from 6% to 8%.

13.31 continued.

December 31, 2014

Accumulated Other Comprehensive Income...............	1,000	
Interest Expense..		1,000

To reclassify a portion of accumulated other comprehensive income to net income for the hedged portion of interest expense on the note payable.

At this point the swap contract account has a debit balance of $926 (= $1,783 + $143 − $1,000). Accumulated other comprehensive income related to this transaction has a credit balance of $926.

Resetting the interest rate on December 31, 2014, to 4% changes the fair value of the swap contract from an asset to a liability. The present value of the $1,000 that Avery Corporation will pay to the counterparty at the end of 2015 when discounted at 4% is $962 (= $1,000 × 0.96154). The entry to revalue the swap contract is:

December 31, 2014

Loss on Revaluation of Swap Contract........................	1,888	
Swap Contract (Asset)		926
Swap Contract (Liability)		962

To measure the swap contract at fair value and recognize a liability on the balance sheet and a loss in other comprehensive income.

December 31, 2015

Interest Expense...	2,000	
Cash		2,000

To recognize interest expense and cash payment at the variable interest rate of 4%: $2,000 = 0.04 × $50,000.

December 31, 2015

Interest on Swap Contract...	38	
Swap Contract		38

To record interest for the increase in the carrying value of the swap contract for the passage of time: $38 = 0.04 × $962.

13.31 continued.

December 31, 2015

Swap Contract..	1,000	
Cash		1,000

To record cash paid to the counterparty because the
interest rate decreased from 8% to 4%.

December 31, 2015

Interest Expense...	1,000	
Accumulated Other Comprehensive Income...........		1,000

To reclassify a portion of accumulated other comprehensive income to net income for the hedged portion
of interest expense on the note payable.

December 31, 2015

Note Payable	50,000	
Cash		50,000

To record repayment of note payable at maturity.

The Swap Contract account has a balance of zero on December 31, 2015
(= $962 + $38 − $1,000). Thus, Avery Corporation makes no entry to close
out the Swap Contract account.

CHAPTER 14

INTERCORPORATE INVESTMENTS IN COMMON STOCK

Questions, Exercises, and Problems: Answers and Solutions

14.1   See the text or the glossary at the end of the book.

14.3   Dividends represent revenues under the fair-value method, or represent a return of capital under the equity method, or are eliminated under the consolidation method.

14.5   When control is present, a parent and a subsidiary operate as a single economic entity. Eliminating intercompany profit and loss in these cases reflects transactions of the economic entity with all other entities. When significant influence is present, the investor and investee operate as economic entity to a lesser extent than when control is present. Thus, the concept of operating as an economic entity, in part, justifies eliminating intercompany profit and loss on equity method investments. Also, the ability to exert significant influence places the firms in a related party arrangement where prices set on intercompany transactions may not reflect arms-length dealings.

14.7   Under the equity method, the change each period in the net assets, or shareholders' equity, of the subsidiary appears on the one line, Investment in Subsidiary, on the balance sheet. When the parent consolidates the subsidiary, changes in the individual assets and liabilities that comprise the net asset change appear in the individual consolidated assets and liabilities. Likewise, under the equity method, the investor's interest in the investee's earnings appears in one line on the income statement, Equity in Earnings of Unconsolidated Subsidiary. When the parent consolidates the subsidiary, the individual revenues and expenses of the subsidiary appear in consolidated revenues and expenses.

14.9   A minority investor in an investee owns less than a controlling financial interest (for example, less than 50% of the voting shares). If a parent has a controlling financial interest, but less than 100% ownership, in an investee,

14.9 continued.

the entities holding the remaining ownership interests in the investee are minority investors (also called noncontrolling investors). Their minority, or noncontrolling, interest appears on the consolidated balance sheet.

14.11 Failing to eliminate the Investment in Subsidiary account will result in double counting the net assets of the subsidiary in the consolidated balance sheet, once as the Investment account on the parent's books and once as the individual net assets on the subsidiary's books.

14.13 Eliminating transactions between affiliated companies ensures that the consolidated financial statements: (1) reflect only transactions with outsiders and (2) reflect those outside transactions once and only once.

14.15 (Cayman Company; equity method entries.) (amounts in US$)

Investment in Stock of Denver Company 550,000
   Cash 550,000

Assets	=	Liabilities	+	Shareholders' Equity	(Class.)
+550,000					
−550,000					

To record acquisition of common stock.

Investment in Stock of Denver Company 120,000
   Equity in Earnings of Denver Company 120,000

Assets	=	Liabilities	+	Shareholders' Equity	(Class.)
+120,000				+120,000	IncSt → RE

To accrue 100% share of Denver Company's earnings.

Cash or Dividends Receivable 30,000
   Investment in Stock of Denver Company 30,000

Assets	=	Liabilities	+	Shareholders' Equity	(Class.)
+30,000					
−30,000					

To accrue dividends received or receivable.

14.17 (Wood Corporation; journal entries to apply the equity method of accounting for investments in securities.) (amounts in US$)

January 2

Investment in Securities (Knox)..................................... 350,000	
Investment in Securities (Vachi)................................... 196,000	
Investment in Securities (Snow).................................... 100,000	
Cash	646,000

Assets	=	Liabilities	+	Shareholders' Equity	(Class.)
+350,000					
+196,000					
+100,000					
−646,000					

December 31

Investment in Securities (Knox)..................................... 35,000	
Investment in Securities (Vachi)................................... 12,000	
Investment in Securities (Snow)	4,800
Equity in Earnings of Affiliates	42,200

Assets	=	Liabilities	+	Shareholders' Equity	(Class.)
+35,000				+42,200	IncSt → RE
+12,000					
−4,800					

(0.50 X $70,000) + (0.30 X $40,000) − (0.20 X $24,000) = $42,200.

December 31

Cash.. 19,500	
Investment in Securities (Knox)............................	15,000
Investment in Securities (Vachi)	4,500

Assets	=	Liabilities	+	Shareholders' Equity	(Class.)
+19,500					
−15,000					
−4,500					

(0.50 X $30,000) + (0.30 X $15,000) = $19,500.

14.19   (Laesch Company; working backward to consolidation relations.) (amounts in US$)

    a. $70,000 = ($156,000 − $100,000)/0.80.

    b.   72.7% = ($156,000 − $100,000)/$77,000.

    c. $56,000 = ($156,000 − $100,000).

14.21   (CAR Corporation; consolidation policy and principal consolidation concepts.) (amounts in US$)

    a.   CAR Corporation should consolidate Alexandre du France Software Systems and R Credit Corporation or, under exceptional circumstances, use the fair value method.

    b.

Charles Electronics	(0.75 x $120,000) =	$ 90,000
Alexandre du France Software Systems .	(0.80 x 60,000) =	48,000
R Credit Corporation	(0.90 x 144,000) =	129,600
Total Income from Subsidiaries		$ 267,600

    c.   Noncontrolling Interest shown under accounting assumed in problem:

Charles Electronics	(0.25 x $120,000) =	$ 30,000
Alexandre du France Software Systems ..	(None) =	—
R Credit Corporation	(None) =	—
		$30,000

CAR Corporation subtracts the noncontrolling interest in computing net income.

    d.   Charles Electronics, no increase because already consolidated.

Alexandre du France Software Systems increase by 80% of net income less dividends:

$$0.80 \times (\$96,000 − \$60,000) = \$28,800.$$

14.21 d. continued.

R Credit Corporation, no increase because equity method results in the same income statement effects as do consolidated statements. Net income of CAR Corporation would be:

$1,228,800 = $1,200,000 (as reported) + $28,800 (increase).

e. Noncontrolling Interest shown if CAR Corporation consolidated all companies:

Charles Electronics .... (0.25 X $120,000) = $ 30,000
Alexandre du France Software Systems . (0.20 X 96,000) = 19,200
R Credit Corporation .... (0.10 X 144,000) = 14,400
$ 63,600

14.23 (Alpha/Omega; working backward from data that has eliminated intercompany transactions.) (amounts in US$)

a. $80,000 = $450,000 + $250,000 – $620,000.

b. $30,000 is Omega's cost; $20,000 is Alpha's cost; $20,000 original cost to Alpha.

Markup on the goods sold from Alpha to Omega, which remain in Omega's inventory, is $10,000 (= $60,000 + $50,000 – $100,000).
Because Alpha priced the goods with markup 50% over its costs, the cost to Alpha to produce goods with markup of $10,000 is $20,000 and the total sales price from Alpha to Omega is $30,000 (= $10,000 + $20,000).

14.25 (Effect of equity method versus consolidation.)

a. (1) When Parent uses the equity method, it recognizes 80% of the net income of Sub. When Parent prepares consolidated financial statements with Sub, it recognizes 100% of the revenues, expenses, and net income of Sub and then subtracts the 20% noncontrolling interest share of net income. Thus, net income is the same whether Parent uses the equity method or consolidates Sub.

14.25 a. continued.

      (2)   Liabilities in the numerator increase by the amount of the liabilities of Sub. Assets in the denominator decrease by the amount in the investment account and increase by the amount of Sub's assets. In this case where there is no excess purchase price, the denominator increases by the liabilities (= assets of Sub minus shareholders' equity) of Sub. Equal increases in the numerator and denominator of a ratio that is initially less than 1.0 result in an increase in the ratio.

b.   (1)   The Parent or investor's share of Sub's net income declines, regardless of whether the amount appears on the single line, Equity in Earnings of Sub, or on multiple revenue and expense lines.

      (2)   Total assets decrease when using the equity method because the investor invests less. Total assets do not decrease when preparing consolidated financial statements because Parent eliminates its Investment in Sub account and consolidates 100% of Sub's assets, regardless of its ownership percentage.

      (3)   The liabilities of Sub do not appear on Parent's balance sheet when it uses the equity method, regardless of the ownership percentage.

      (4)   Total liabilities do not change when preparing consolidated financial statements because Parent consolidates 100% of Sub's liabilities, regardless of its ownership percentage.

      (5)   Shareholders' equity decreases when using the equity method because Parent owns less of the net income, dividends, and shareholders' equity of Sub. The shareholders' equity on the consolidated balance sheet is the shareholders' equity of Parent only. Parent eliminates the shareholders' equity of Sub when preparing consolidated financial statements in its entry to eliminate the Investment in Sub account and recognize the noncontrolling interest.

14.25 b. continued.

      (6)   Assets and liabilities do not change with the decrease in ownership percentage because consolidated financial statements reflect 100% of Sub's assets and liabilities. The change in the ownership percentage affects the amount of the noncontrolling interest in Sub's net assets.

14.27   (Ely Company and Sims Company; preparing a consolidated balance sheet.) (amounts in US$)

	Ely Company	Sims Company	Consolidated
Assets			
Cash..	$ 12,000	$ 5,000	$ 17,000
Receivables..............................	25,000	15,000	32,500
Investment in Sims Company..........................	78,000	—	—
Other Assets.............................	85,000	80,000	183,000
Total Assets	$ 200,000	$ 100,000	$ 232,500
Liabilities and Shareholders' Equity			
Current Liabilities.................	$ 45,000	$ 40,000	$ 77,500
Common Stock	50,000	10,000	50,000
Retained Earnings	105,000	50,000	105,000
Total Liabilities and Shareholders' Equity...	$ 200,000	$ 100,000	$ 232,500

The elimination entries (not required) are as follows:

Common Stock	10,000	
Retained Earnings	50,000	
Other Assets (Goodwill)...	18,000	
Investment in Sims Company...............................		78,000

Assets	=	Liabilities	+	Shareholders' Equity	(Class.)
+18,000				−10,000	ContriCap
−78,000				−50,000	ContriCap

To eliminate investment account, the shareholders' equity of Sims Company, and recognize the excess price as an asset.

14.27 continued.

Current Liabilities.. 7,500
    Receivables 7,500

Assets	=	Liabilities	+	Shareholders' Equity	(Class.)
−7,500		−7,500			IncSt → RE

To eliminate intercompany advances.

14.29   (Peak Company and Valley Company; equity method and consolidated financial statements.) (amounts in US$)

a. **January 1**
    Investment in Valley Company.............................. 50,000
        Cash.. 50,000

Assets	=	Liabilities	+	Shareholders' Equity	(Class.)
+50,000					
−50,000					

To record acquisition of 100% of Valley Company.

December 31
Investment in Valley Company.............................. 10,000
    Equity in Earnings of Valley Company............... 10,000

Assets	=	Liabilities	+	Shareholders' Equity	(Class.)
+10,000				+10,000	IncSt → RE

To recognize share of Valley Company's earnings.

December 31
Cash.. 4,000
    Investment in Valley Company.......................... 4,000

Assets	=	Liabilities	+	Shareholders' Equity	(Class.)
+4,000					
−4,000					

To recognize dividend received from Valley Company.

14.29 continued.

b.

	Peak Company	Valley Company	Consolidated
Assets			
Cash.................................	$ 33,000	$ 6,000	$ 39,000
Accounts Receivable........	42,000	20,000	54,000
Investment in Valley Company (Using the Equity Method)............	56,000	—	—
Other Assets....................	123,000	85,000	208,000
Total Assets	$254,000	$111,000	$ 301,000
Liabilities and Shareholders' Equity			
Accounts Payable	$ 80,000	$ 25,000	$ 97,000
Bonds Payable.................	50,000	30,000	80,000
Common Stock.................	10,000	5,000	10,000
Retained Earnings...........	114,000	51,000	114,000
Total Liabilities and Shareholders' Equity	$254,000	$111,000	$ 301,000
Sales Revenue	$ 400,000	$ 125,000	$ 525,000
Equity in Earnings of Valley Company..........	10,000	—	—
Cost of Goods Sold...........	(320,000)	(90,000)	(410,000)
Selling and Administrative Expense.................	(44,000)	(20,000)	(64,000)
Income Tax Expense	(12,000)	(5,000)	(17,000)
Net Income......................	$ 34,000	$ 10,000	$ 34,000

The elimination entries (not required) are as follows:

Common Stock... 5,000
Retained Earnings... 51,000
   Investment in Valley Company...........................   56,000

Assets	=	Liabilities	+	Shareholders' Equity	(Class.)
–56,000				–5,000	ContriCap
				–51,000	RE

To eliminate the investment account and the shareholders' equity accounts of Valley Company.

14-9

14.29 b. continued.

An alternative elimination entry using amounts before closing entries is as follows:

Common Stock..	5,000	
Retained Earnings..	45,000	
Equity in Earnings of Valley Company	10,000	
Dividends Declared		4,000
Investment in Valley Company..........................		56,000

Assets	=	Liabilities	+	Shareholders' Equity	(Class.)
–56,000				–5,000	ContriCap
				–45,000	RE
				–10,000	IncSt → RE
				+4,000	RE

To eliminate the investment account and the shareholders' equity accounts of Valley Company.

c. **January 1**

Investment in Valley Company...............................	70,000	
Cash...		70,000

Assets	=	Liabilities	+	Shareholders' Equity	(Class.)
+70,000					
–70,000					

To record acquisition of 100% of Valley Company.

December 31

Investment in Valley Company...............................	10,000	
Equity in Earnings of Valley Company...............		10,000

Assets	=	Liabilities	+	Shareholders' Equity	(Class.)
+10,000				+10,000	IncSt → RE

To recognize share of Valley Company's earnings.

14.29 c. continued.

December 31

Cash.. 4,000

   Investment in Valley Company 4,000

Assets	=	Liabilities	+	Shareholders' Equity	(Class.)
+4,000					
−4,000					

To recognize dividend received from Valley Company.

December 31

Selling and Administrative Expenses...................... 2,000

   Investment in Valley Company........................... 2,000

Assets	=	Liabilities	+	Shareholders' Equity	(Class.)
−2,000				−2,000	

To recognize acquisition of excess cost: $2,000 = $20,000/10$.

d. and e.

	Peak Company	Valley Company	Consolidated
Assets			
Cash.................................	$ 13,000	$ 6,000	$ 19,000
Accounts Receivable........	42,000	20,000	54,000
Investment in Valley Company (Using the Equity Method)............	74,000[a]	—	—
Other Assets....................	123,000	85,000	226,000
Total Assets	$252,000	$111,000	$ 299,000
Liabilities and Shareholders' Equity			
Accounts Payable	$ 80,000	$ 25,000	$ 97,000
Bonds Payable.................	50,000	30,000	80,000
Common Stock................	10,000	5,000	10,000
Retained Earnings...........	112,000[b]	51,000	112,000
Total Liabilities and Shareholders' Equity	$252,000	$111,000	$ 299,000

14.29 d. and e. continued.

Sales Revenue	$ 400,000	$ 125,000	$ 525,000
Equity in Earnings of Valley Company	10,000	—	—
Cost of Goods Sold	(320,000)	(90,000)	(410,000)
Selling and Administrative Expense	(46,000)c	(20,000)	(66,000)
Income Tax Expense	(12,000)	(5,000)	(17,000)
Net Income	$ 32,000	$ 10,000	$ 32,000

a$74,000 = $70,000 + $10,000 – $4,000 – $2,000.

b$112,000 = $114,000 – $2,000 amortization.

c$46,000 = $44,000 + $2,000 amortization.

The elimination entry (not required) is as follows:

Common Stock	5,000	
Retained Earnings	51,000	
Other Assets	18,000	
Investment in Valley Company		74,000

Assets	=	Liabilities	+	Shareholders' Equity	(Class.)
+18,000				–5,000	ContriCap
–74,000				–51,000	RE

To eliminate the investment account and the shareholders' equity accounts of Valley Company.

14.29 d. and e. continued.

Alternative elimination entries using amounts before closing entries are as follows:

Common Stock..	5,000	
Retained Earnings...	45,000	
Equity in Earnings of Valley Company..................	10,000	
Other Assets..	18,000	
Dividends Declared		4,000
Investment in Valley Company..........................		74,000

Assets	=	Liabilities	+	Shareholders' Equity	(Class.)
+18,000				−5,000	ContriCap
−74,000				−45,000	RE
				−10,000	IncSt → RE
				+4,000	RE

To eliminate the investment account and the shareholders' equity accounts of Valley Company.

Accounts Payable	8,000	
Accounts and Notes Receivable		8,000

Assets	=	Liabilities	+	Shareholders' Equity	(Class.)
−8,000		−8,000			

To eliminate intercompany advance.

14.31 (Ganton; effect of intercorporate investment policies on financial statements.) (amounts in millions of US$)

a. Ganton's acquisition cost of its investments in the bottlers exceeds the carrying value of the net assets of the bottlers. Ganton attributes the excess cost to long-term tangible or intangible assets. Note that consolidated Other Noncurrent Assets of $71,116 million exceeds the sum of the amounts on Ganton's books of $23,875 and the bottlers' books of $44,636 by $2,605 million. The portion attributable to Ganton's acquisition of bottlers is $785 million. The remainder of $1,820 (= $2,605 − $785) relates to the amount for the external interest in the bottlers. Thus, Ganton owns 30.134% (= $785/$2,605) of the bottlers and the external interest owns 69.9%. The amount for the noncontrolling interest in the net assets of the bottlers of $16,899 million comprises the following:

Noncontrolling Interest in Carrying Value of Bottlers Net Assets: 0.69866 × $21,583	$ 15,079
Excess of Fair Value over Carrying Value of Net Assets Attributed to the Noncontrolling Interest	1,820
Total Noncontrolling Interest	$ 16,899

b. (1) **Equity Method**
Liabilities to Assets Ratio: $21,525/$43,269 = 49.7%.
Debt-Equity Ratio: $8,300/$21,744 = 38.2%

(2) **Consolidation**
Liabilities to Assets Ratio: $58,829/$97,472 = 60.4%.
Debt-Equity Ratio: $31,674/$38,643 = 82.0%

c. The bottlers have a heavier proportion of noncurrent assets and noncurrent liabilities than does Ganton. By owning less that 50% of the bottlers, Ganton does not have to consolidate them, resulting in lower debt ratios.

CHAPTER 15

SHAREHOLDERS' EQUITY: CAPITAL CONTRIBUTIONS AND DISTRIBUTIONS

Questions, Exercises, and Problems: Answers and Solutions

15.1   See the text or the glossary at the end of the book.

15.3   Seniority means that, in the event of bankruptcy, the preferred shareholders are ahead of the common shareholders for claims on the firm's assets. A common claim that the preferred shareholders have, which is senior to any claim by common shareholders, is any declared but unpaid dividends.

15.5   The greater the volatility of the stock price, the larger is the potential excess of the market price over the exercise price on the exercise date and the greater the benefit to the employee. The longer the time between the grant date and the exercise date, the more time that elapses for the market price to increase. Offsetting the value of this increased benefit element is the longer time to realize the benefit, which reduces the present value of the option. Stock option valuation models discount the expected benefit element in a stock option to a present value. The larger the discount rate, the smaller is the present value of the benefit.

15.7   The accounting for each of these transactions potentially involves transfers between contributed capital and retained earnings accounts and clouds the distinction between capital transactions and income transactions. The accounting for stock options results in a reduction in net income and retained earnings and an increase in contributed capital. The accounting for stock dividends results in a reduction in retained earnings and an increase in contributed capital. The purchase of treasury stock represents a reduction in both contributed capital and accumulated earnings. The reissuance of treasury stock at a "loss" may result in a debit to both contributed capital and retained earnings. Thus, the Common Stock and Additional Paid-In Capital accounts do not reflect just capital transactions and Retained Earnings does not reflect just income transactions.

15.9 The managers of a firm have knowledge of the plans and risks of the firm that external investors may not possess. Although laws prevent firms from taking advantage of this "inside information," inclusion of gains from treasury stock transactions in net income might motivate firms to buy and sell treasury stock to improve reported earnings. Excluding these gains from net income removes this incentive. Also, the accounting for the acquisition of treasury stock (that is, a reduction from total shareholders' equity) has the same effect on shareholders' equity as a retirement of the capital stock. The reissue of the treasury stock for more than its acquisition cost does not result in a gain any more than the issue of common stock for more than par value represents a gain.

15.11 (Carter, Inc.; issuing common stock.) (amounts in US$)

December 1, 2013

Cash (= 100,000 shares × $18 per share)..................... 1,800,000
    Common Stock—Par Value 100,000
    Additional Paid-In Capital 1,700,000

Assets	=	Liabilities	+	Shareholders' Equity	(Class.)
+1,800,000				+100,000	ContriCap
				+1,700,000	ContriCap

15.13 (Grable, Inc.; journal entries for dividends.) (amounts in US$)

a. Retained Earnings (Dividends Declared) 19,500
    Dividends Payable—Preferred Stock 19,500

Assets	=	Liabilities	+	Shareholders' Equity	(Class.)
		+19,500		−19,500	RE

Dividend of $1.50 per share on 13,000 shares.

b. Dividends Payable—Preferred Stock 19,500
    Cash... 19,500

Assets	=	Liabilities	+	Shareholders' Equity	(Class.)
−19,500		−19,500			

15.13 continued.

    c.   Retained Earnings (Dividends Declared) 300,000
           Common Stock   300,000

Assets	=	Liabilities	+	Shareholders' Equity	(Class.)
				−300,000	RE
				+300,000	ContriCap

    d.   No entry.

15.15   (Danos Corporation; journal entries for treasury stock transactions.) (amounts in US$)

    a.   Treasury Stock—Common 300,000
           Cash (= 10,000 X $30)   300,000

Assets	=	Liabilities	+	Shareholders' Equity	(Class.)
−300,000				−300,000	ContriCap

    b.   Cash (= 6,000 X $32)... 192,000
       Additional Paid-In Capital (Common Stock
          Options) (= 6,000 X $6) 36,000
           Treasury Stock—Common (= 6,000 X $30)......   180,000
           Additional Paid-In Capital..............................   48,000

Assets	=	Liabilities	+	Shareholders' Equity	(Class.)
+192,000				−36,000	ContriCap
				+180,000	ContriCap
				+48,000	ContriCap

Odd-numbered Solutions

15.15 continued.

c. Treasury Stock—Common 266,000
        Cash (= 7,000 X $38)   266,000

Assets	=	Liabilities	+	Shareholders' Equity	(Class.)
−266,000				−266,000	ContriCap

d. Land... 300,000
        Treasury Stock—Common [= (4,000 X $30) +
        (4,000 X $38)]   272,000
        Additional Paid-In Capital....................................   28,000

Assets	=	Liabilities	+	Shareholders' Equity	(Class.)
+300,000				+272,000	ContriCap
				+28,000	ContriCap

e. Cash (= 3,000 X $36).. 108,000
    Additional Paid-In Capital......................................   6,000
        Treasury Stock—Common (= 3,000 X $38)..........   114,000

Assets	=	Liabilities	+	Shareholders' Equity	(Class.)
+108,000				−6,000	ContriCap
				+114,000	ContriCap

15.17   (Intelliant; accounting for stock options.) (amounts in US$)

The value of the stock options on January 1, 2013, is $142.434 (= 24.6 X $5.79) million. Intelliant amortizes this value as an expense of $47.478 (= $142.434/3) million for 2013, 2014, and 2015. Intelliant recognizes no additional expense when employees exercise their options in 2016.

15.19 (Watson Corporation; journal entries for employee stock options.) (amounts in US$)

December 31, 2014, 2015, and 2016

Compensation Expense (= $75,000/3)...................... 25,000	
Additional Paid-In Capital (Stock Options)...........	25,000

Assets	=	Liabilities	+	Shareholders' Equity	(Class.)
				−25,000	IncSt → RE
				+25,000	ContriCap

April 30, 2017

Cash (= 15,000 × $25).................................	375,000	
Additional Paid-In Capital (Stock Options)		
[= (15,000/20,000) × $75,000]........................	56,250	
Common Stock (= 15,000 × $10)		150,000
Additional Paid-In Capital [= $56,250 +		
(15,000 × $15)].............................		281,250

Assets	=	Liabilities	+	Shareholders' Equity	(Class.)
+375,000				−56,250	ContriCap
				+150,000	ContriCap
				+281,250	ContriCap

September 15, 2018

Cash (= 5,000 × $25)	125,000	
Additional Paid-In Capital (Stock Options) [= (5,000/		
20,000) × $75,000]	18,750	
Common Stock (= 5,000 × $10)		50,000
Additional Paid-In Capital [= $18,750 +		
(5,000 × $15)]		93,750

Assets	=	Liabilities	+	Shareholders' Equity	(Class.)
+125,000				−18,750	ContriCap
				+50,000	ContriCap
				+93,750	ContriCap

15.21   (Symantec; accounting for conversion of bonds.) (amounts in US$)

Carrying Value Method

Convertible Bonds Payable 10,255,000

    Common Stock (= 100,000 × $10)   1,000,000

    Additional Paid-In Capital (Plug)   9,255,000

Assets	=	Liabilities	+	Shareholders' Equity	(Class.)
		−10,225,000		+1,000,000	ContriCap
				+9,255,000	ContriCap

Fair Value Method

Convertible Bonds Payable 10,255,000

Loss on Conversion of Bonds (Plug)   245,000

    Common Stock (= 100,000 × $10)   1,000,000

    Additional Paid-In Capital (= 100,000 × $95)........   9,500,000

Assets	=	Liabilities	+	Shareholders' Equity	(Class.)
		−10,255,000		−245,000	IncSt → RE
				+1,000,000	ContriCap
				+9,500,000	ContriCap

15.23   (Alpharm; journal entries for stock warrants.) (amounts in US$)

December 7, 2008

Cash.. 46,180,000

    Convertible Preferred Stock....................................   43,450,000

    Additional Paid-In Capital (Stock Warrants).......   2,730,000

Assets	=	Liabilities	+	Shareholders' Equity	(Class.)
+46,180,000				+43,450,000	ContriCap
				+2,730,000	ContriCap

To record issuance of convertible preferred stock with stock warrants.

15.23 continued.

January 15, 2013

Convertible Preferred Stock 62,533,000

    Common Stock (5,269,705 × $0.01)   52,697

    Additional Paid-In Capital   62,480,303

Assets	=	Liabilities	+	Shareholders' Equity	(Class.)
				–62,533,000	ContriCap
				+52,697	ContriCap
				+62,480,303	ContriCap

To record conversion of preferred stock with accumulated dividends into common stock. $62,533,000 = $43,450,000 + $19,083,000.

15.25   (Journal entries for the issuance of common stocks.) (amounts in US$)

a.   Inventory... 175,000

     Land... 220,000

     Building.. 1,400,000

     Equipment 405,000

        Common Stock (= 20,000 × $10)   200,000

        Additional Paid-In Capital..................................   2,000,000

Assets	=	Liabilities	+	Shareholders' Equity	(Class.)
+175,000				+200,000	ContriCap
+220,000				+2,000,000	ContriCap
+1,400,000					
+405,000					

b.   Cash (= 10,000 × $100) 1,000,000

     Preferred Stock...   1,000,000

Assets	=	Liabilities	+	Shareholders' Equity	(Class.)
+1,000,000				+1,000,000	

15.25 continued.

c. Cash (= 5,000 X $24)... 120,000
Additional Paid-In Capital (Common Stock
    Warrants) (= 5,000 X $8)..................................... 40,000
        Common Stock (= 5,000 X $1) 5,000
        Additional Paid-In Capital............................. 155,000

Assets	=	Liabilities	+	Shareholders' Equity	(Class.)
+120,000				−40,000	ContriCap
				+5,000	ContriCap
				+155,000	ContriCap

d. Preferred Stock (= 10,000 X $50) 500,000
        Common Stock (= 20,000 X $10) 200,000
        Additional Paid-In Capital................................. 300,000

Assets	=	Liabilities	+	Shareholders' Equity	(Class.)
				−500,000	ContriCap
				+200,000	ContriCap
				+300,000	ContriCap

15.27   (Fisher Company; reconstructing transactions involving shareholders' equity.) (amounts in US$)

a. $60,000 par value/$10 per share = 6,000 shares.

b. $7,200/360 = $20 per share.

c. 600 − 360 = 240 shares.

d. If the Additional Paid-In Capital is $31,440, then $30,000 [= 6,000 X ($15 − $10)] represents contributions in excess of par value on original issue of 6,000 shares. Then, $1,440 (= $31,440 − $30,000) represents the credit to Additional Paid-In Capital when it reissued the treasury shares.

The $1,440 represents 240 shares reissued times the excess of reissue price over acquisition price:

$$240(\$X - \$20) = \$1,440, \text{ or } X = \$26.$$

The shares were reissued for $26 each.

15.27 continued.

e. (1) Cash (= 6,000 × $15) 90,000
      Common Stock ($10 Par Value)................. 60,000
      Additional Paid-In Capital........................ 30,000

Assets	=	Liabilities	+	Shareholders' Equity	(Class.)
+90,000				+60,000	ContriCap
				+30,000	ContriCap

(2) Treasury Stock—Common 12,000
      Cash (= 600 × $20) 12,000

Assets	=	Liabilities	+	Shareholders' Equity	(Class.)
−12,000				−12,000	ContriCap

(3) Cash (= 240 × $26) 6,240
      Treasury Stock—Common (= 240 × $20)..... 4,800
      Additional Paid-In Capital......................... 1,440

Assets	=	Liabilities	+	Shareholders' Equity	(Class.)
+6,240				+4,800	ContriCap
				+1,440	ContriCap

(4a) Cash.. 10,000
      Securities Available for Sale 6,000
      Realized Gain on Sale of Securities
      Available for Sale...................................... 4,000

Assets	=	Liabilities	+	Shareholders' Equity	(Class.)
+10,000				+4,000	IncSt → RE
−6,000					

15.27 e. continued.

(4b) Securities Available for Sale 2,000
Unrealized Gain on Securities Available
for Sale (Accumulated Other
Comprehensive Income) 2,000

Assets	=	Liabilities	+	Shareholders' Equity	(Class.)
+2,000				+2,000	OCI → AOCI

f. The realized gain appears in the income statement and the unrealized gain appears in a statement of other comprehensive income or in reconciliation of accumulated other comprehensive income.

15.29 (Lowen Corporation; accounting for stock options.) (amounts in US$)

Compensation expense reduces net income each year as follows:

2013: zero compensation because all benefits occur after the granting of the stock option.

2014:	0.5(5,000 X $2.40)	$ 6,000
2015:	[0.5(5,000 X $2.40) + 0.5(6,000 X $3.00)]	15,000
2016:	[0.5(6,000 X $3.00) + 0.5(7,000 X $3.14)]	19,990
2017:	[0.5(7,000 X $3.14) + 0.5(8,000 X $3.25)]	23,990
	Total Compensation Expense	$ 64,980

15.31 (Microtel Corporation; reconstructing transactions affecting shareholders' equity.) (amounts in millions of US$)

(1) Cash... 6,783
Common Stock and Additional Paid-In
Capital... 6,783

Assets	=	Liabilities	+	Shareholders' Equity	(Class.)
+6,783				+6,783	ContriCap

To issue common stock for cash.

15.31 continued.

(2) Common Stock and Additional Paid-In Capital...   6,162
     Retained Earnings...   21,212
         Cash...   27,374

Assets	=	Liabilities	+	Shareholders' Equity	(Class.)
–27,374				–6,162	ContriCap
				–21,212	RE

To repurchase common stock for more than its initial issue price.

(3) Compensation Expense...   889
         Additional Paid-In Capital...............................   889

Assets	=	Liabilities	+	Shareholders' Equity	(Class.)
				–889	IncSt → RE
				+889	ContriCap

To record stock-based compensation expense.

(4) Revenues and Gains Net of Expenses and Losses ..   14,065
         Retained Earnings...   14,065

Assets	=	Liabilities	+	Shareholders' Equity	(Class.)
				–14,065	IncSt → RE
				+14,065	RE

To close revenues, gain, expense, and loss accounts to retained earnings.

(5) Retained Earnings...   3,837
         Cash...   3,837

Assets	=	Liabilities	+	Shareholders' Equity	(Class.)
–3,837				–3,837	RE

To declare and pay cash dividends.

Odd-numbered Solutions

15.31 continued.

(6) Marketable Securities 326

    Net Unrealized Gains and Losses on

      Marketable Securities 326

Assets	=	Liabilities	+	Shareholders' Equity	(Class.)
+326				+326	OCI → AOCI

To record net unrealized gains and losses for changes in fair value of marketable securities.

(7) Derivative Securities................................... 14

    Net Unrealized Gains and Losses on

      Derivatives 14

Assets	=	Liabilities	+	Shareholders' Equity	(Class.)
+14	or	−14		+14	OCI → AOCI

To record net unrealized gains and losses for changes in fair value derivatives.

15.33 (Busch Corporation; journal entries for changes in shareholders' equity.) (amounts in millions of US$)

(1) Cash... 292.3

    Common Stock 8.8

    Additional Paid-In Capital............................... 283.5

Assets	=	Liabilities	+	Shareholders' Equity	(Class.)
+292.3				+8.8	ContriCap
				+283.5	ContriCap

To record the issuance of common stock to employees under stock option plans.

15.33 continued.

(2)   Compensation Expense.. 136.3
          Additional Paid-In Capital.................................   136.1
          Treasury Stock—Common...................................   0.2

Assets	=	Liabilities	+	Shareholders' Equity	(Class.)
				−136.3	IncSt → RE
				+136.1	ContriCap
				+0.2	ContriCap

To record the amortized cost of employees stock options. The reason for the credit to Treasury Stock is not explained by Busch.

(3)   Revenues, Gains, Expenses, and Losses................. 2,115.3
          Retained Earnings..   2,115.3

Assets	=	Liabilities	+	Shareholders' Equity	(Class.)
				−2,115.3	IncSt → RE
				+2,115.3	RE

To close revenue and expense accounts to retained earnings.

(4)   Retained Earnings... 932.4
          Cash..   932.4

Assets	=	Liabilities	+	Shareholders' Equity	(Class.)
−932.4				−932.4	RE

To record the declaration and payment of cash dividends.

(5)   Treasury Stock—Common....................................... 2,707.2
          Cash..   2,707.2

Assets	=	Liabilities	+	Shareholders' Equity	(Class.)
−2,707.2				−2,707.2	ContriCap

To record repurchase of common stock held as treasury stock.

15.33 continued.

(6) Net Unrealized Gains and Losses on Marketable
    Securities 0.3
        Marketable Securities 0.3

Assets	=	Liabilities	+	Shareholders' Equity	(Class.)
−0.3				−0.3	OCI → AOCI

To record net unrealized loss on marketable securities.

(7) Net Unrealized Gains and Losses on Cash Flow
    Hedges 2.0
        Derivative Securities................................... 2.0

Assets	=	Liabilities	+	Shareholders' Equity	(Class.)
−2.0	or	+2.0		−2.0	OCI → AOCI

To record net unrealized loss on cash flow hedges.

(8) Pension Liability... 205.2
        Pension Liability Adjustment 205.2

Assets	=	Liabilities	+	Shareholders' Equity	(Class.)
		+205.2		+205.2	OCI → AOCI

To reduce pension liability for a reduction in the minimum pension liability or for changes in actuarial assumptions, actuarial performance, or prior cost and
increase in other comprehensive income.

CHAPTER 16

STATEMENT OF CASH FLOWS: ANOTHER LOOK

Problems and Cases: Answers and Solutions

16.1   (Effects of transactions on statement of cash flows.) (amounts in US$)

a. The journal entry to record this transaction is:

Retained Earnings...	15,000	
Dividends Payable..		3,000
Cash..		12,000

	ΔCash	=	ΔL	+	ΔSE	–	ΔN\$A
Financing	–$12,000	=	$3,000	+	–$15,000	–	$0

The credit to the Cash account reduces Line (11) by $12,000. Paying dividends is a financing activity, so Line (10) increases by $12,000.

b. The journal entry to record this transaction is:

Cash..	75,000	
Bank Loan Payable		75,000

	ΔCash	=	ΔL	+	ΔSE	–	ΔN\$A
Financing	+$75,000	=	$75,000	+	$0	–	$0

The debit to the Cash account increases Line (11) by $75,000. Borrowing is a financing activity so Line (8) increases by $75,000.

16.1 continued.

c. The journal entry to record this transaction is:

Cash... 20,000
Accumulated Depreciation.................................... 35,000
   Machinery... 40,000
   Gain on Sale of Machinery.............................. 15,000

	ΔCash	=	ΔL +	ΔSE −	ΔN\$A
Investing	$20,000	=	$0 +	$15,000 −	−$5,000

The debit to the Cash account results in an increase in Line (11) of $20,000. Selling machinery is an investing activity so Line (6) increases by $20,000. The gain on the sale increases net income on Line (3) by $15,000. Because the full cash proceeds is an investing activity, Line (5) increases by $15,000 to subtract from net income a revenue that did not provide an operating source of cash.

d. The journal entry for this transaction is:

Rent Expense... 28,000
   Cash... 28,000

	ΔCash	=	ΔL +	ΔSE −	ΔN\$A
Operations	−$28,000	=	$0 +	−$28,000 −	$0

The credit to the Cash account reduces Line (11) by $28,000. The recognition of rent expense reduces net income on Line (3) by $28,000. Expenditure matched the expense, so Line (2) shows an increase in the amount subtracted of $28,000.

e. The journal entry to record this transaction is:

Marketable Securities 39,000
   Cash... 39,000

	ΔCash	=	ΔL +	ΔSE −	ΔN\$A
Investing	−$39,000	=	$0 +	$0 −	$39,000

The credit to the Cash account reduces Line (11) by $39,000. Purchasing marketable securities is an investing transaction so Line (7) increases by $39,000.

16.1 continued.

f. The journal entry to record this transaction is:

Accumulated Depreciation..................................... 14,000
   Truck.. 14,000

	ΔCash	=	ΔL	+	ΔSE	–	ΔN\$A
	\$0	=	\$0	+	\$0	–	\$0

Because this transaction affects neither the Cash account nor net income, it does not appear on the statement of cash flows.

g. The journal entry to record this event is:

Unrealized Holding Loss of Marketable
   Securities (Other Comprehensive Income) 8,000
      Marketable Securities 8,000

	ΔCash	=	ΔL	+	ΔSE	–	ΔN\$A
	\$0	=	\$0	+	–\$8,000	–	–\$8,000

Because this entry does not affect either the Cash account or net income, it does not appear on the statement of cash flows. The firm discloses in a supplementary schedule or note the write down of marketable equity securities totaling $8,000.

h. The journal entry to record this transaction is:

Interest Expense.. 15,000
   Bonds Payable.. 500
   Cash... 14,500

	ΔCash	=	ΔL	+	ΔSE	–	ΔN\$A
Operations	–\$14,500	=	\$500	+	–\$15,000	–	\$0

The credit to the Cash account results in a decrease in Line (11) of $14,500. The recognition of interest expense reduces net income on Line (3) by $15,000. Because the firm used only $14,500 of cash for this expense, Line (4) increases by $500 for the portion of the expense that did not use cash. Line (2) increased the amount to be subtracted by the amount of the expense paid in cash, $14,500.

16.1 continued.

    i.   The journal entry for this event is:

Goodwill Impairment Loss 22,000
    Goodwill 22,000

ΔCash	=	ΔL	+	ΔSE	–	ΔN$A
$0	=	$0	+	–$22,000	–	–$22,000

This entry does not involve the Cash account so Line (11) does not change. The recognition of the impairment loss reduces net income on Line (3) by $22,000. Because this loss requires no cash outflow, Line (4) increases by $22,000 to convert net income to cash flow from operations.

16.3   (Effects of transactions on statement of cash flows.) (amounts in US$)

    a.   The journal entry to record this event is:

Contracts in Process... 15,000
    Contract Revenue 15,000

ΔCash	=	ΔL	+	ΔSE	–	ΔN$A
$0	=	$0	+	$15,000	–	$15,000

This entry does not affect the Cash account so Line (11) does not change. The recognition of contract revenue increases net income on Line (3) by $15,000. Because this revenue does not result in a change in cash, Line (5) increases by $15,000 to convert net income to cash flow from operations.

    b.   The journal entry to record this transaction is:

Land.. 50,000
    Donated Capital... 50,000

ΔCash	=	ΔL	+	ΔSE	–	ΔN$A
$0	=	$0	+	$50,000	–	$50,000

16.3 b. continued.

This transaction affects neither the Cash account [Line (11)] nor net income [Line (3)] and, therefore, does not appear on the statement of cash flows. The firm discloses in a supplementary schedule or note the donation of land by a governmental agency totaling $50,000.

c. The journal entry to record this event is:

Unrealized Holding Loss on Investments in
    Securities (Other Comprehensive Income) 8,000
        Investments in Securities 8,000

ΔCash	=	ΔL	+	ΔSE	–	ΔN$A
$0	=	$0	+	–$8,000	–	–$8,000

This transaction affects neither the Cash account [Line (11)] nor net income [Line (3)] so would not appear on the statement of cash flows. The firm discloses in a supplementary schedule or note the write down of marketable equity investments totaling $8,000.

d. The journal entry to record the recognition of depreciation is:

Inventories 60,000
    Accumulated Depreciation 60,000

The journal entry to record the sale of the inventory items is:

Cost of Goods Sold... 60,000
    Inventories 60,000

ΔCash	=	ΔL	+	ΔSE	–	ΔN$A
$0	=	$0	+	–$60,000	–	–$60,000

These entries do not affect the Cash account so Line (11) does not change. The recognition of cost of goods sold containing depreciation reduces net income on Line (3) by $60,000. Because this expense does not use cash, Line (4) increases by $60,000 to convert net income to cash flow from operations.

        Odd-numbered Solutions

16.3 continued.

e. The journal entry to record this transaction is:

Warranty Expense.. 35,000
    Estimated Warranty Liability......................... 35,000

	ΔCash	=	ΔL	+	ΔSE	–	ΔN$A
	$0	=	$35,000	+	–$35,000	–	$0

This entry does not affect the Cash account so Line (11) does not change. The recognition of warranty expense reduces net income on Line (3) by $35,000. Because this expense does not use cash, Line (4) increases by $35,000 to convert net income to cash flow from operations.

f. The journal entry to record this transaction is:

Estimated Warranty Liability.............................. 28,000
    Cash... 28,000

	ΔCash	=	ΔL	+	ΔSE	–	ΔN$A
Operations	–$28,000	=	–$28,000	+	$0	–	$0

The credit to the Cash account reduces Line (11) by $28,000. Honoring warranties is an operating item so Line (2) increases the amount to be subtracted. This entry does not affect net income on Line (3) this period. Thus, Line (5) increases by $28,000 to convert net income to cash flow from operations.

g. The journal entry to record this event is:

Income Tax Expense 80,000
Deferred Tax Liability.. 20,000
    Cash... 100,000

	ΔCash	=	ΔL	+	ΔSE	–	ΔN$A
Operations	–$100,000	=	–$20,000	+	–$80,000	–	$0

16.3 g. continued.

The credit to the Cash account results in a reduction in Line (11) of $100,000. Line (2) increases the amount to be subtracted by $100,000. The recognition of income tax expense reduces net income on Line (3) by $80,000. Because the firm used more cash this period than the amount of income tax expense, Line (5) increases by $20,000 when converting net income to cash flow from operations.

h.   The journal entry to record this event is:

Loss from Writedown of Inventories 18,000
    Inventories   18,000

$$\Delta \text{Cash} \quad = \quad \Delta L \ + \quad \Delta SE \ - \quad \Delta N\$A$$
$$\$0 \quad = \quad \$0 \ + \ -\$18,000 \ - \ -\$18,000$$

This entry does not affect the Cash account so Line (11) does not change. The recognition of the writedown reduces net income on Line (3) by $18,000. Because the writedown did not use cash, Line (4) increases by $18,000 to convert net income to cash flow from operations.

16.5 (Metals Company deriving direct method presentation of cash flow from operations using data from T-account work sheet.) (amounts in millions of US$)

(a) (The letters here correspond to the column header letters in the exhibit below.) Copy Income Statement and Cash Flow from Operations

(b) Copy Information from T-Account Work Sheet Next to Related Income Statement Item

(c)-(d) Sum Across Rows to Derive Direct Receipts and Expenditures

Operations	(a)	Indirect Method (b)	Changes in Related Balance Sheet Accounts from T-Account Work Sheet (c)	Direct Method (d)	From Operations: Receipts Less Expenditures
Sales Revenues	$20,465.0	$74.6	= Accounts Receivable Decrease	20,539.6	Receipts from Customers
Gain on Sale of Marketable Equity Securities	20.8	(20.8)	Gain Produces No Operating Cash	—	
Equity in Earnings of Affiliates	214.0	(47.1)	Metals Company's Share of Earnings Retained by Affiliates	166.9	Receipts for Equity Method Investments
Cost of Goods Sold	(9,963.3)	664.0	Depreciation on Manufacturing Facilities	(9,464.3)	Payments for Inventory
		33.9	= Accounts Payable Increase		
		(198.9)	= Increase in Inventories		
General and Administrative Expenses	(5,570.2)	(40.3)	= Prepayments Increase	(5,721.3)	Payments for General and Administrative Services
		(110.8)	= Decrease in Other Current Liabilities		
Interest Expense	(2,887.3)	—		(2,887.3)	Payments for Interest
Income Tax Expense	(911.6)	82.0	Deferred Income Taxes Uses no Cash this Period	(829.6)	Payment for Income Taxes
Net Income	= $1,367.4	= 1,367.4	Totals	$1,804.0	= Cash Flow from Operations
		$1,804.0	= Cash Flow from Operations Derived via Indirect Method		Derived via Direct Method

16.7 (Warren Corporation; preparing a statement of cash flows.) (amounts in US$)

a.

		Cash		
		√ 223,200		

Operations

Net Income	(5)	234,000	
Loss on Sale of Machinery	(1b)	15,600	
Amortize Patent	(2b)	5,040	
Decrease in Accounts Receivable	(7)	18,000	
Bad Debt Expense	(8)	2,400	
Decrease in Inventories	(9)	66,000	
Depreciation Expense	(11)	106,800	
Amortize Leasehold Improvements	(12)	10,800	
Increase in Accounts Payable	(13)	153,360	

Investing

Sale of Machinery	(1b)	57,600	463,200	(1a)	Acquisition of Machinery
			2,400	(2a)	Payment for Patent Defense
			180,000	(10)	Acquisition of Securities

Financing

		13,200	(3)	Retirement of Preferred Stock
		60,000	(15)	Provision for Current Portion of Serial Bonds

	√ 174,000	

16-9

16.7 a. continued.

Accounts Receivable			Allowance for Uncollectible Accounts				Inventory		
√ 327,600					20,400 √	√	645,600		
	3,600 (6)	(6)	3,600		2,400 (8)			66,000	(9)
	18,000 (7)								
√ 306,000					19,200 √	√	579,600		

Securities Held for Plant Expansion			Machinery and Equipment (Cost)			Accumulated Depreciation			
√ -0-			√ 776,400					446,400 √	
(10) 180,000			(1a) 463,200	127,200 (1b)		(1b)	54,000	106,800 (11)	
√ 180,000			√ 1,112,400					499,200 √	

Leasehold Improvements			Allowance for Amortization			Patents		
√ 104,400				58,800 √		√ 36,000		
				10,800 (12)		(2a) 2,400	5,040 (2b)	
√ 104,400				69,600 √		√ 33,360		

Accounts Payable			Dividends Payable			Bonds Payable (Current)		
	126,000 √			— √			60,000 √	
	153,360 (13)			48,000 (4)		(15) 60,000	60,000 (14)	
	279,360 √			48,000 √			60,000 √	

6% Serial Bonds Payable			Preferred Stock			Common Stock		
	360,000 √			120,000 √			600,000 √	
(14) 60,000			(3) 12,000					
	300,000 √			108,000 √			600,000 √	

Retained Earnings		
	321,600 √	
(4) & (5) 48,000	234,000 (5)	
(3) 1,200		
	506,400 √	

16.7 continued.

b.
WARREN CORPORATION
Statement of Cash Flows
For the Year Ending June 30, 2014

Operations:

Net Income	$ 234,000	
Loss on Sale of Machinery	15,600	
Depreciation	106,800	
Amortization of Leasehold Improvements	10,800	
Amortization of Patents	5,040	
Bad Debt Expense	2,400	
Decrease in Accounts Receivable	18,000	
Decrease in Inventories	66,000	
Increase in Accounts Payable	153,360	
Cash Flow from Operations		$ 612,000
Investing:		
Sale of Machinery	$ 57,600	
Payment of Legal Fee for Patent Defense	(2,400)	
Acquisition of Securities for Plant Expansion	(180,000)	
Acquisition of Machinery	(463,200)	
Cash Flow from Investing		(588,000)
Financing:		
Retirement of Serial Bonds	$ (60,000)	
Retirement of Preferred Stock	(13,200)	
Cash Flow from Financing		(73,200)
Net Change in Cash		$ (49,200)
Cash, January 1, 2014		223,200
Cash, June 30, 2014		$ 174,000

16.9   (Biddle Corporation; preparing a statement of cash flows.)   (amounts in US$)

a.
Cash

√ 45,000

Operations

Income from Continuing Operations	(14)	60,500	6,000	(3)	Gain on Retirement of Bonds Net of Income Taxes	
Loss on Sale of Equipment	(4)	2,000	35,000	(7)	Increase in Accounts Receivable	
Depreciation	(9)	10,000				
Amortization	(10)	1,500	20,000	(8)	Increase in Inventories	
Increase in Accounts Payable	(11)	30,000				
Deferred Income Taxes	(13)	20,000	5,000	(12)	Decrease in Accrued Liabilities	

Investing

Sale of Equipment	(4)	9,500	42,500	(6)	Acquisition of Land	

Financing

		19,000	(3)	Retirement of Bonds, Including Income Taxes	
		1,000	(5)	Dividends	

√ 50,000

Accounts Receivable—Net		Inventories		Land	
√ 70,000		√ 110,000		√ 100,000	
(7) 35,000		(8) 20,000		(2) 20,000	
				(6) 42,500	
√ 105,000		√ 130,000		√ 162,500	

16.9 a. continued.

	Plant and Equipment				Accumulated Depreciation			Patents	
√ 316,500					50,000	√	√ 16,500		
	26,500 (4)	(4)	15,000	10,000	(9)			1,500 (10)
√ 290,000					45,000	√	√ 15,000		

	Accounts Payable		Accrued Liabilities			Deferred Income Taxes	
	100,000 √		105,000	√		50,000	√
	30,000 (11)	(12) 5,000				20,000 (13)	
	130,000 √		100,000	√		70,000	√

	Long-Term Bonds		Common Stock			Additional Paid-In Capital	
	90,000 √		105,000	√		85,000	√
(3) 25,000			10,500	(1)		21,000	(1)
			9,500	(2)		10,500	(2)
	65,000 √		125,000	√		116,500	√

	Retained Earnings	
	73,000	√
(1) 31,500	60,500	(14)
(5) 1,000		
	101,000	√

16-13

16.9 continued.

b.
BIDDLE CORPORATION
Statement of Cash Flows
For the Year Ended December, 2014

Operations:		
Net Income..	$ 60,500	
Subtract Gain on Sale of Repurchase of		
Bonds	(6,000)	
Add Back Loss on Sale of Equipment............	2,000	
Depreciation	10,000	
Amortization	1,500	
Deferred Income Taxes....................................	20,000	
Increase in Accounts Payable.........................	30,000	
Increase in Accounts Receivable	(35,000)	
Increase in Inventories	(20,000)	
Decrease in Accrued Liabilities.....................	(5,000)	
Cash Flow from Operations		$ 58,000
Investing:		
Sale of Equipment...	$ 9,500	
Acquisition of Land...	(42,500)	
Cash Flow from Investing		(33,000)
Financing:		
Retirement of Bonds	$ (19,000)	
Dividends..	(1,000)	
Cash Flow from Financing		(20,000)
Net Change in Cash		$ 5,000
Cash, January 1, 2014		45,000
Cash, December 31, 2014.................................		$ 50,000

Supplementary Information
During 2014, Biddle Corporation issued common stock with a market value of $20,000 in the acquisition of land.

16.11 (Airlines Corporation; preparing and interpreting the statement of cash flows.) (amounts in millions of US$)

a. T-account work sheet for 2013.

Cash

√	1,087		

Operations

(1)	324	106	(4)
(3)	517	147	(7)
(11)	56	39	(8)
(15)	42	67	(9)
(17)	12	49	(16)

Investing

(4)	1,199	1,568	(2)
(10)	40	957	(6)

Financing

(12)	325	110	(13)
(18)	4	98	(19)
√	465		

Marketable Securities		Accounts Receivable		Inventories	
√	—	√	741	√	210
(5)	85	(7)	147	(8)	39
(6)	957				
√	1,042	√	888	√	249

Prepayments		Property, Plant, and Equipment			Accumulated Depreciation		
√	112	√	7,710			3,769	√
(9)	67	(2)	1,568	1,574 (4)	(4) 481	517	(3)
√	179	√	7,704			3,805	√

16.11 a. continued.

Other Assets		Accounts Payable		Short-Term Borrowing	
√ 610			540 √		121 √
	40 (10)		56 (11)		325 (12)
√ 570			596 √		446 √

Current Portion Long-Term Debt		Advances from Customers		Other Current Liabilities	
	110 √		619 √		1,485 √
(13) 110	84 (14)		42 (15)	(16) 49	
	84 √		661 √		1,436 √

Long-Term Debt		Deferred Tax Liability		Other Noncurrent Liabilities	
	1,418 √		352 √		715 √
(14) 84			12 (17)		4 (18)
	1,334 √		364 √		719 √

Common Stock		Unrealized Holding Gain on Marketable Securities		Retained Earnings	
	119 √		— √		1,188 √
			85 (5)		324 (1)
	119 √		85 √		1,512 √

Additional Paid-In Capital		Treasury Stock	
	48 √	√ 14	
		(19) 98	
	48 √	√ 112	

16.11 a. continued.

a. T-account work sheet for 2014.

		Cash		
√	465			

		Operations		
(1)	101	286	(4)
(3)	560	25	(7)
(15)	182	74	(8)
(16)	390	30	(9)
(18)	4	44	(11)

		Investing		
(4)	1,697	2,821	(2)
		17	(6)
		35	(10)

		Financing		
(12)	1	84	(13)
(17)	230		
(19)	2		
(20)	5		
√	221		

Marketable Securities		Accounts Receivable		Inventories	
√	1,042	√	888	√	249
(5)	7	(7)	25	(8)	74
(6)	17				
√	1,066	√	913	√	323

Prepayments		Property, Plant, and Equipment		Accumulated Depreciation	
√	179	√	7,704		3,805 √
(9)	30	(2)	2,821 1,938 (4)	(4)	527 560 (3)
√	209	√	8,587		3,838 √

16-17

16.11 a. continued.

Other Assets			Accounts Payable			Short-Term Borrowing		
√	570			596	√		446	√
(10)	35		(11)	44			1	(12)
√	605			552	√		447	√

Current Portion Long-Term Debt			Advances from Customers			Other Current Liabilities		
		84 √			661 √			1,436 √
(13)	84	89 (14)			182 (15)			390 (16)
		89 √			843 √			1,826 √

Long-Term Debt			Deferred Tax Liability			Other Noncurrent Liabilities		
		1,334 √			364 √			719 √
(14)	89	230 (17)			4 (18)			2 (19)
		1,475 √			368 √			721 √

Common Stock			Additional Paid-In Capital			Unrealized Holding Gain on Marketable Securities		
		119 √			48 √			85 √
		1 (20)			4 (20)			7 (5)
		120 √			52 √			92 √

Retained Earnings			Treasury Stock		
		1,512 √	√	112	
		101 (1)			
		1,613 √	√	112	

16.11 continued.

b. **Comparative Statement of Cash Flows for Airlines Corporation**
(amounts in millions of US$)

	2014	2013
Operations:		
Net Income..	$ 101	$ 324
Depreciation Expense......................................	560	517
Deferred Income Taxes	4	12
Gain on Sale of Property, Plant, and Equipment	(286)	(106)
(Increase) Decrease in Accounts Receivable...	(25)	(147)
(Increase) Decrease in Inventories	(74)	(39)
(Increase) Decrease in Prepayments..............	(30)	(67)
Increase (Decrease) in Accounts Payable	(44)	56
Increase (Decrease) in Advances from Customers	182	42
Increase (Decrease) in Other Current Liabilities..	390	(49)
Cash Flow from Operations	$ 778	$ 543
Investing:		
Sale of Property, Plant, and Equipment	$ 1,697	$ 1,199
Acquisition of Property, Plant, and Equipment	(2,821)	(1,568)
Acquisition of Marketable Securities............	(17)	(957)
(Increase) Decrease in Other Noncurrent Assets	(35)	40
Cash Flow from Investing	$(1,176)	$ (1,286)
Financing:		
Increase in Short-Term Borrowing.................	$ 1	$ 325
Increase in Long-Term Borrowing..................	230	—
Increase in Common Stock.............................	5	—
Decrease in Long-Term Borrowing................	(84)	(110)
Acquisition of Treasury Stock........................	—	(98)
Increase in Other Noncurrent Liabilities	2	4
Cash Flow from Financing................................	$ 154	$ 121
Net Change in Cash	$ (244)	$ (622)
Cash, January 1	465	1,087
Cash, December 31...	$ 221	$ 465

16.11 continued.

c. During 2013, cash flow from operations exceeded net income primarily because of the non-cash expense for depreciation. Cash flows from operations and from the sale of property, plant, and equipment were sufficient to finance capital expenditures. Airlines Corporation used the excess cash flow as well as cash from additional short-term borrowing to repay long-term debt and reacquire treasury stock. It invested the remaining excess cash flow in short-term marketable securities. Although the balance in the cash account declined during 2013, the combined balance in cash and marketable securities actually increased.

Net income declined in 2014 relative to 2013 but cash flow from operations increased. The increase occurred because Airlines Corporation received increased cash advances from customers and stretched its other current liabilities. Cash flow from operations and from the sale of property, plant, and equipment were insufficient to finance capital expenditures. Airlines Corporation increased long-term borrowing and decreased the balance in its cash account to finance these capital expenditures.

One additional item to note for Airlines Corporation is the significant turnover of aircraft each year. The airline sold older aircraft at a gain and replaced them with newer aircraft.

16.13   (Breda Enterprises, Inc.; preparing a statement of cash flows.) (amounts in US$)

BREDA ENTERPRISES, INC.
Statement of Cash Flows
For the Year Ended December 31, 2014

Operations:		
Net Income (1)	$ 90,000	
Adjustments for Non-cash Transactions:		
Decrease in Merchandise Inventory (3)	4,000	
Increase in Accounts Payable (3)	12,000	
Loss on Sale of Equipment (4)	13,000	
Depreciation Expense (4)	42,000	
Amortization of Leasehold Asset (5)	5,000	
Loss on Conversion of Bonds (8)	15,000	
Increase in Accounts Receivable (Net) (2)	(10,600)	
Increase in Notes Receivable (2)	(15,000)	
Increase in Interest Receivable (2) [(0.08 × $15,000) × (1/6)]	(200)	
Decrease in Advances from Customers (2)	(2,700)	
Realized Gain on Marketable Securities (7)	(4,600)	
Interest Expense Greater than Cash Paid for Interest = Amortization of Bond Premium (8)	(1,500)	
Cash Flow from Operations		$ 146,400
Investing:		
Sale of Equipment (4)	$ 25,000	
Sale of Marketable Securities (7)	9,100	
Purchase of Equipment (4) ($31,000 + $38,000 − $26,000)	(43,000)	
Cash Flow from Investing		(8,900)
Financing:		
Reduction of Lease Liability (5)	$ (2,400)	
Dividends (6)	(24,000)	
Cash Flow from Financing		(26,400)
Change in Cash		$ 111,100

16.15 (Canned Soup Company; interpreting the statement of cash flows.)

a. Canned uses suppliers and other creditors to finance its working capital needs. Consumer foods is a mature industry in the United States, so Canned's modest growth rate does not require large incremental investments in accounts receivable and inventories.

b. (1) Capital expenditures have declined slightly each year, suggesting little need to add productive capacity.

(2) Depreciation expense is a growing percentage of acquisitions of property, plant, and equipment, suggesting slower growth in manufacturing capacity.

(3) Canned trades a substantial amount of marketable securities each year. Mature, profitable firms tend to accumulate cash beyond their operating needs and invest in marketable securities until they need cash.

(4) Canned acquired another business in 2013. Firms in mature industries grow by acquiring other firms. Canned financed this acquisition in part by selling marketable securities.

c. (1) Increases in long-term debt approximately equal repayments of long-term debt, particularly for 2012 and 2013. Mature firms tend to roll over debt as long as they remain in the no-growth phase.

(2) Canned repurchased a portion of its common stock with excess cash.

(3) Dividends have grown in line with increases in net income and represent approximately a 37% payout rate relative to net income.

16.17 (Cypress Corporation; interpreting the statement of cash flows.)

a. Although net income increased between 2011 and 2013, the firm increased accounts receivable and inventories to support this growth. It stretched its creditors somewhat to finance the buildup of accounts receivable and inventories, but not sufficiently to keep cash from operations from decreasing.

16.17 continued.

b. The principal factors causing cash flow from operations to increase in 2013 is an increase in net income. Inventories decreased and the firm stretched its payable somewhat as well. The principal factors causing the increased cash flow from operations in 2015 are increased and decreased accounts receivable and decreased inventories, partially offset by decreases in accounts payable and other liabilities.

c. The firm has repaid both short- and long-term debt, likely reducing its debt service payments. It invested excess cash in marketable securities. It also substantially increased its dividend. Even with these actions, cash on the balance sheet increased significantly, particularly in 2015.

This page is intentionally left blank

CHAPTER 17

SYNTHESIS AND EXTENSIONS

Exercises and Problems: Answers and Solutions

17.1   (Identifying accounting principles.)

   a.   FIFO cost flow assumption.

   b.   Allowance method.

   c.   Equity method.

   d.   Capital or financing lease method.

   e.   Weighted-average cost-flow assumption.

   f.   Effective interest method.

   g.   Cash flow hedge.

   h.   Market value method.

   i.   Percentage-of-completion method.

   j.   Allowance method.

   k.   Fair value hedge.

   l.   Operating lease method.

   m.   FIFO cost-flow assumption.

   n.   Market value method for securities available for sale.

   o.   Straight-line method.

Odd-numbered Solutions

17.1 continued.

      p.   FIFO cost-flow assumption.

      q.   Operating lease method.

      r.   LIFO cost-flow assumption.

      s.   Capital or financing lease method.

      t.   LIFO cost-flow assumption.

17.3   (Campbell Incorporated; calculating earnings per share.) (amounts in thousands of US$)

      a.   Basic earnings per share:

          2012: $1.75 per share = $1,200,472/687,910

          2013: $2.07 per share = $1,456,091/702,987

      b.   Diluted earnings per share:

          2012: $1.72 per share = $1,200,472/699,012

          2013: $2.04 per share = $1,456,091/713,456

      c.   Diluted earnings per share are smaller than basic earnings per share because the diluted number of shares exceeds the number of basic shares.

17.5   (Kennett Corporation; calculating weighted-average shares outstanding.)

Period	Shares Outstanding	Fraction of Year	Product
January–March	214.6	25.00%	53.7
April–August	250.8 (= 214.6 + 36.2)	41.67%	104.5
September–December	278.2 (= 250.8 + 27.4)	33.33%	92.7
Weighted Average Outstanding		100.00%	**250.9**

      a.   Kennett had 278.2 million common shares outstanding as of December 31, 2013.

17.5 continued.

    b. Kennett's weighted-average number of common shares is 250.9 million, calculated above.

17.7   (Company A/Company B; interpreting changes in earnings per share.) (amounts in US$)

    a. **Company A Earnings Per Share:**

2012 .... $\dfrac{\$100{,}000}{100{,}000 \text{ Shares}} = \$1 \text{ per Share}$

2013 .... $\dfrac{\$100{,}000}{100{,}000 \text{ Shares}} = \$1 \text{ per Share}$

      Company B Earnings Per Share:

2012 .... $\dfrac{\$100{,}000}{100{,}000 \text{ Shares}} = \$1 \text{ per Share}$

2013 .... $\dfrac{\$110{,}000}{100{,}000 \text{ Shares}} = \$1.10 \text{ per Share}$

    b. Company A: No growth [= ($1.00/$1.00) – 1.0].
       Company B: 10% [= ($1.10/$1.00) – 1.0] annual growth.

    c. Company B: This result is misleading. Comparisons of growth in earnings per share are valid only if firms employ equal amounts of assets in the business. The rates of return both on assets and on shareholders' equity are better measures of growth performance. Earnings per share results do not, in general (as in this problem), take earnings retention into account.

    d. The problem states that both Company A and Company B earned a ROE of 10% each year. Thus, using the change in ROE as the performance criterion, both companies performed the same. Specifically, both Company A and Company B had no change in ROE between 2012 and 2013.

            Odd-numbered Solutions

17.9   (Union Cable Company; journal entries to correct errors and adjust for changes in estimates.) (amounts in US$)

a. Retained Earnings.. 12,000
        Patent (or Accumulated Amortization)..............   12,000

Assets	=	Liabilities	+	Shareholders' Equity	(Class.)
−12,000				−12,000	RE

To correct error from neglecting to amortize patent during previous year.

b. Accumulated Depreciation...................................... 7,000
        Retained Earnings.......................................   4,000
        Retained Earnings.......................................   3,000

Assets	=	Liabilities	+	Shareholders' Equity	(Class.)
+7,000				+4,000	RE
				+3,000	RE

To correct error in recording the sale of a machine by eliminating the balance in accumulated depreciation relating to the machine sold and converting a $4,000 loss on the sale to a $3,000 gain. (The two credits to Retained Earnings could be netted to form a single $7,000 credit to Retained Earnings.)

c. Depreciation Expense... 50,000
        Accumulated Depreciation................................   50,000

Assets	=	Liabilities	+	Shareholders' Equity	(Class.)
−50,000				−50,000	IncSt → RE

To record depreciation expense for 2012. Carrying value on January 1, 2012 is $1,600,00 [= $2,400,000 − ($80,000 x 10)]. The revised annual depreciation is $50,000 (= $1,600,000/32).

17.9 continued.

d. Bad Debt Expense.. 10,000
   Allowance for Uncollectible Accounts................. 10,000

Assets	=	Liabilities	+	Shareholders' Equity	(Class.)
–10,000				–10,000	IncSt → RE

To adjust the balance in the allowance account to the amount needed to cover estimated uncollectibles.

17.11 (Tuck Corporation; comprehensive review problem.) (amounts in US$)

a. Balance in Marketable Equity Securities on December 31,
   2012 .... $ 125,000
   Less Cost of Marketable Equity Securities Sold................. (35,000)
   Plus Decrease in Unrealized Loss on Marketable
   Securities.. 4,000
   Plus Cost of Marketable Equity Securities Purchased .... _____?_____
   Balance in Marketable Equity Securities on December 31,
   2013 .... $ 141,000

The cost of marketable equity securities purchased is $47,000.

b. Cost of Marketable Equity Securities Sold.......................... $ 35,000
   Less Loss on Sale of Marketable Equity Securities .... (8,000)
   Sales Proceeds... $ 27,000

c. Balance in Allowance Account on December 31, 2012......... $ 128,800
   Plus Provision for Estimated Uncollectible Accounts .... ?
   Less Write-Offs of Specific Customers' Accounts .... (63,000)
   Balance in Allowance Account on December 31, 2013......... $ 210,400

The provision for estimated uncollectibles is $144,600.

d.

	LIFO	Difference	FIFO
Beginning Inventory	$1,257,261	$ 430,000	$1,687,261
Purchases.............................	2,848,054	—	2,848,054
Available	$4,105,315	$ 430,000	$4,535,315
Less Ending Inventory.........	(1,525,315)	(410,000)	(1,935,315)
Cost of Goods Sold...............	$2,580,000	$ 20,000	$2,600,000

17.11 continued.

e. Unrealized Loss on Investments in Securities 5,000
    Investments in Securities 5,000

Assets	=	Liabilities	+	Shareholders' Equity	(Class.)
−5,000				−5,000	OCI → AOCI

To recognize unrealized loss on investments in securities.

f. Dividend revenue of $8,000. The unrealized loss of $5,000 (see Part *e*.) is not included in the calculation of net income for 2013.

g. Investment in Davis Corporation 87,000
    Equity in Earnings of Affiliates 87,000

Assets	=	Liabilities	+	Shareholders' Equity	(Class.)
+87,000				+87,000	IncSt → RE

To recognize share of Davis Corporation's earnings in 2013; 0.40 × $217,500 = $87,000.

Cash 24,000
    Investment in Davis Corporation 24,000

Assets	=	Liabilities	+	Shareholders' Equity	(Class.)
+24,000					
−24,000					

To recognize dividend received from Davis Corporation; 0.40 × $60,000 = $24,000.

Investment in Davis Corporation 20,000
    Cash 20,000

Assets	=	Liabilities	+	Shareholders' Equity	(Class.)
+20,000					
−20,000					

To record additional investment in Davis Corporation.

17.11 continued.

h. Cash.. 7,000
    Accumulated Depreciation.................................. 19,000
        Equipment.. 23,000
        Gain on Sale of Equipment................................ 3,000

Assets	=	Liabilities	+	Shareholders' Equity	(Class.)
+7,000				+3,000	IncSt → RE
+19,000					
−23,000					

i. Present Value of Lease Payment at Signing .... $ 10,000
    Present Value of 19 Lease Payments Due on January 2 of
        Each Subsequent Year at 8%; $10,000 × 9.6036 96,036
    Total.. $ 106,036

j. Balance in Rental Fees Received in Advance on December
        31, 2012 .... $ 46,000
    Plus Cash Received for Rentals During 2013 .... ?
    Less Rental Fees Earned During 2013.............................. (240,000)
    Balance in Rental Fees Received in Advance on December
        31, 2013 .... $ 58,000

Cash received during 2013 totaled $252,000.

k. Balance in Estimated Warranty Liability on December
        31, 2012 .... $75,200
    Plus Estimated Warranty Cost Provision for 2013 46,800
    Less Cost of Actual Warranty Services........................... (?)
    Balance in Estimated Warranty Liability on December
        31, 2013 .... $78,600

Warranty costs incurred during 2013 totaled $43,400.

l. First 6 Months: 0.025 × $1,104,650.00 .... $27,616.25
    Second 6 Months: 0.025 × $1,102,266.25[a] 27,556.66
        Total Interest Expense....................................... $55,172.91

[a]$1,104,650.00 − ($30,000.00 − $27,616.25) = $1,102,266.25.

17.11 continued.

m. Interest Expense.. 20,996
  Mortgage Payable 19,004
    Cash 40,000

Assets	=	Liabilities	+	Shareholders' Equity	(Class.)
−40,000		−19,004		−20,996	IncSt → RE

To record mortgage interest and principal payment; $20,996 = 0.07 × ($262,564 + $37,383).

n. Present Value of Payment on January 1, 2013...................... $10,000
  Present Value of Seven Remaining Lease Payments
    ($10,000 × 5.20637)... 52,064
    Total $62,064

o. Capitalized Lease Obligation, December 31, 2012 .... $62,064
  Lease Payment on January 1, 2013 .... (10,000)
  Interest Expense for 2013 (0.08 × $52,064)........................... 4,165
    Total ($10,000 + $46,229)... $56,229

p. Income Tax Expense 150,000
  Income Tax Payable 135,000
  Deferred Tax Liability ($145,000 − $130,000) .. 15,000

Assets	=	Liabilities	+	Shareholders' Equity	(Class.)
		+135,000		−150,000	IncSt → RE
		+15,000			

q. Income Tax Payable—Current, December 31, 2012 .... $ 140,000
  Provision for Current Taxes Payable (See Part p.) 135,000
  Less Cash Payments Made During 2013............................. (?)
  Income Tax Payable—Current, December 31, 2013 .... $ 160,000

Cash payments for income taxes during 2013 were $115,000.

r. $\dfrac{\text{Deferred Tax Expense Relating to Depreciation}}{\text{Income Tax Rate}} = \dfrac{\$12,000}{0.30} = \$40,000$

17.11 continued.

s. Convertible Preferred Stock (5,000 X $100) 500,000
    Common Stock (25,000 X $10)........................... 250,000
    Additional Paid-In Capital 250,000

Assets	=	Liabilities	+	Shareholders' Equity	(Class.)
				−500,000	ContriCap
				+250,000	ContriCap
				+250,000	ContriCap

To record conversion of preferred into common stock.

t. Treasury Stock 8,800
    Cash 8,800

Assets	=	Liabilities	+	Shareholders' Equity	(Class.)
−8,800				−8,800	ContriCap

To record purchases of treasury stock.

Cash.. 25,200
    Treasury Stock.. 21,600[a]
    Additional Paid-In Capital .... 3,600[b]

Assets	=	Liabilities	+	Shareholders' Equity	(Class.)
+25,200				+21,600	ContriCap
				+3,600	ContriCap

To record the sale of treasury stock.

[a]1,800 shares X $12 = $21,600.

[b]Additional Paid-In Capital on December 31, 2012............ $ 130,000
Plus Amount Arising from Conversion of Preferred
    Stock.. 250,000
Plus Amount Arising from Issue of Common Stock........... 200,000
Plus Amount Arising from Sale of Treasury Stock .... ?
Additional Paid-In Capital on December 31, 2013............ $ 583,600

The additional paid-in capital arising from the treasury stock sales is $3,600.

This page is intentionally left blank

APPENDIX

TIME VALUE OF CASH FLOWS: COMPOUND INTEREST CONCEPTS AND APPLICATIONS

Questions, Exercises, and Problems: Answers and Solutions

A.1   See the text or the glossary at the end of the book.

A.3   In simple interest, only the principal sum earns interest. In compound interest, interest is earned on the principal plus amounts of interest not paid or withdrawn.

A.5   The timing of the first payment for an annuity due is *now* (at the beginning of the first period), whereas that for an ordinary annuity is at the *end* of the first period. The future value of an annuity due is computed as of one year after the final payment, but for an ordinary annuity is computed as of the time of the last payment.

A.7   Present values increase when interest rates decrease, and present values decrease when interest rates increase, regardless of the time period.

A.9   The formula assumes that the growth [represented by the parameter g in the formula $1/(r - g)$] continues forever. That is a long time. The formula assumes also that the discount and growth rates remain constant. In our experience, more harm results from assuming the growth persists forever than from the other assumptions.

A.11   a. $150,000 × 0.62741 = $94,112.

b. $150,000 × 0.54027 = $81,041.

A.13   a.   ¥45,000,000/10.63663 = ¥4.23 million.

b.   ¥45,000,000/12.29969 = ¥3.66 million.

A.15   a.   £145,000/4.62288 = £31,366.

b.   £145,000/4.11141 = £35,268.

A.17   (Effective interest rates.)

    a.   12% per period; 5 periods.

    b.   6% per period; 10 periods.

    c.   3% per period; 20 periods.

    d.   1% per period; 60 periods.

A.19   (amounts in US$)

    a. $100 X 0.30832 = $30.83.

    b. $250 X 0.53063 = $132.66.

    c. $1,000 X 0.78757 = $787.57.

A.21   (amounts in US$)

    a. $1,000(1.00 + 0.94340) + $2,000(4.21236 − 0.94340) + $2,500(6.80169 − 4.21236) = $14,955.

    b. $1,000(1.00 + 0.92593) + $2,000(3.99271 − 0.92593) + $2,500(6.24689 − 3.99271) = $13,695.

    c. $1,000(1.00 + 0.90909) + $2,000(3.79079 − 0.90909) + $2,500(5.75902 − 3.79079) = $12,593.

A.23   (amounts in US$)

    a. $3,000/(0.06 − 0.02) = $75,000.

    b. $3,000/(0.08 − 0.02) = $50,000.

    c.   [$3,000/(0.06 − 0.02)] X 0.79209 = $59,406.75.

    d.   [$3,000/(0.08 − 0.02)] X 0.73503 = $36,751.50.

A.25   (amounts in US$)

7.00%. Note that $100,000/$55,307 = 1.80809. See Appendix Table 4, 2-period row and observe 1.80809 in the 7% column.

A.27   (amounts in US$)

a. $16\% = (\$67{,}280/\$50{,}000)^{1/2} - 1$.

b.

Year (1)	Carrying Value Start of Year (2)	Interest for Year = (2) X 0.16 (3)	Amount (Reducing) Increasing Carrying Value (4)	Carrying Value End of Year = (2) + (3) + (4) (5)
1	$ 50,000	$ 8,000		$ 58,000
2	58,000	9,280	$ (67,280)	-0-

A.29   (Find equivalent annual rate offered for purchase discounts.) (amounts in US$)

a.   Terms of sale of 2/10, net/30 on a $100 gross invoice price, for example, mean that the interest rate is 2/98 for a 20-day period, because if the discount is not taken, a charge of $2 is levied for the use of $98. The $98 is used for 20 days (= 30 − 10), so the number of compounding periods in a year is 365/20 = 18.25. The expression for the exact rate of interest implied by 2/10, net 30 is $(1 + 2/98)^{(365/20)} - 1 = 1.020408^{18.25} - 1 = 44.59\%$.

b.   Appendix Table 1 can be used. Use the 2% column and the 18-period row to see that the rate implied by 2/10, net 30 must be at least 42.825% (= 1.42825 − 1).

A.31   (amounts in US$)

Present value of future proceeds = 0.85282 X $30,000 + C = $30,000; where C represents the present value of the foregone interest payments. Appendix Table 2, 16-period row, 1% column = 0.85282.

$C = \$30{,}000 - \$25{,}585 = \$4{,}415$.

A.33   (amounts in US$)

Present value of deposit = $3.00.

Present value of $3.00, recorded 20 periods, have discounted at 0.50% per period = $3.00 X 0.90506 = $2.72.

Loss of $0.28 (= $3.00 − $2.72) in foregone interest vs. Loss of $1.20 in price.

Net advantage of returnables is $0.92.

A.35   (Oberweis Dairy.) (amounts in US$)

$1,800/12 = $150 saved per month. $6,000/$150 = 40.0.

Present value of annuity of $1 discounted at 1% for 50 periods = 39.19612.

The present value of the annuity is $40 when the annuity lasts between 51 and 52 periods. Oberweis Dairy will recoup its investment in about 52 months, a bit more than four years.

A.37   (Friendly Loan Company; finding implicit interest rates; truth-in-lending laws reduce the type of deception suggested by this problem.) (amounts in US$)

The effective interest rate is 19.86% and must be found by trial and error. The time line for this problem is

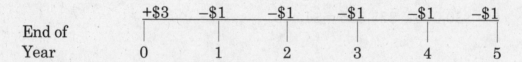

```
        +$6,000      −$2,000−$2,000    −$2,000−$2,000    −$2,000
End of    |            |      |          |      |          |
Year      0            1      2          3      4          5
```

Dividing every number in the above time line by 2,000, we get a time line that is equivalent, at least in terms of the implied interest rate, to

```
        +$3      −$1      −$1      −$1      −$1      −$1
End of   |        |        |        |        |        |
Year     0        1        2        3        4        5
```

Scanning Appendix Table 4, 5-period column, one finds the factor 2.99061, which is approximately 3.00, in the 20% column, so one can easily see that the implied interest rate is about 20% per year. The 3.00 is the +$3 cash inflow shown in the above time line for End of Year 0.

A.39 (Lynch Company/Bages Company; computation of present value of cash flows; untaxed acquisition, no change in tax basis of assets.) (amounts in US$)

a. $440,000 = $390,000 + $50,000 = $700,000 − $260,000.

b. $3,745,966 = $440,000 × 8.51356; see Appendix Table 4, 20-period column, 10% row.

A.41 (American Basketball Association/National Basketball Association; valuation of intangibles with perpetuity formulas.) (amounts in millions of US$)

a. $50 million = $4 million/0.08.

b. Increase.

c. $68 million = ($4 million × 1.02)/(0.08 − 0.02) = $4.08 million/(0.08 − 0.02).

d. Increase.

e. Decrease.

Odd-numbered Solutions

A.43 (Gulf Coast Manufacturing; choosing between investment alternatives.) (amounts in US$)

	Basic Data Repeated from Problem		Present Value Computations			
	Lexus	Mercedes-Benz	Factor	Source [B]	Lexus	Mercedes-Benz
Initial Cost at the Start of 2013	$60,000	$45,000	1.00000		$60,000	$45,000
Initial Cost at the Start of 2016		48,000	0.75131	T[2, 3, 0.10]		36,063
Trade-in Value						
End of 2015		23,000	0.75131	T[2, 3, 0.10]		(17,280)
End of 2018 [A]	16,000	24,500	0.56447	T[2, 6, 0.10]	(9,032)	(13,830)
Estimated Annual Cash Operating Costs, Except Major Servicing	4,000	4,500	4.35526	T[4, 6, 0.10]	17,421	19,599
Estimated Cash Cost of Major Servicing						
End of 2016	6,500		0.68301	T[2, 4, 0.10]	4,440	
End of 2014 and End of 2017		2,500	0.82645	T[2, 2, 0.10]		2,066
			0.62092	T[2, 5, 0.10]		1,552
Sum of Present Values of All Costs					$72,829	$73,170

[A] At this time, Lexus is 6 years old; second Mercedes-Benz is 3 years old.

[B] $T[i, j, r]$ means Table i (= Appendix Table 2 or Appendix Table 4), row j, interest rate r.

a. Strategy L, buying one Lexus has lower present value of costs, but the difference is so small that we'd encourage the CEO to go with his whim, whatever it may be. Also, the relatively new theory of real options will likely prefer Strategy M because it gives the owner more choices at the end of the third year.

b. Depreciation plays no role, so long as we ignore income taxes. Only cash flows matter.

This page is intentionally left blank

This page is intentionally left blank

This page is intentionally left blank

This page is intentionally left blank

This page is intentionally left blank

A-11

This page is intentionally left blank

This page is intentionally left blank

A-13

This page is intentionally left blank